Devils and Realist

vol.11

story by Madoka Takadono
art by Utako Yukihiro

SEVEN SEAS ENTERTAINMENT PRESENTS

Devils and Realist

art by UTAKO YUKIHIRO / story by MADOKA TAKADONO VOLUME 11

TRANSLATION
Jocelyne Allen

COPY EDITING
Danielle King

LETTERING
Roland Amago

LAYOUT
Bambi Eloriaga-Amago

COVER DESIGN
Nicky Lim

PROOFREADER
Lee Otter

PRODUCTION MANAGER
Lissa Pattillo

EDITOR-IN-CHIEF
Adam Arnold

PUBLISHER
Jason DeAngelis

MAKAI OUJI: DEVILS AND REALIST VOL. 11

First published in Japan in 2015 by ICHIJINSHA Inc., Tokyo.
English translation rights arranged with ICHIJINSHA Inc., Tokyo, Japan.

ISBN: 978-1-626923-52-2

Printed in Canada

First Printing: November 2016

10 9 8 7 6 5 4 3 2 1

FOLLOW US ONLINE: ***www.gomanga.com***

READING DIRECTIONS

This book reads from ***right to left***, Japanese style. If this is your first time reading manga, you start reading from the top right panel on each page and take it from there. If you get lost, just follow the numbered diagram here. It may seem backwards at first, but you'll get the hang of it! Have fun!!

1
2
3
4
5
6
7
8
9

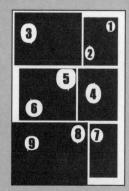

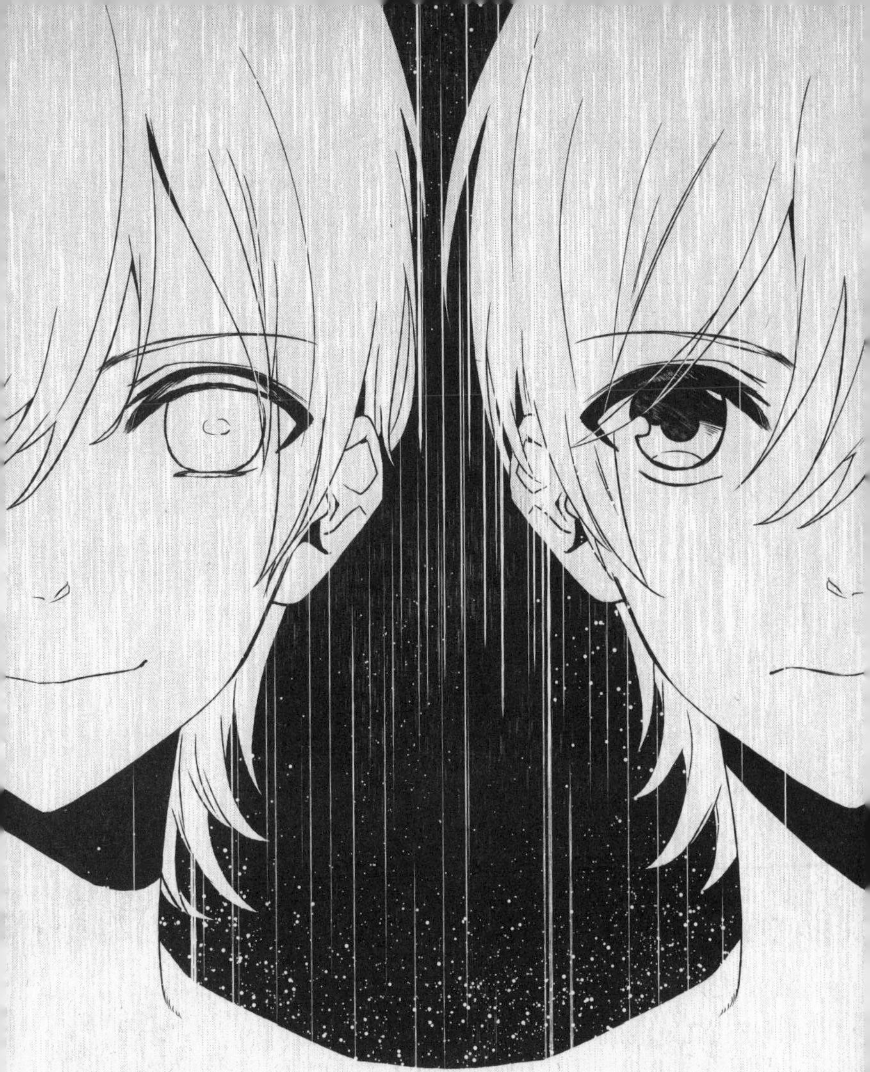

Pillar 61

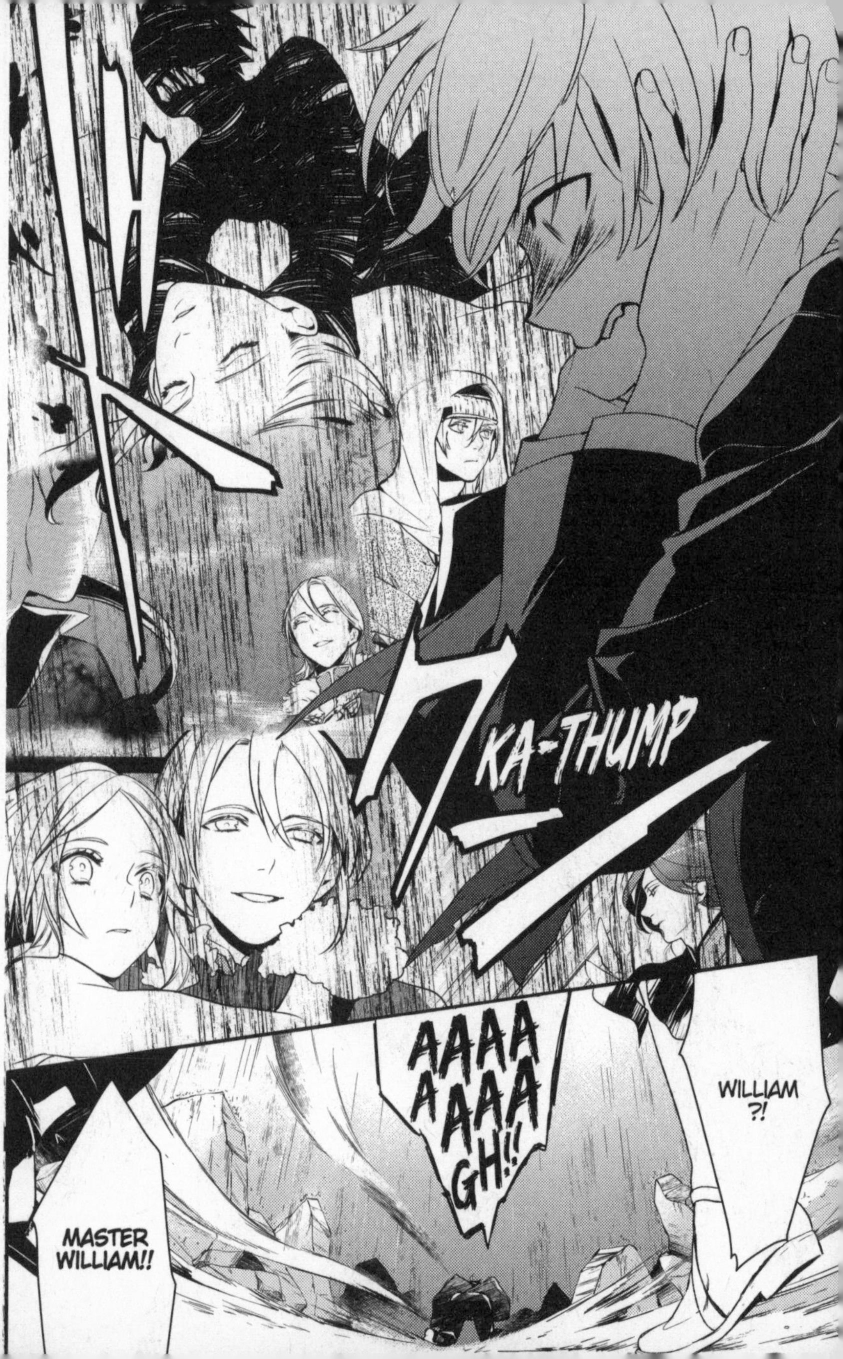
KA-THUMP
WILLIAM ?!
AAAA AAAA GH!!
MASTER WILLIAM!!

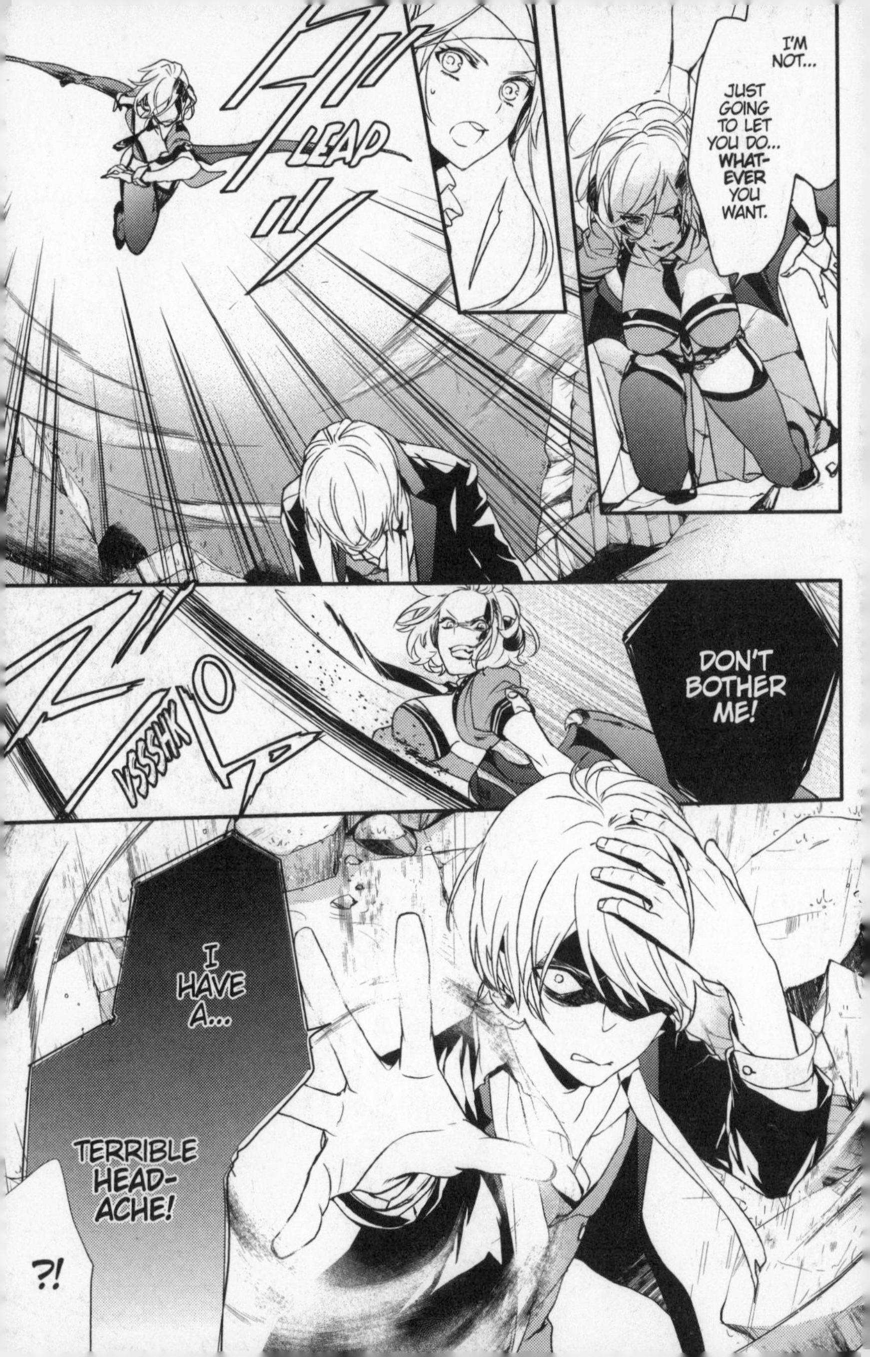
I'M NOT...
JUST GOING TO LET YOU DO... WHATEVER YOU WANT.
LEAP
DON'T BOTHER ME!
VSSSHK
I HAVE A...
TERRIBLE HEADACHE!
?!

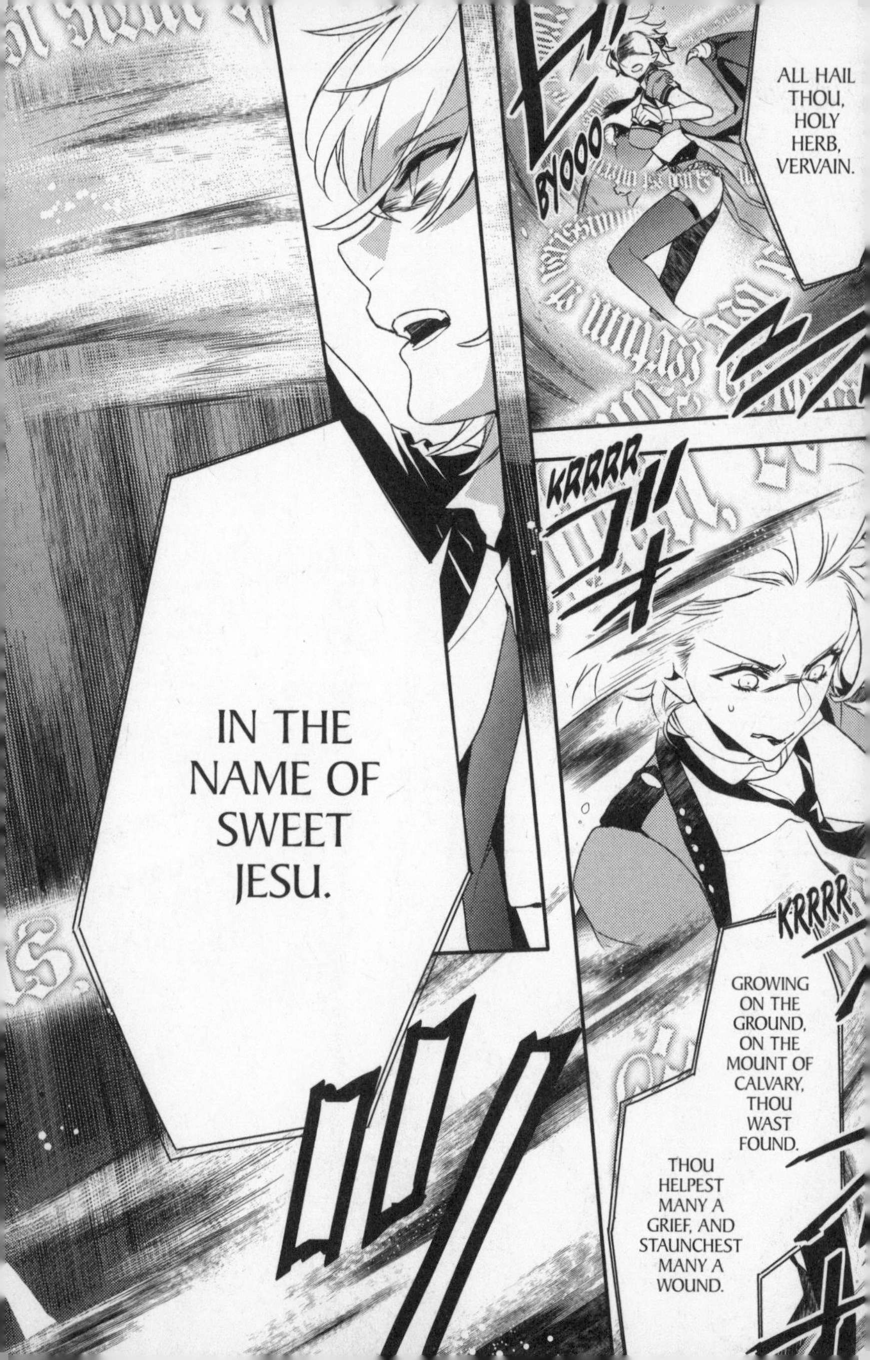
BYOOO
ALL HAIL THOU, HOLY HERB, VERVAIN.
KRRRR
KRRRR
GROWING ON THE GROUND, ON THE MOUNT OF CALVARY, THOU WAST FOUND.
THOU HELPEST MANY A GRIEF, AND STAUNCHEST MANY A WOUND.
IN THE NAME OF SWEET JESU.

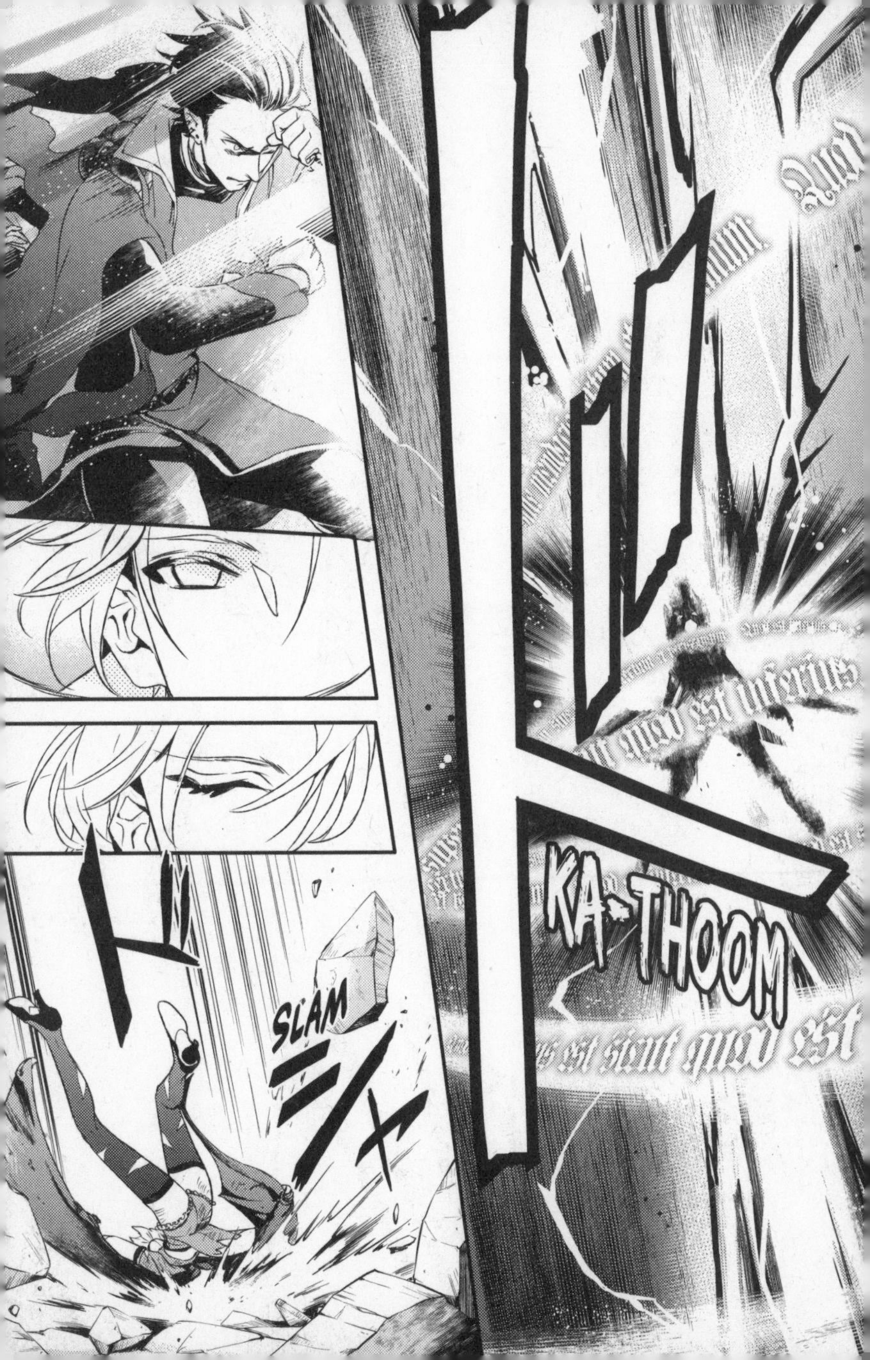
KA-THOOM
SLAM

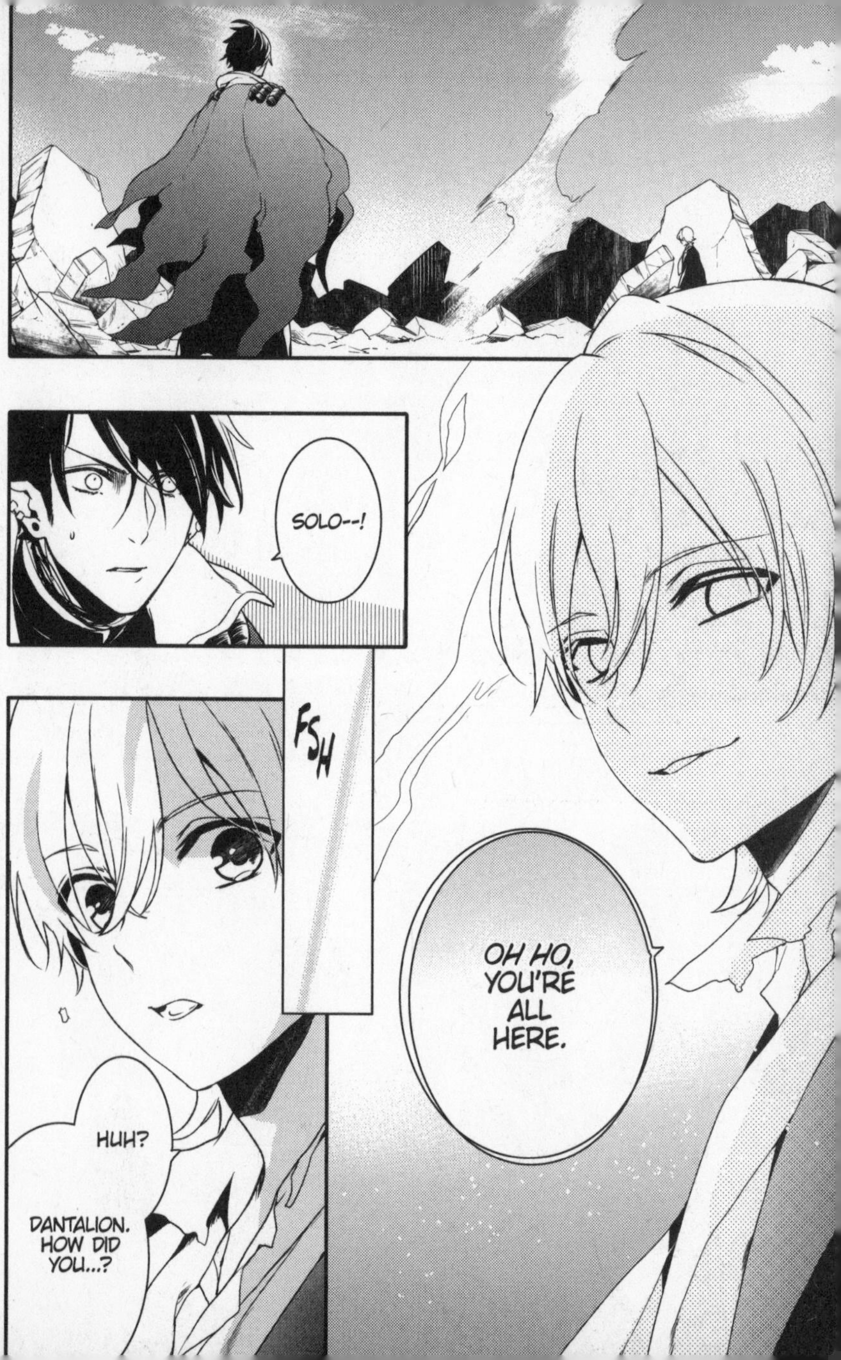
OH HO, YOU'RE ALL HERE.
SOLO--!
FSH
HUH?
DANTALION. HOW DID YOU...?

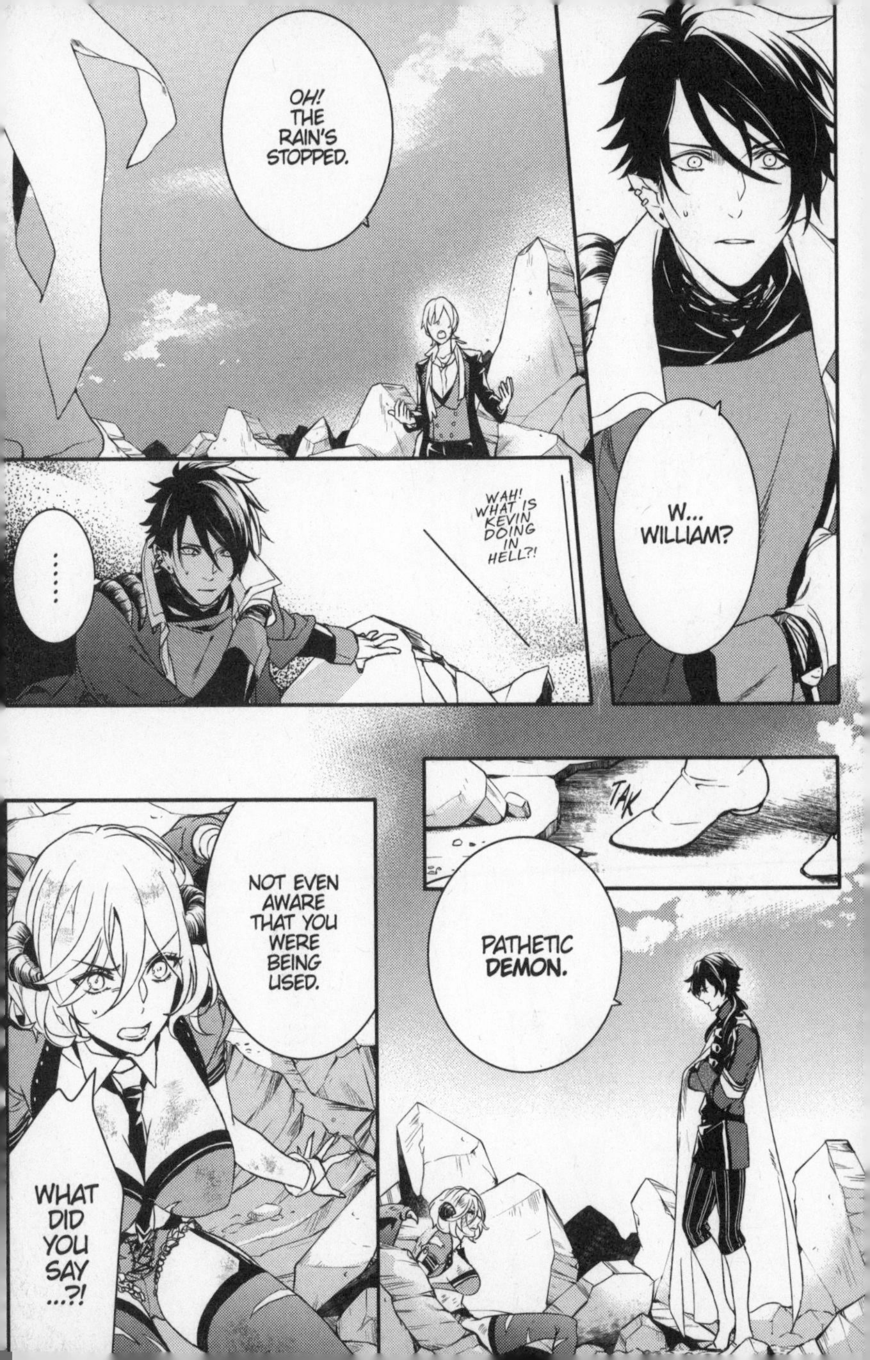
W... WILLIAM?
OH! THE RAIN'S STOPPED.
WAH! WHAT IS KEVIN DOING IN HELL?!
......
TAK
PATHETIC DEMON.
NOT EVEN AWARE THAT YOU WERE BEING USED.
WHAT DID YOU SAY ...?!

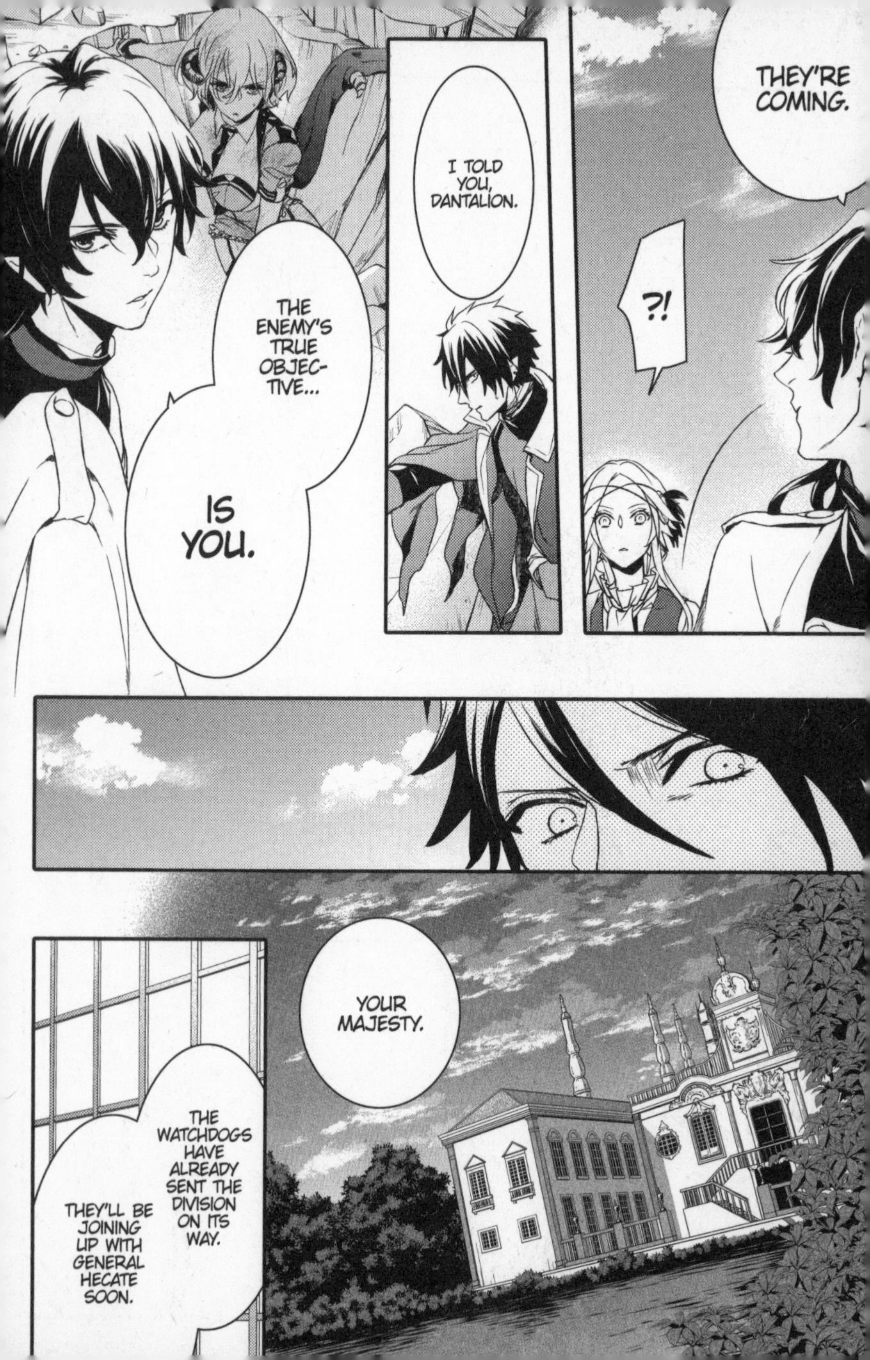
THEY'RE COMING.
?!
I TOLD YOU, DANTALION.
THE ENEMY'S TRUE OBJECTIVE...
IS YOU.
YOUR MAJESTY.
THE WATCHDOGS HAVE ALREADY SENT THE DIVISION ON ITS WAY.
THEY'LL BE JOINING UP WITH GENERAL HECATE SOON.

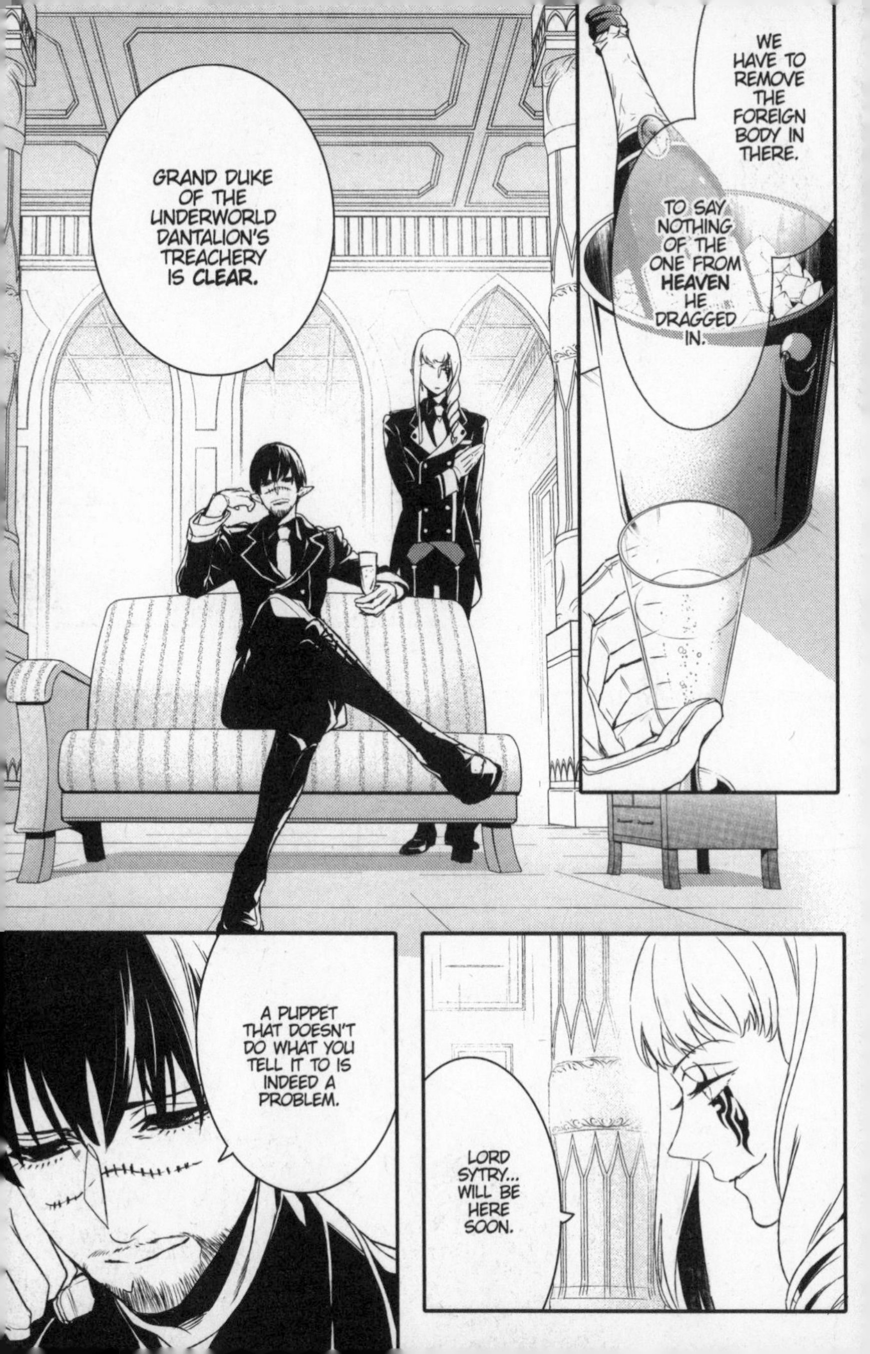
WE HAVE TO REMOVE THE FOREIGN BODY IN THERE.
TO SAY NOTHING OF THE ONE FROM HEAVEN HE DRAGGED IN.
GRAND DUKE OF THE UNDERWORLD DANTALION'S TREACHERY IS CLEAR.
LORD SYTRY... WILL BE HERE SOON.
A PUPPET THAT DOESN'T DO WHAT YOU TELL IT TO IS INDEED A PROBLEM.

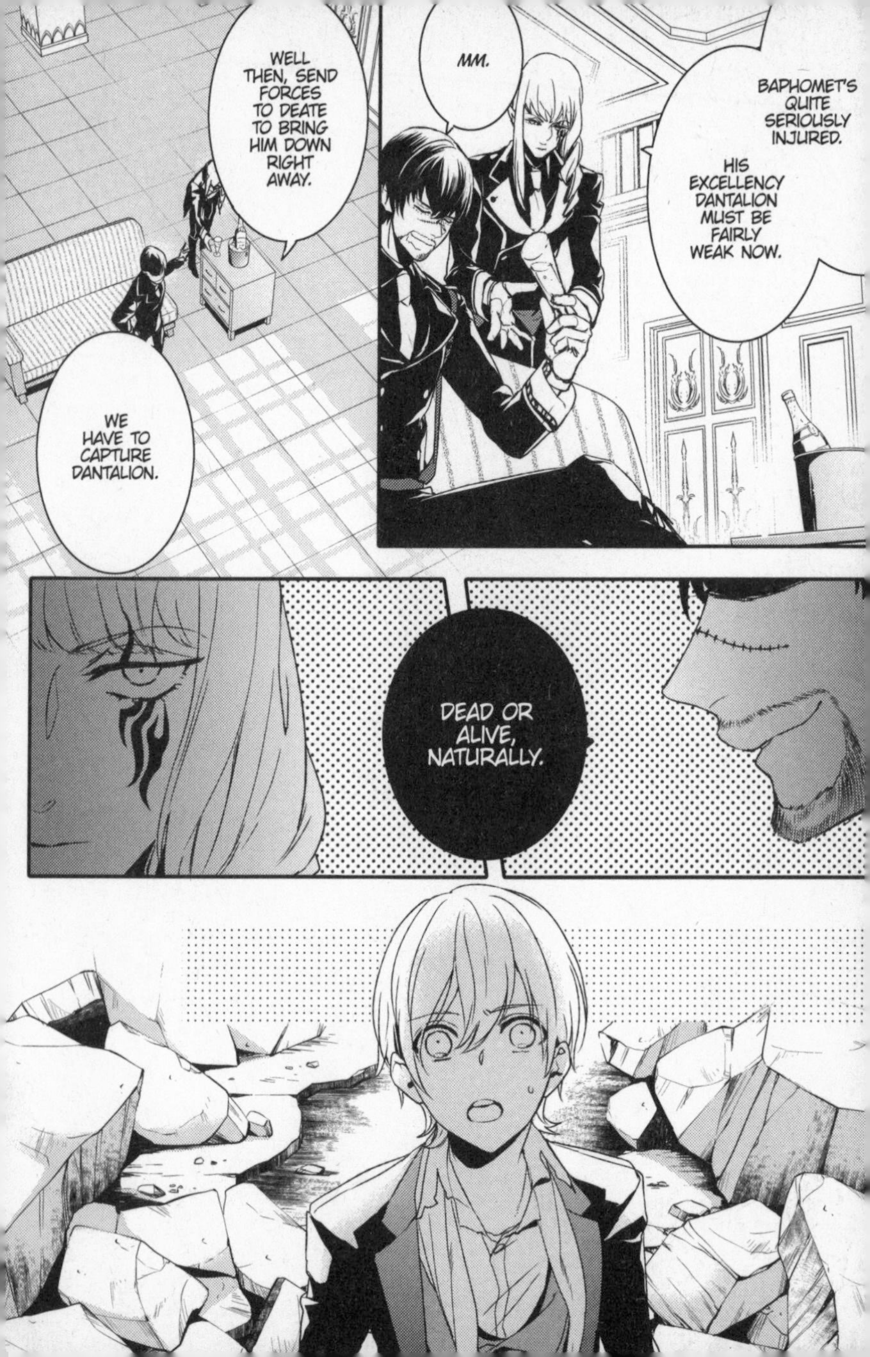
BAPHOMET'S QUITE SERIOUSLY INJURED.
HIS EXCELLENCY DANTALION MUST BE FAIRLY WEAK NOW.
MM.
WELL THEN, SEND FORCES TO DEATE TO BRING HIM DOWN RIGHT AWAY.
WE HAVE TO CAPTURE DANTALION.
DEAD OR ALIVE, NATURALLY.

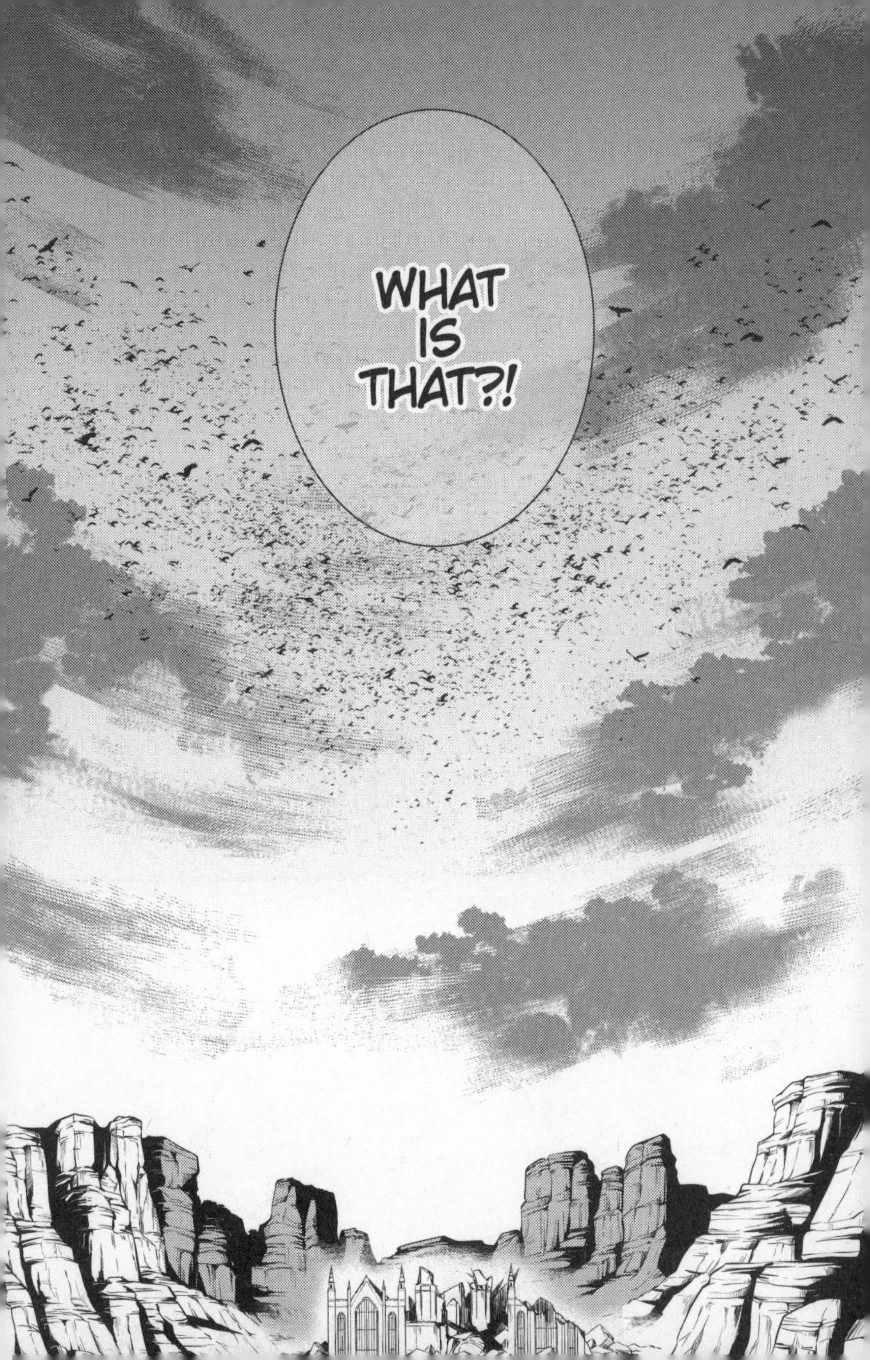
WHAT IS THAT?!

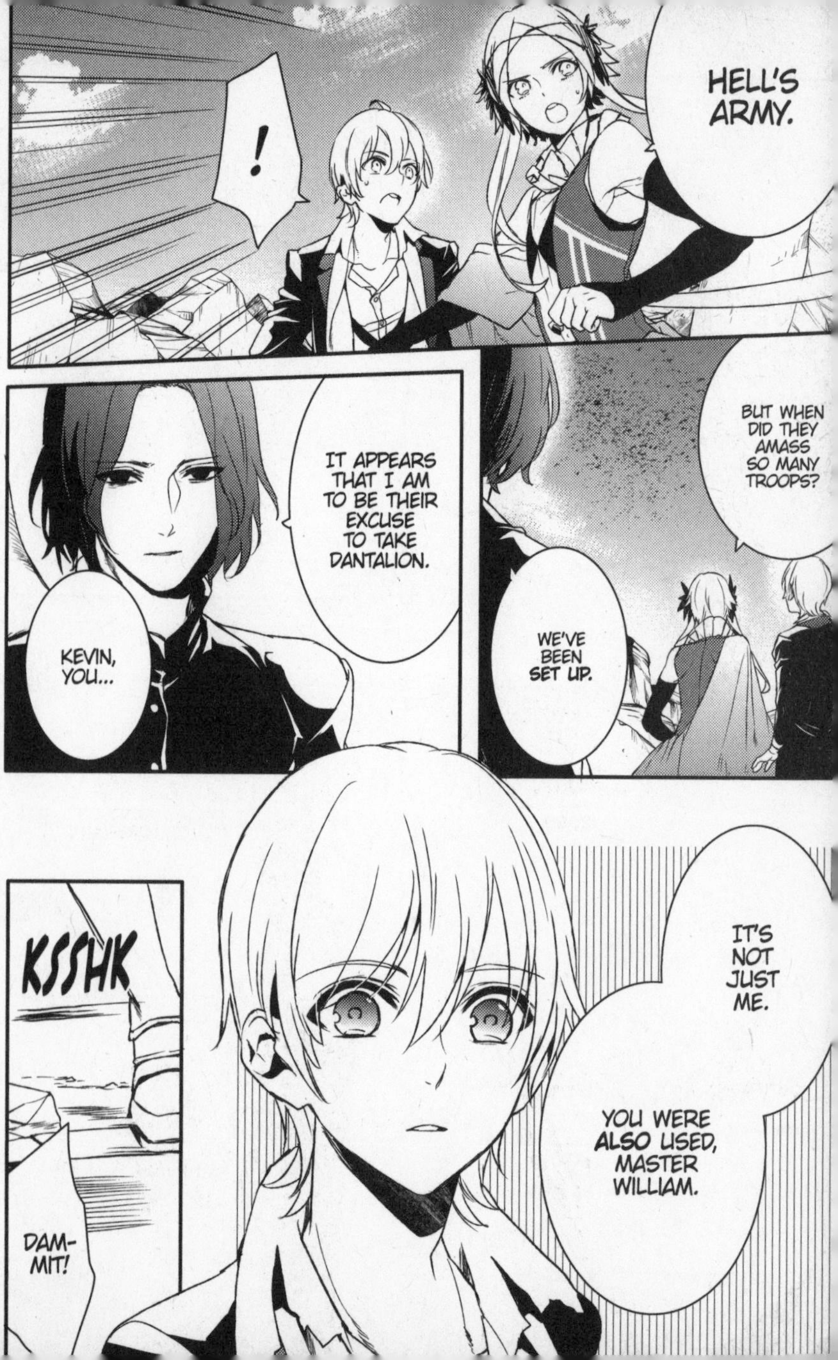
HELL'S ARMY.
!
BUT WHEN DID THEY AMASS SO MANY TROOPS?
WE'VE BEEN SET UP.
IT APPEARS THAT I AM TO BE THEIR EXCUSE TO TAKE DANTALION.
KEVIN, YOU...
IT'S NOT JUST ME.
YOU WERE ALSO USED, MASTER WILLIAM.
KSSHK
DAM-MIT!

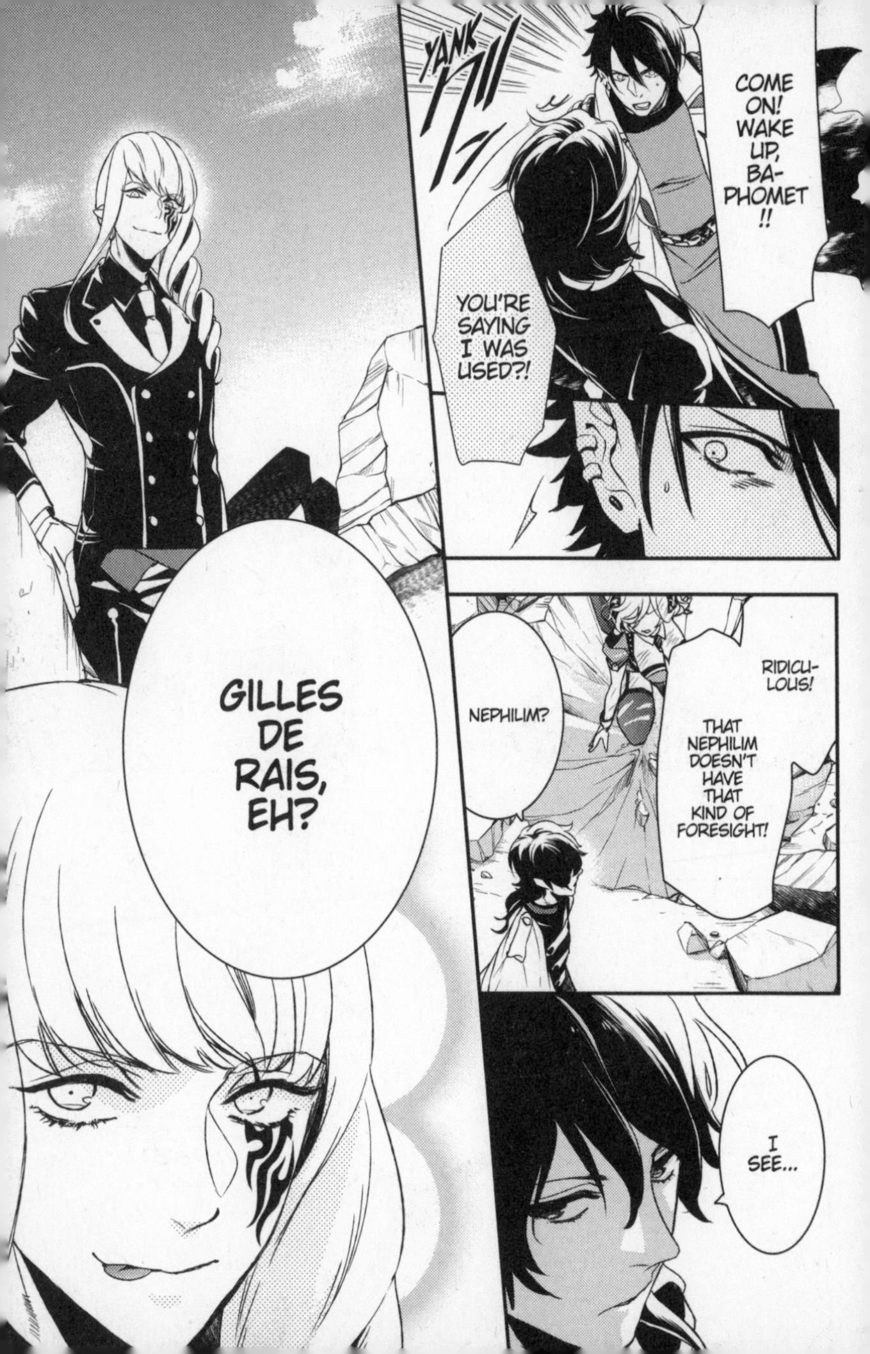
COME ON! WAKE UP, BA-PHOMET!!
YANK
YOU'RE SAYING I WAS USED?!
RIDICULOUS!
THAT NEPHILIM DOESN'T HAVE THAT KIND OF FORESIGHT!
NEPHILIM?
I SEE...
GILLES DE RAIS, EH?

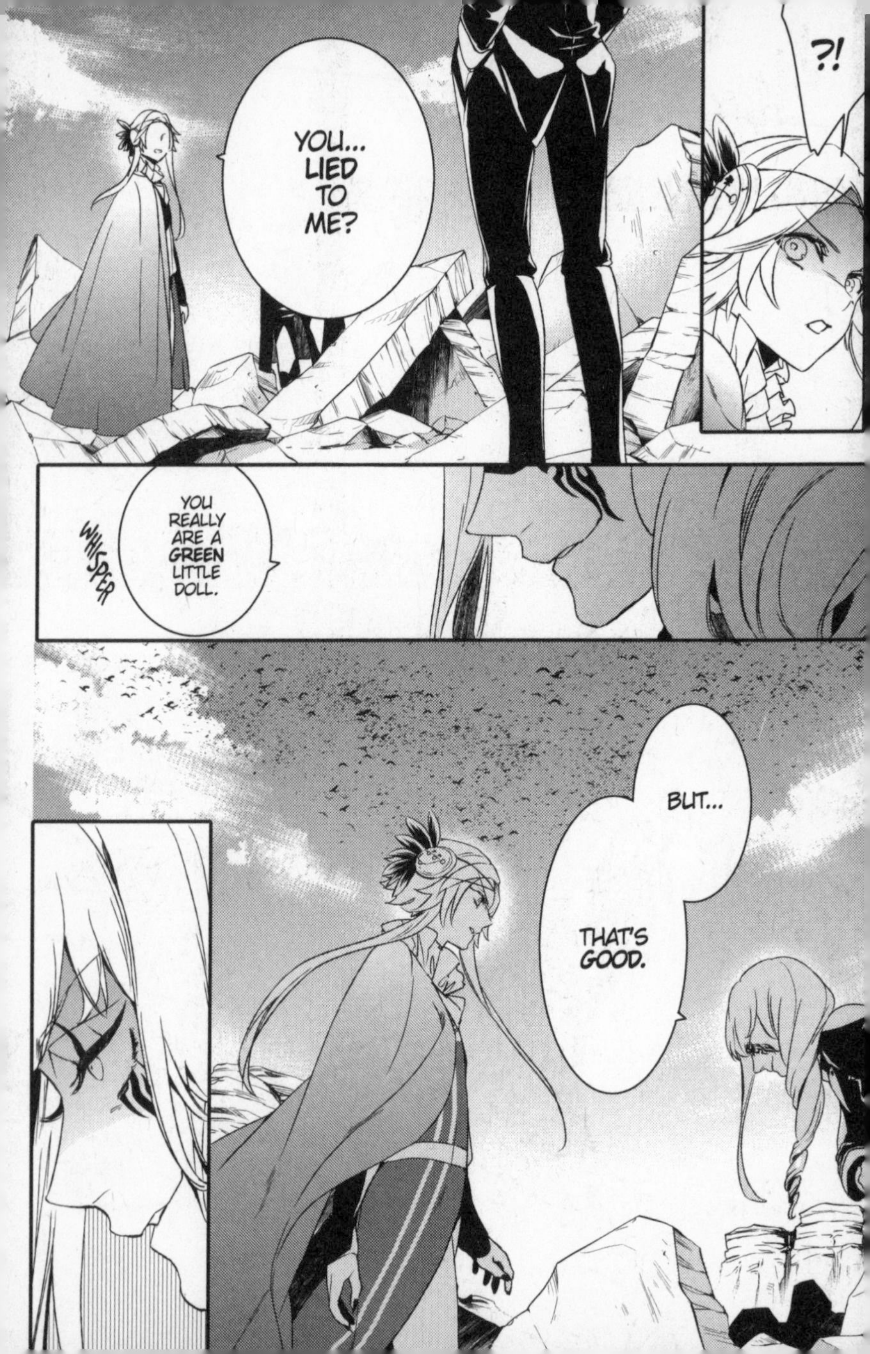
?!
YOU... LIED TO ME?
YOU REALLY ARE A GREEN LITTLE DOLL.
WHISPER
BUT...
THAT'S GOOD.

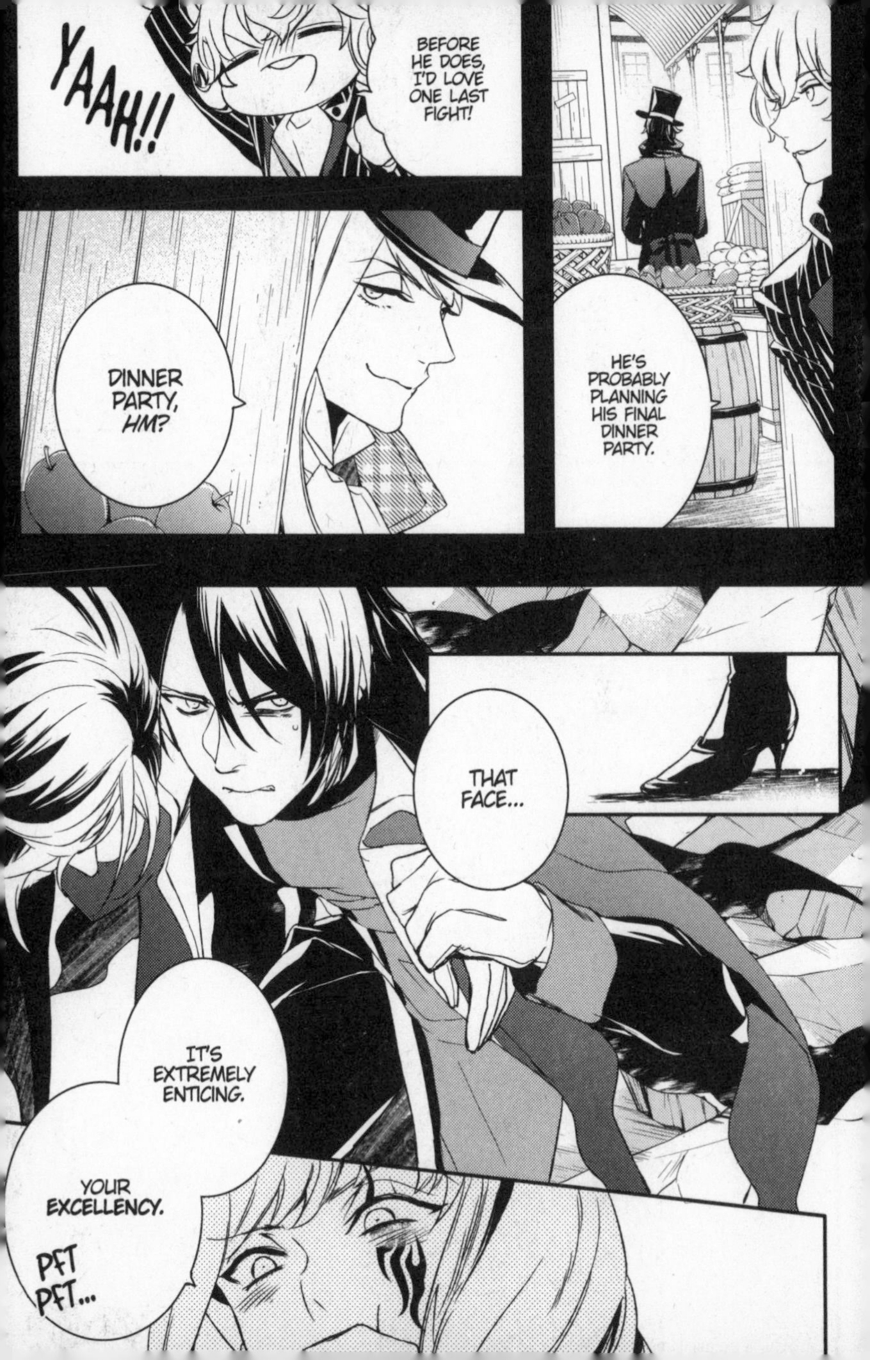
HE'S PROBABLY PLANNING HIS FINAL DINNER PARTY.
BEFORE HE DOES, I'D LOVE ONE LAST FIGHT!
YAAH!!
DINNER PARTY, *HM?*
THAT FACE...
IT'S EXTREMELY ENTICING.
YOUR EXCELLENCY.
PFT PFT...

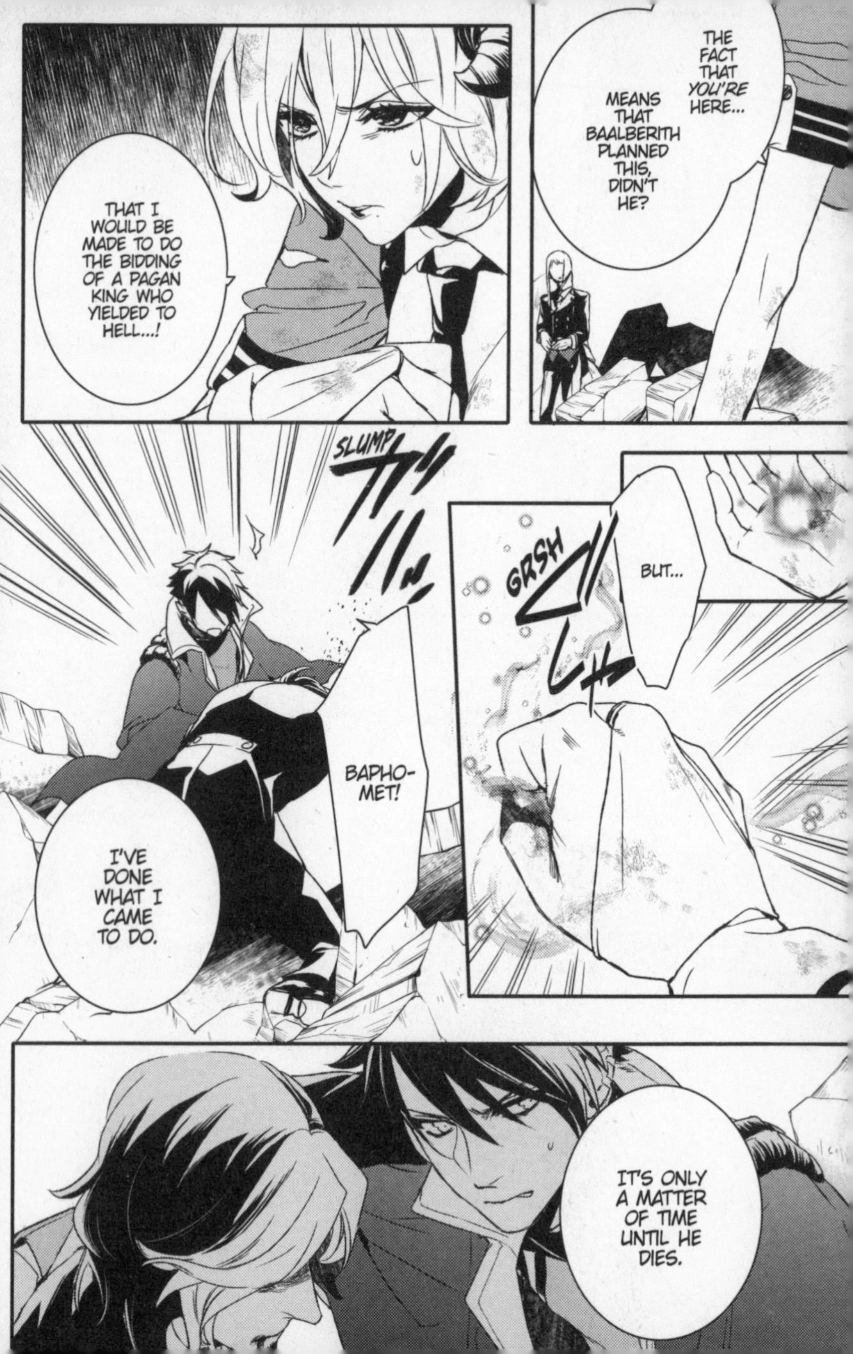
THE FACT THAT YOU'RE HERE...
MEANS THAT BAALBERITH PLANNED THIS, DIDN'T HE?
THAT I WOULD BE MADE TO DO THE BIDDING OF A PAGAN KING WHO YIELDED TO HELL...!
BUT...
GRSH
SLUMP
BAPHOMET!
I'VE DONE WHAT I CAME TO DO.
IT'S ONLY A MATTER OF TIME UNTIL HE DIES.

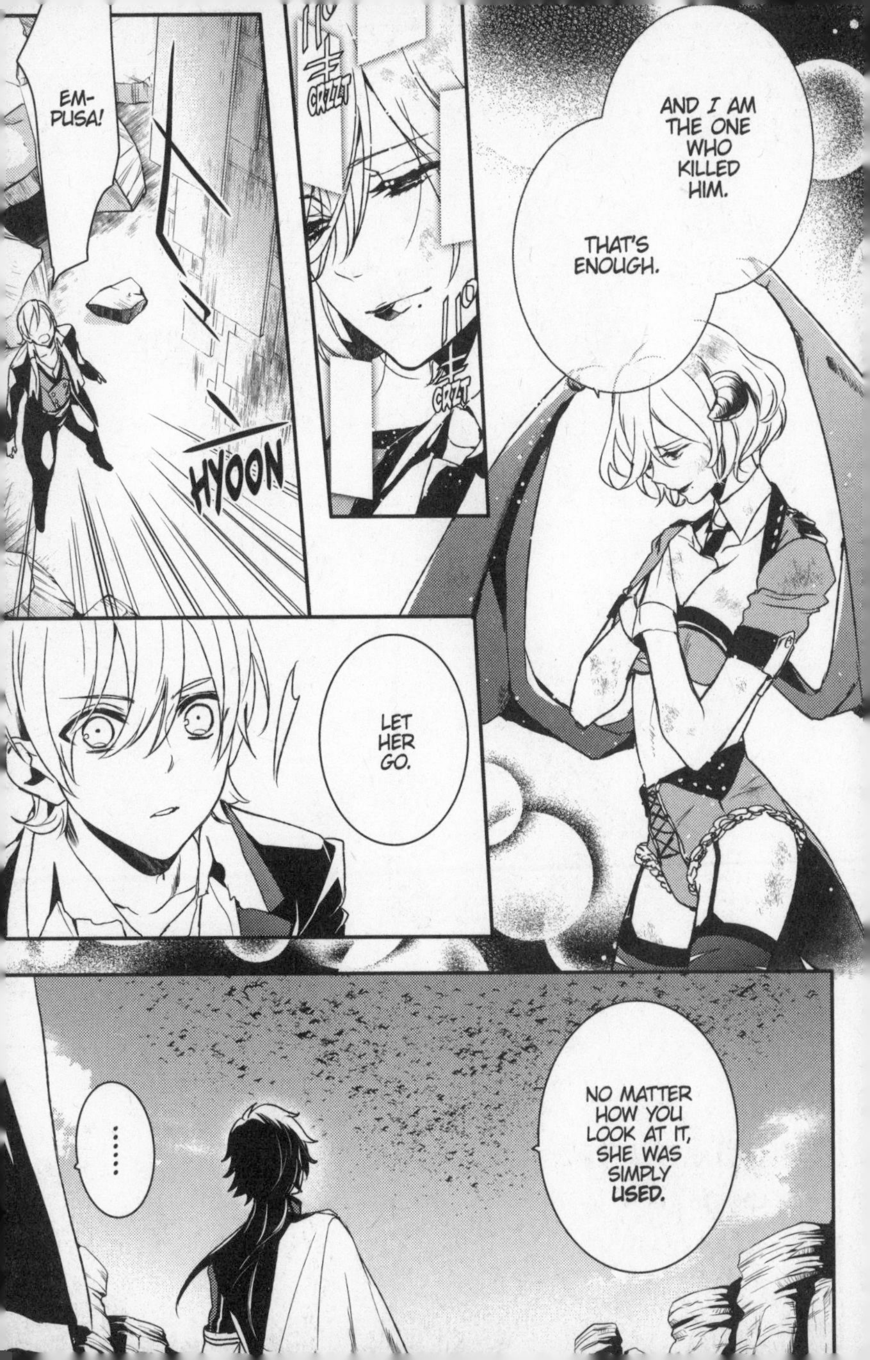
AND I AM THE ONE WHO KILLED HIM.
THAT'S ENOUGH.
CRZZT
CRZZT
EM-PUSA!
HYOON
LET HER GO.
NO MATTER HOW YOU LOOK AT IT, SHE WAS SIMPLY USED.
......

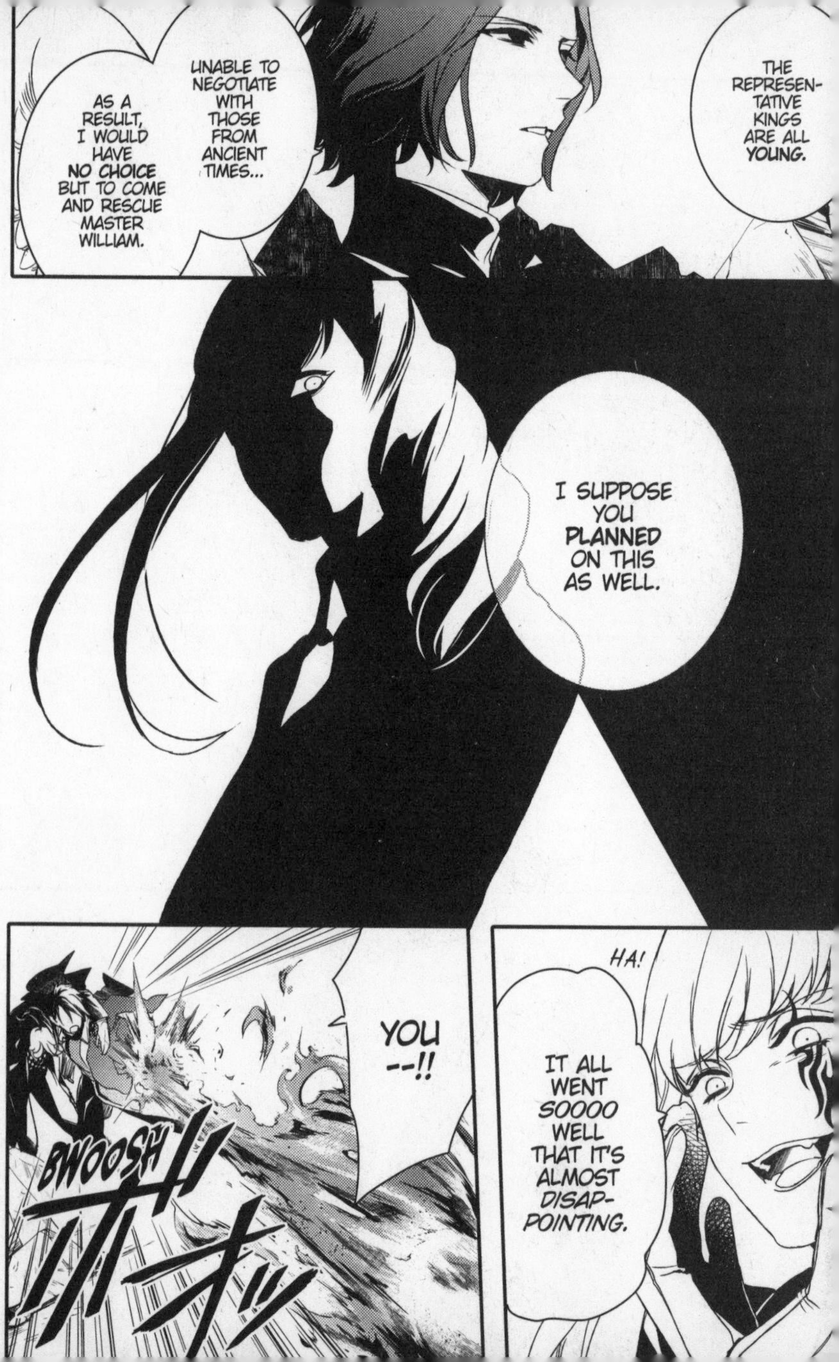
THE REPRESEN-TATIVE KINGS ARE ALL YOUNG.
UNABLE TO NEGOTIATE WITH THOSE FROM ANCIENT TIMES...
AS A RESULT, I WOULD HAVE NO CHOICE BUT TO COME AND RESCUE MASTER WILLIAM.
I SUPPOSE YOU PLANNED ON THIS AS WELL.
HA!
IT ALL WENT SOOOO WELL THAT IT'S ALMOST DISAP-POINTING.
YOU --!!
BWOOSH

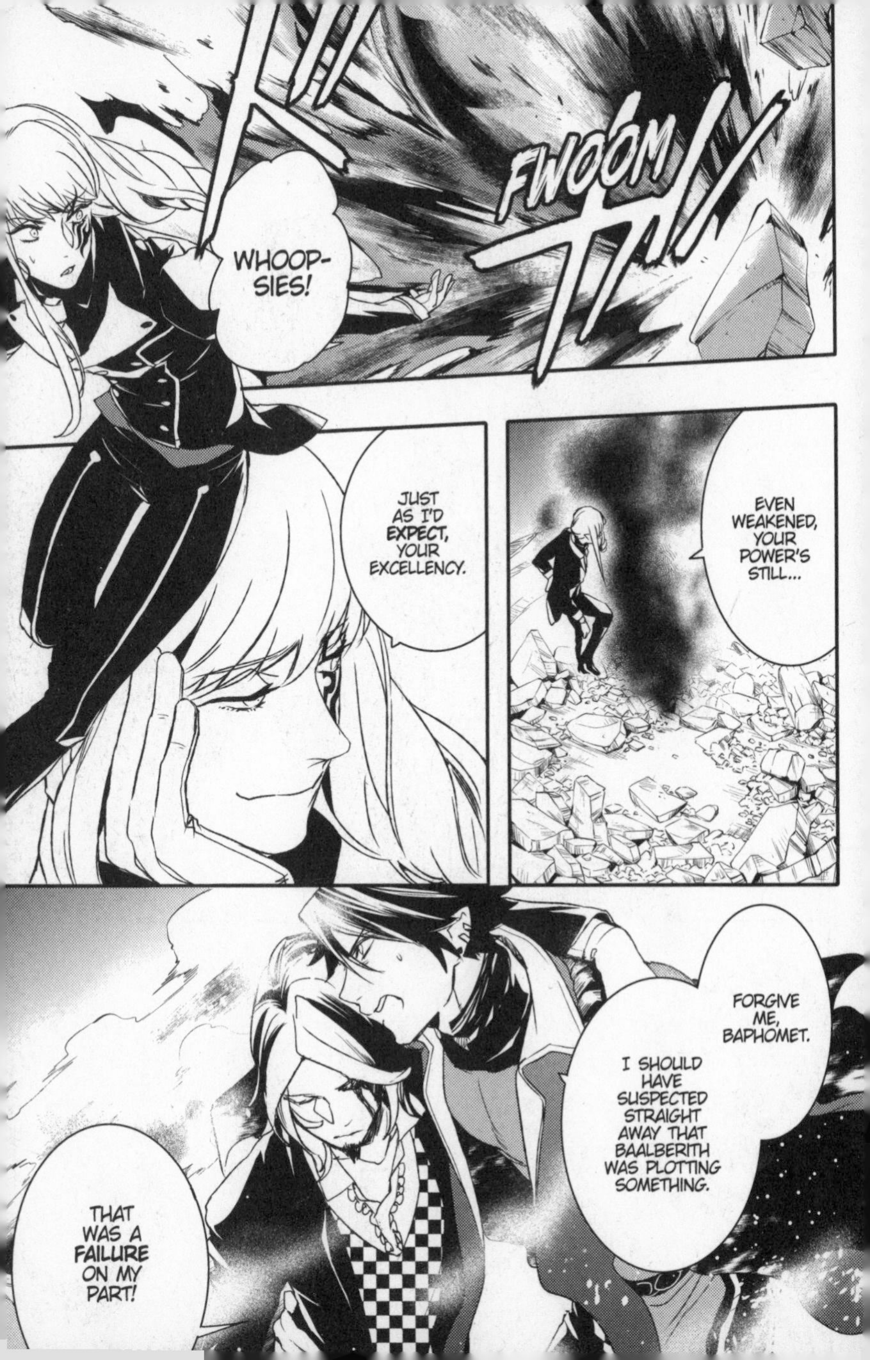
FWOOM
WHOOPSIES!
EVEN WEAKENED, YOUR POWER'S STILL...
JUST AS I'D EXPECT, YOUR EXCELLENCY.
FORGIVE ME, BAPHOMET.
I SHOULD HAVE SUSPECTED STRAIGHT AWAY THAT BAALBERITH WAS PLOTTING SOMETHING.
THAT WAS A FAILURE ON MY PART!

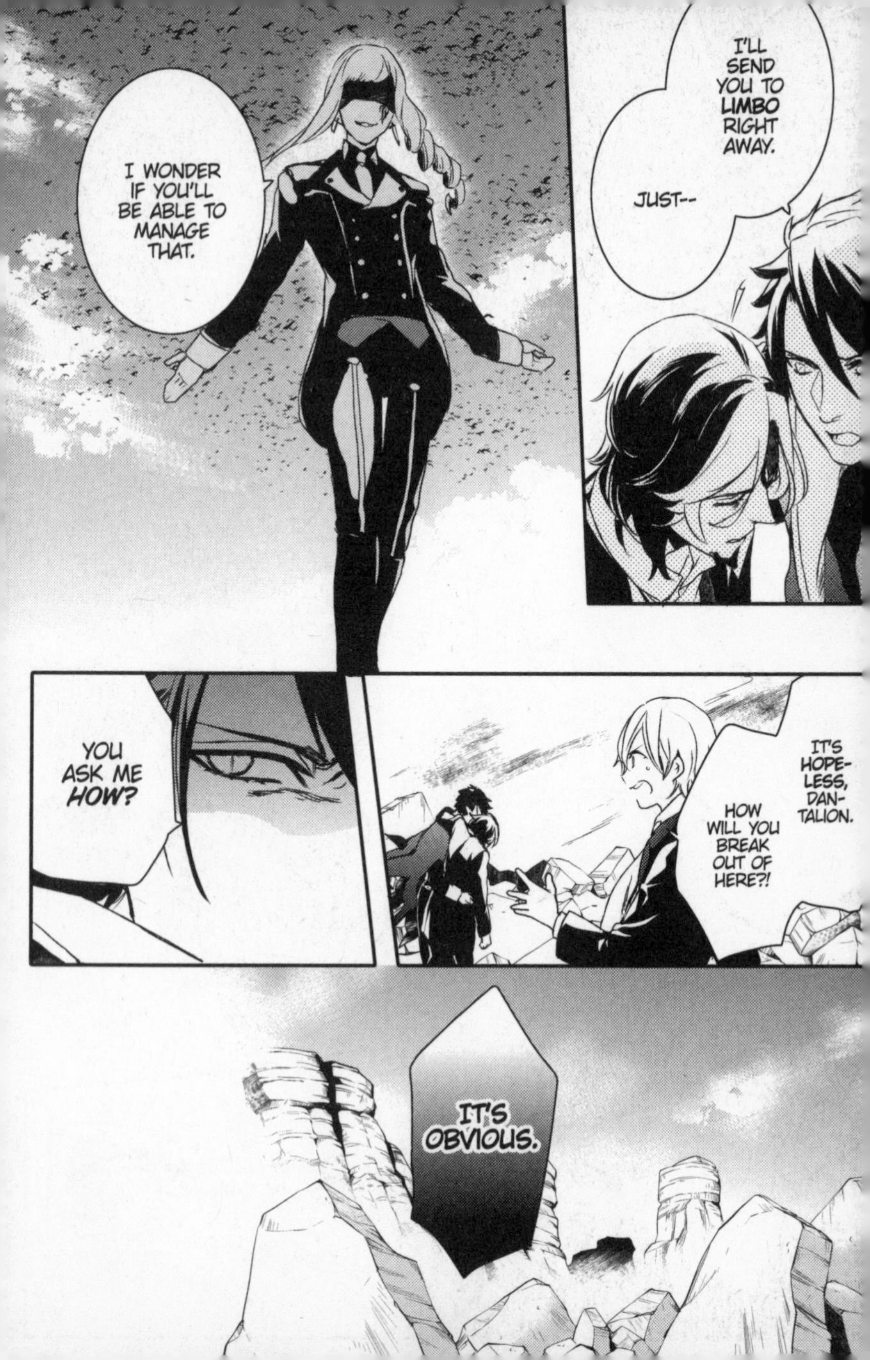
I'LL SEND YOU TO LIMBO RIGHT AWAY.
JUST--
I WONDER IF YOU'LL BE ABLE TO MANAGE THAT.
IT'S HOPE-LESS, DAN-TALION.
HOW WILL YOU BREAK OUT OF HERE?!
YOU ASK ME *HOW*?
IT'S OBVIOUS.

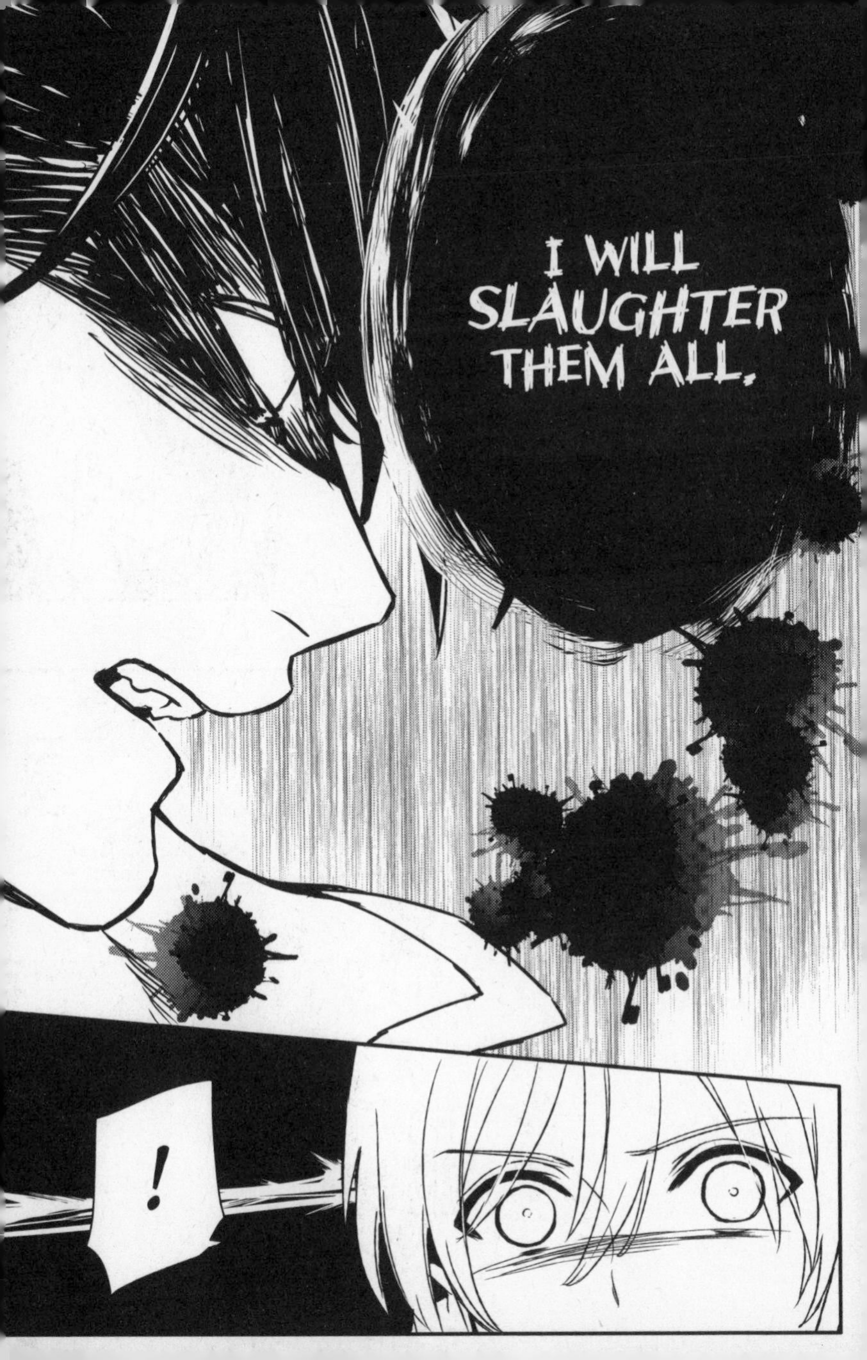
I WILL SLAUGHTER THEM ALL.
!

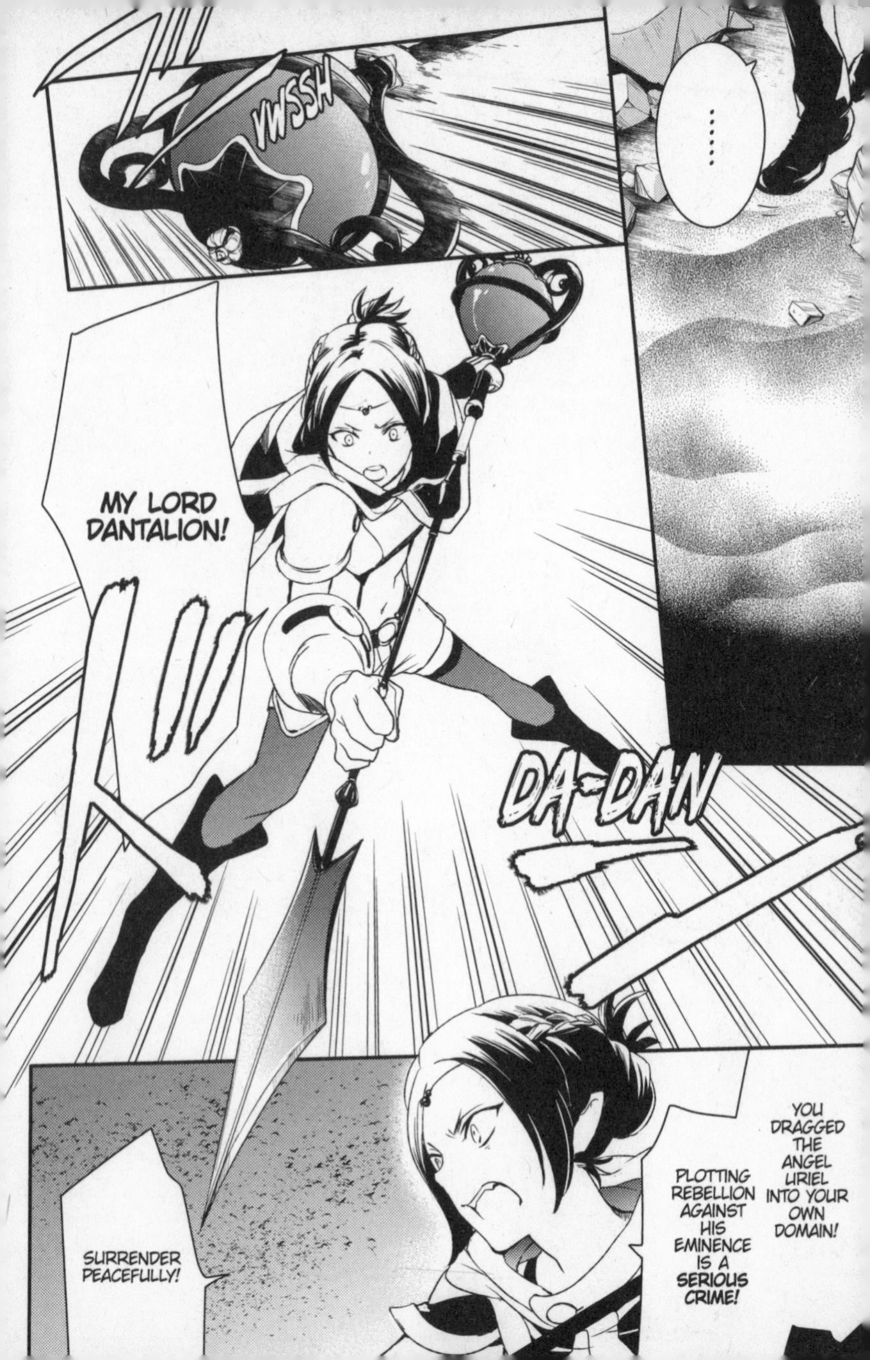
......
VWSSH
MY LORD DANTALION!
DA-DAN
YOU DRAGGED THE ANGEL URIEL INTO YOUR OWN DOMAIN!
PLOTTING REBELLION AGAINST HIS EMINENCE IS A SERIOUS CRIME!
SURRENDER PEACEFULLY!

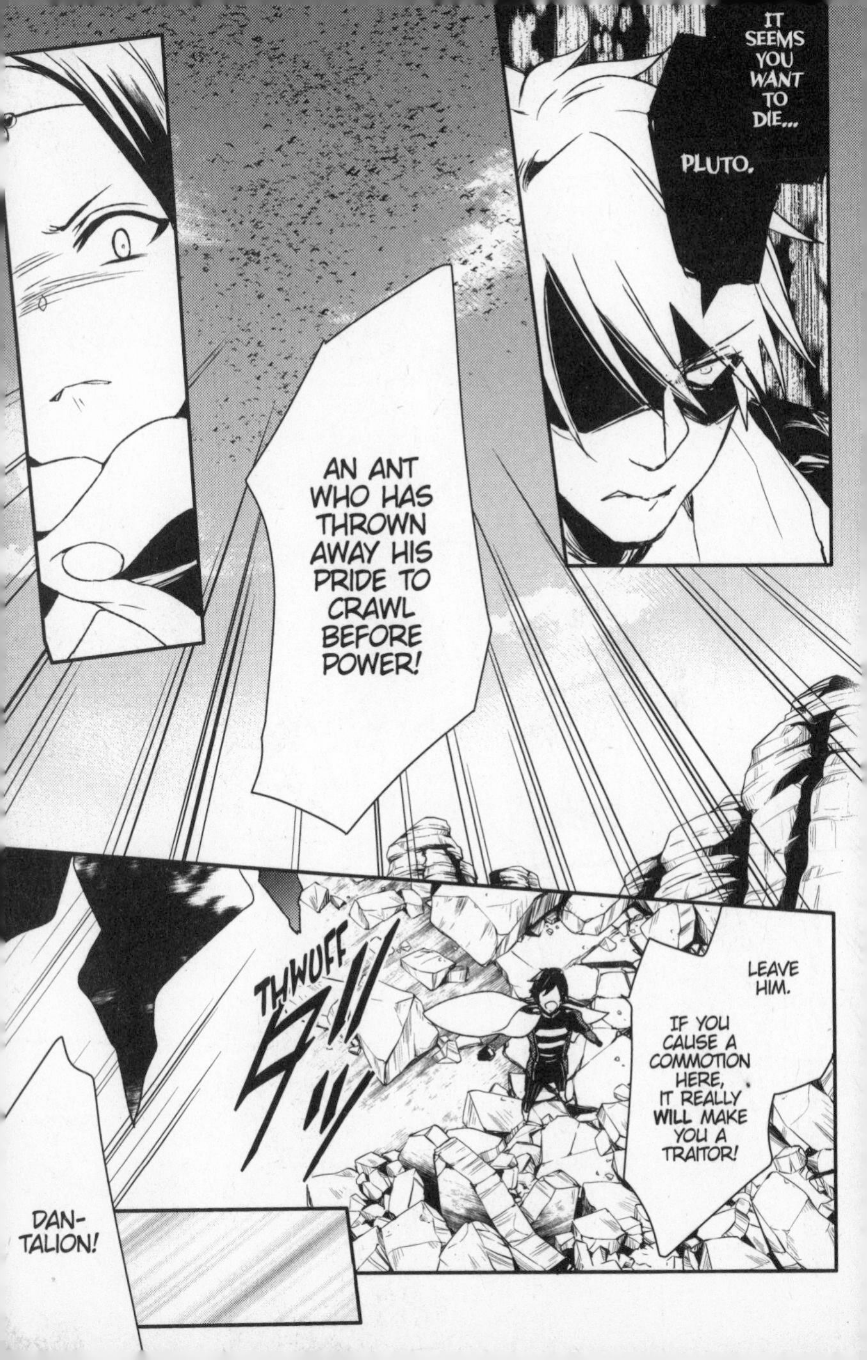
IT SEEMS YOU WANT TO DIE...
PLUTO.
AN ANT WHO HAS THROWN AWAY HIS PRIDE TO CRAWL BEFORE POWER!
LEAVE HIM.
IF YOU CAUSE A COMMOTION HERE, IT REALLY WILL MAKE YOU A TRAITOR!
THWUFF
DAN-TALION!

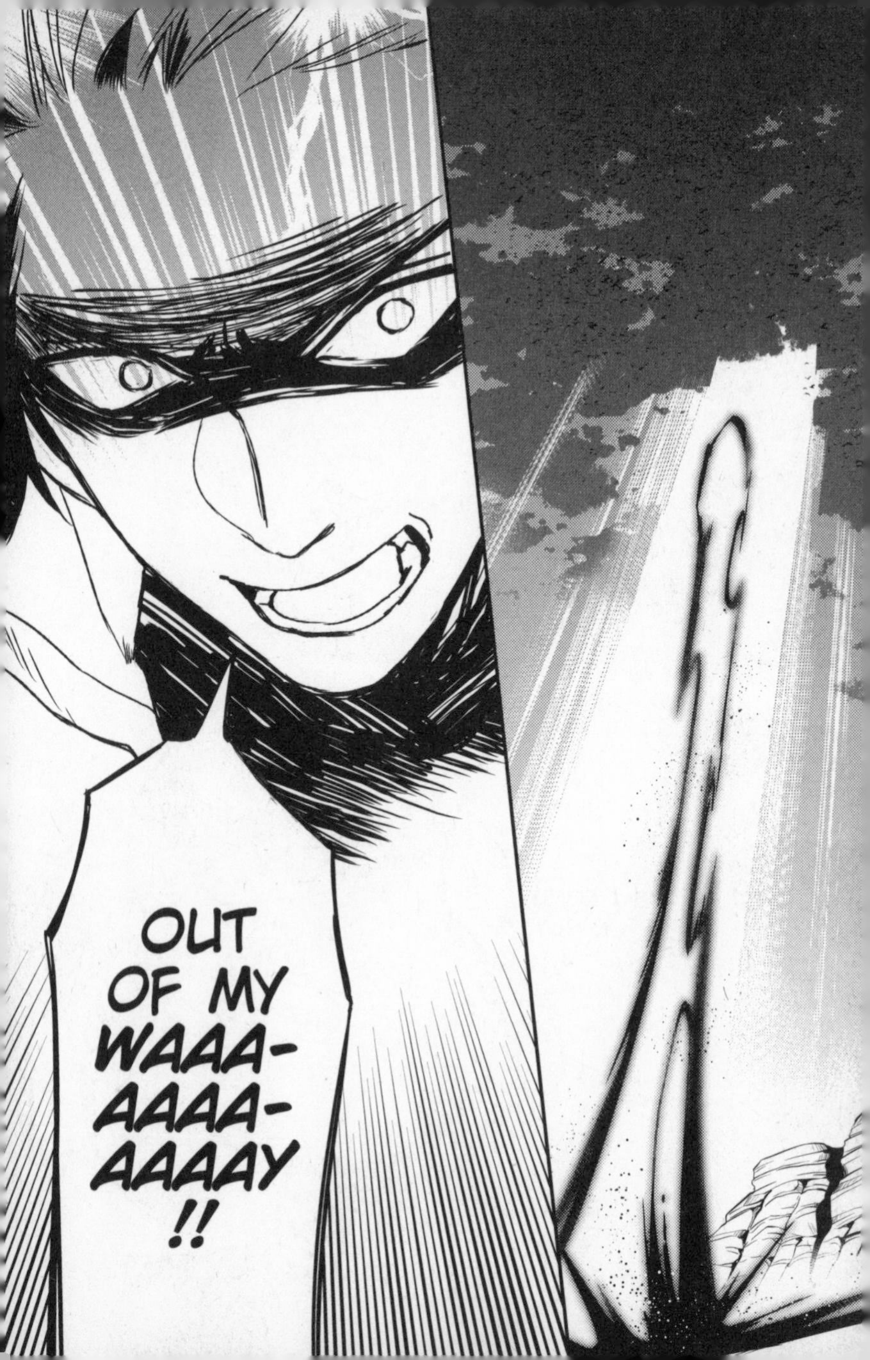
OUT OF MY WAAAA-AAAA-AAAAY !!

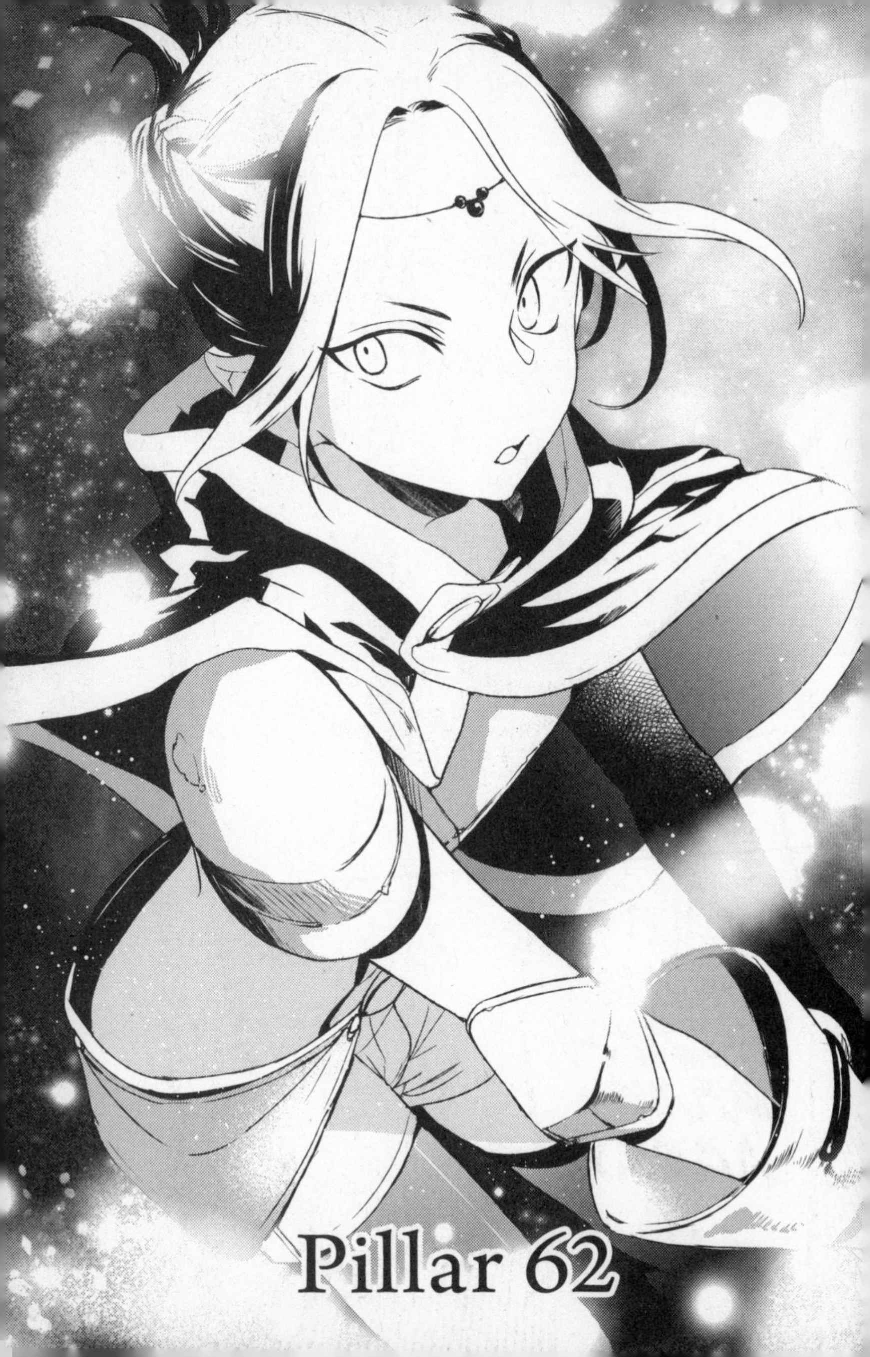
Pillar 62

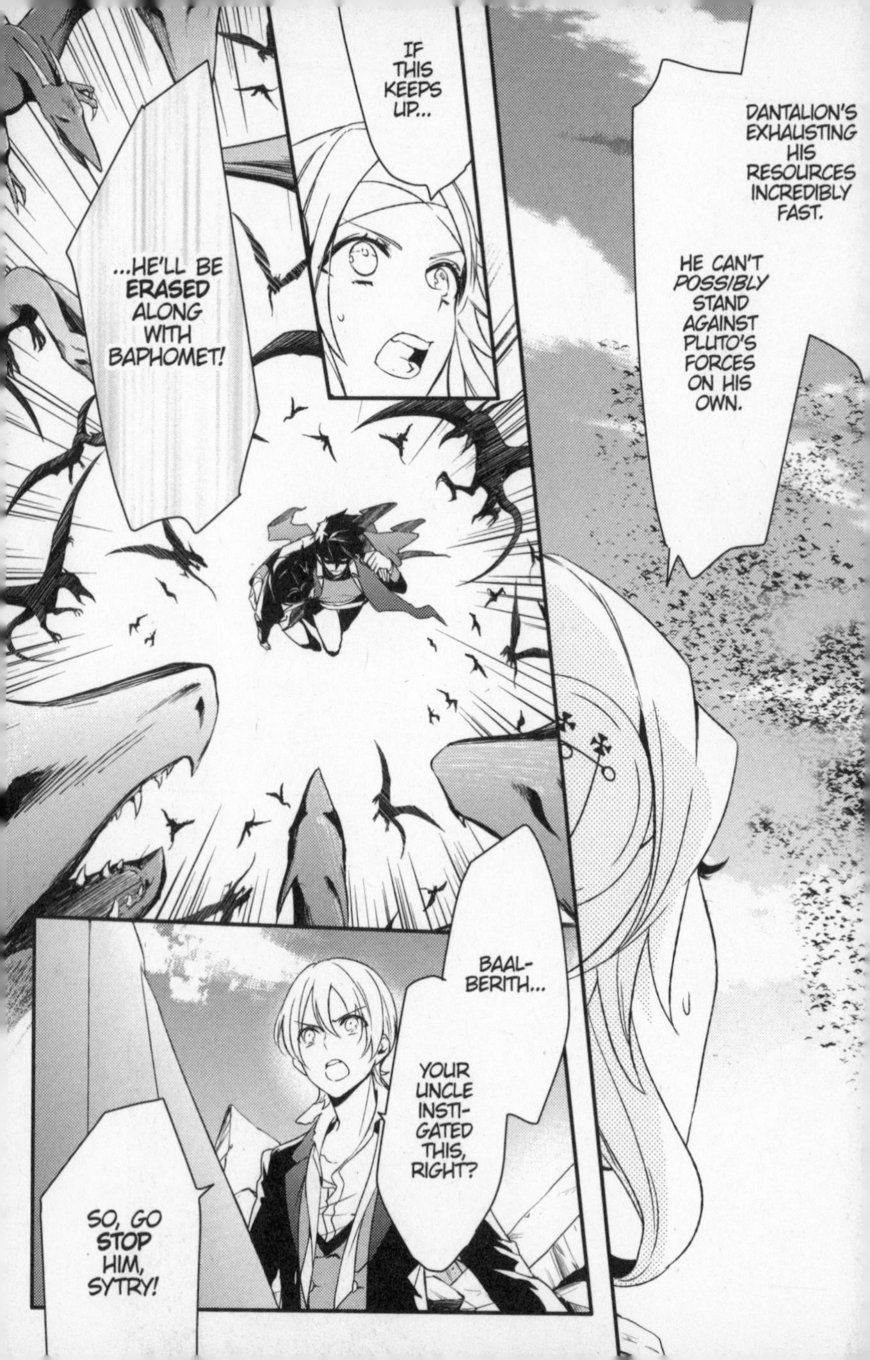
DANTALION'S EXHAUSTING HIS RESOURCES INCREDIBLY FAST.
HE CAN'T *POSSIBLY* STAND AGAINST PLUTO'S FORCES ON HIS OWN.
IF THIS KEEPS UP...
...HE'LL BE **ERASED** ALONG WITH BAPHOMET!
BAAL-BERITH...
YOUR UNCLE INSTIGATED THIS, RIGHT?
SO, GO STOP HIM, SYTRY!

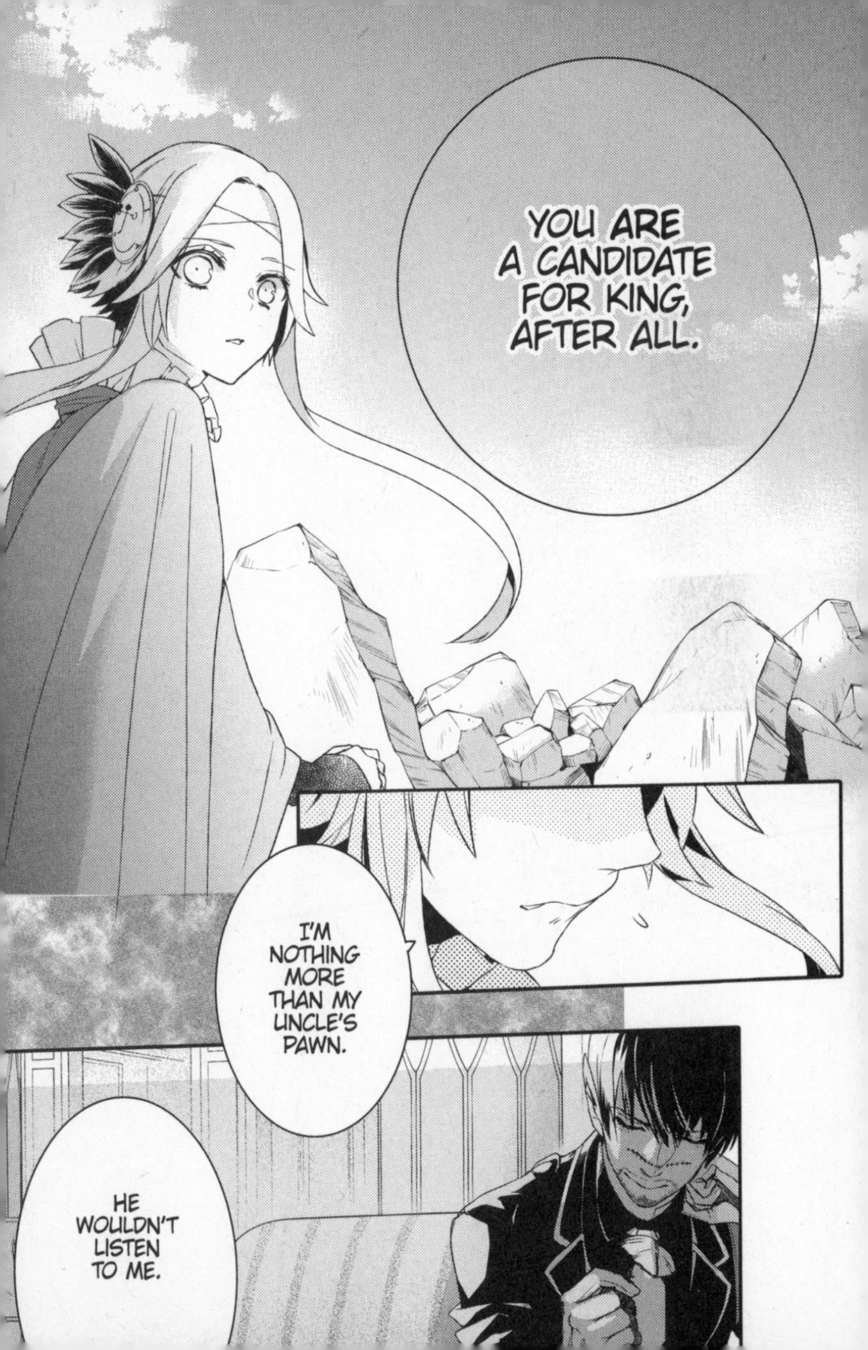
YOU ARE A CANDIDATE FOR KING, AFTER ALL.
I'M NOTHING MORE THAN MY UNCLE'S PAWN.
HE WOULDN'T LISTEN TO ME.

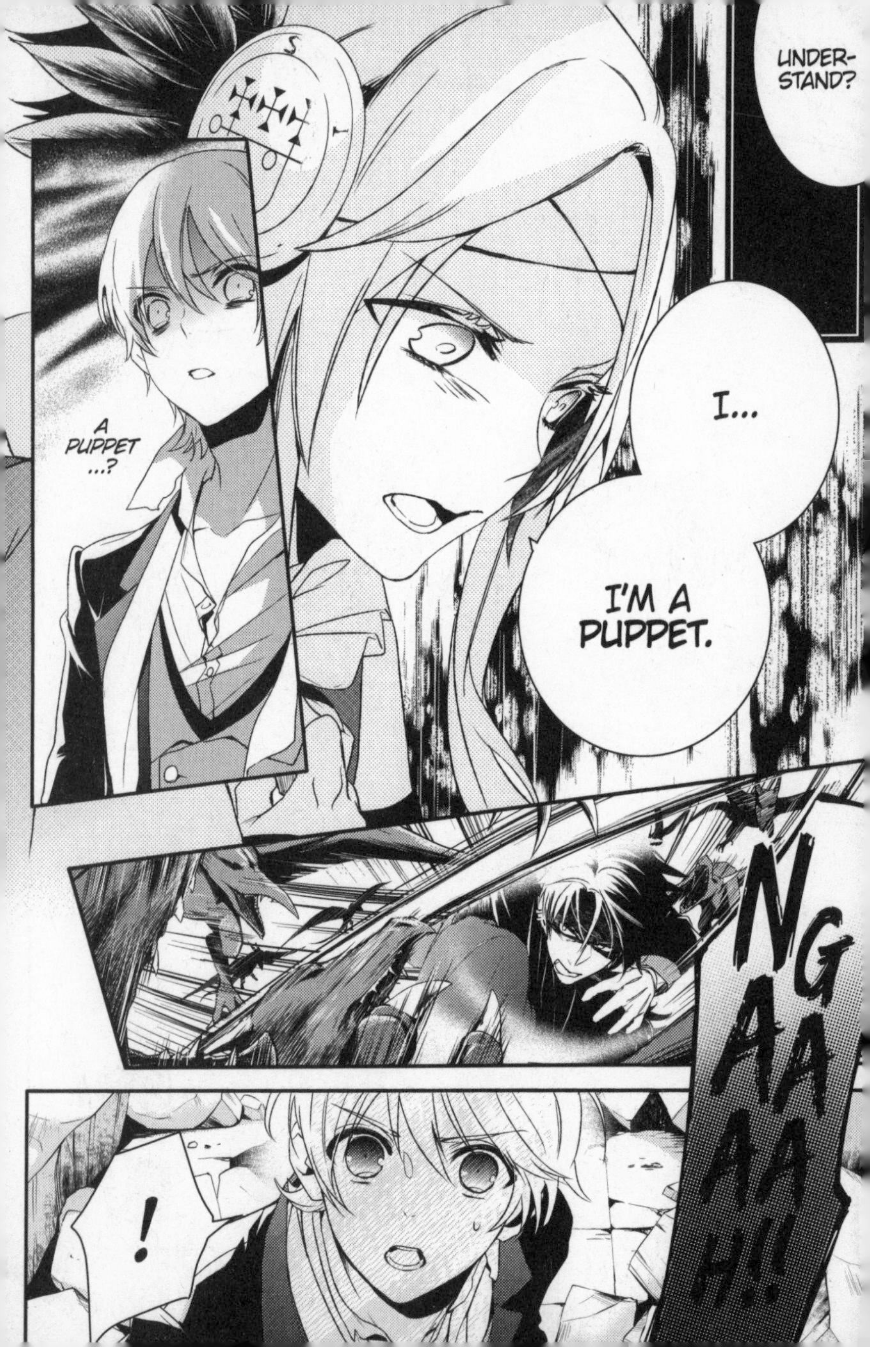
UNDER-STAND?
I...
I'M A PUPPET.
A PUPPET ...?
NGAAAAAH!!
!

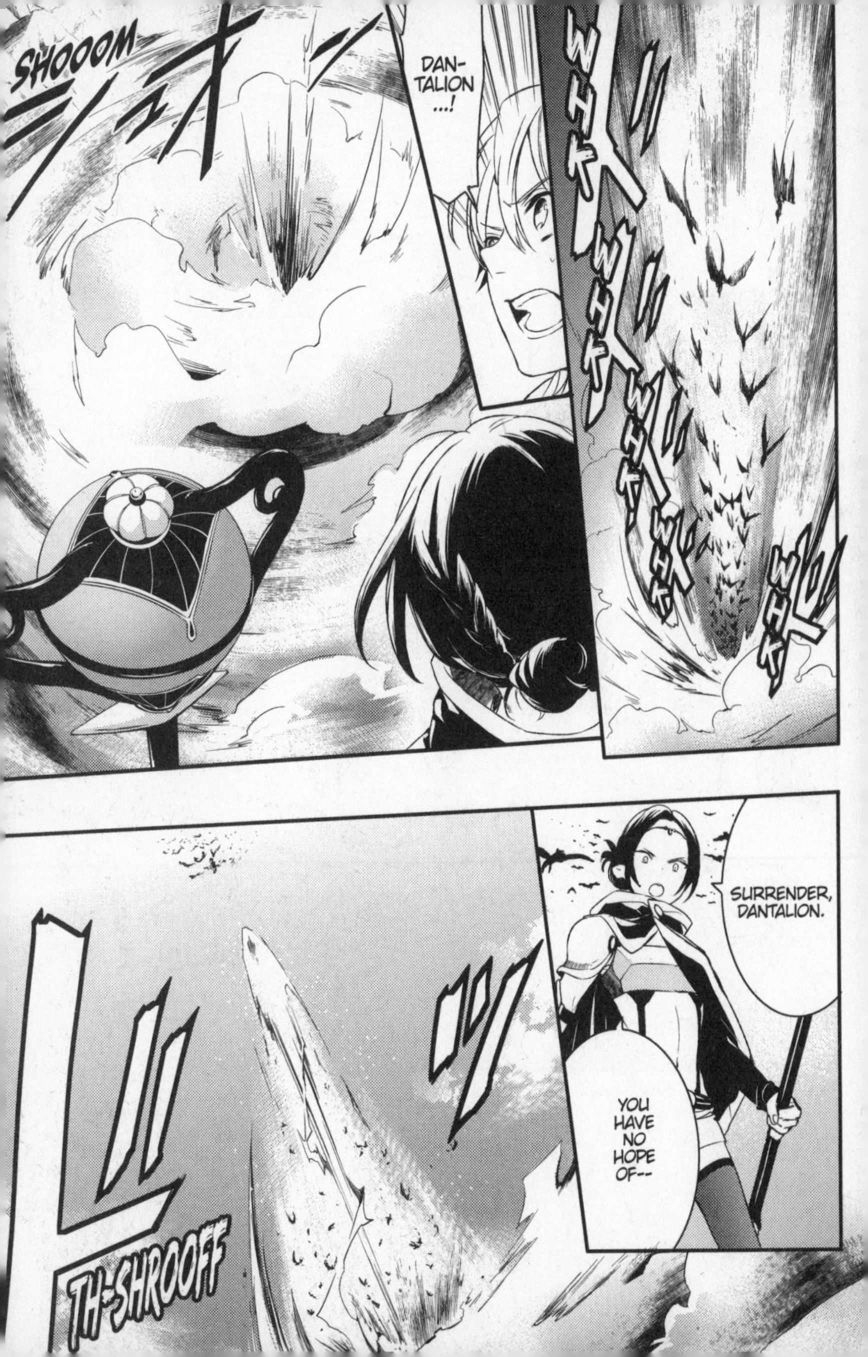
WHK
WHK
WHK
WHK
WHK
DAN-TALION ...!
SHOOOM
SURRENDER, DANTALION.
YOU HAVE NO HOPE OF--
TH-SHROOFF

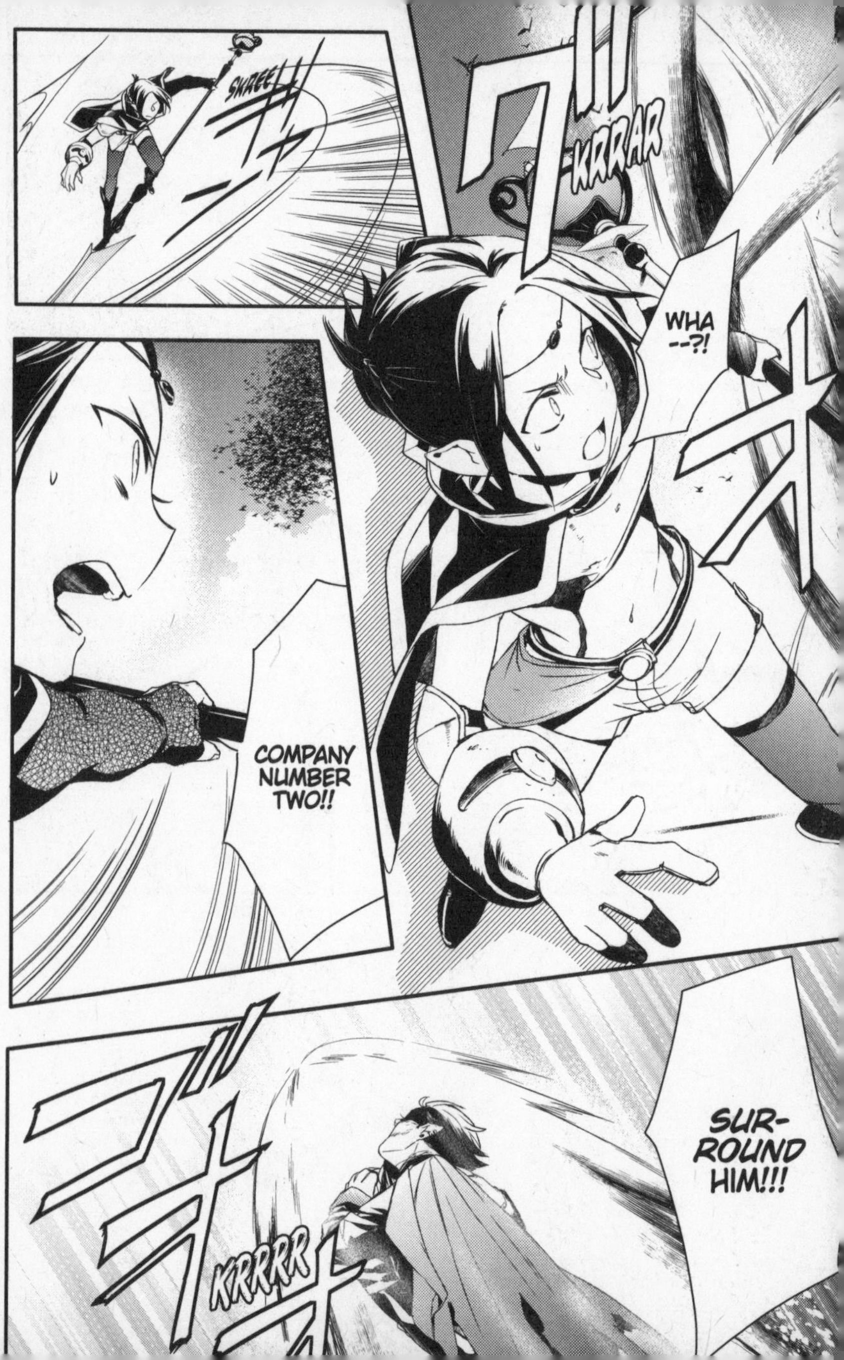
KRRAR
WHA--?!
SKREE
COMPANY NUMBER TWO!!
SUR-ROUND HIM!!!
KRRRR

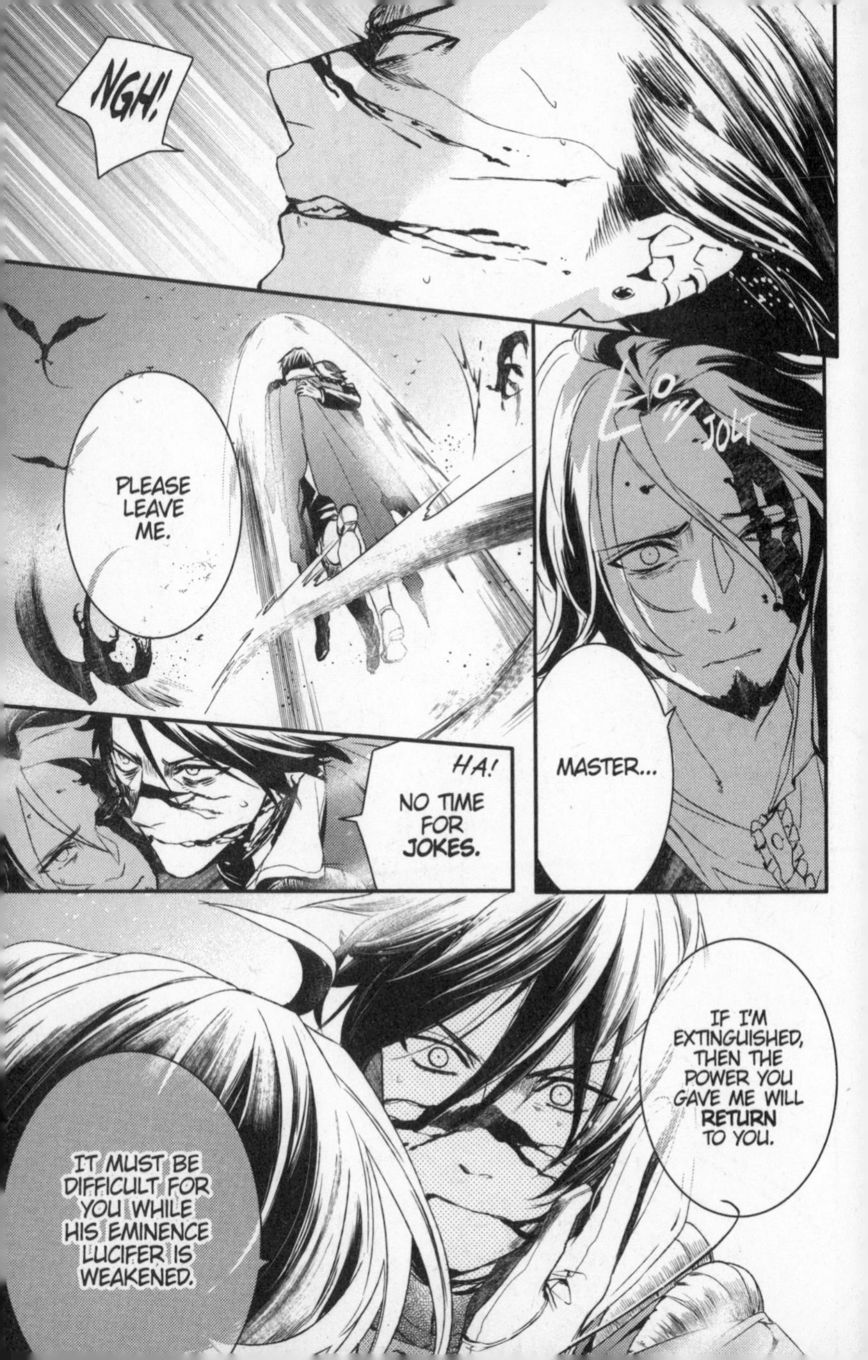
NGH!
JOLT
MASTER...
PLEASE LEAVE ME.
HA! NO TIME FOR JOKES.
IF I'M EXTINGUISHED, THEN THE POWER YOU GAVE ME WILL RETURN TO YOU.
IT MUST BE DIFFICULT FOR YOU WHILE HIS EMINENCE LUCIFER IS WEAKENED.

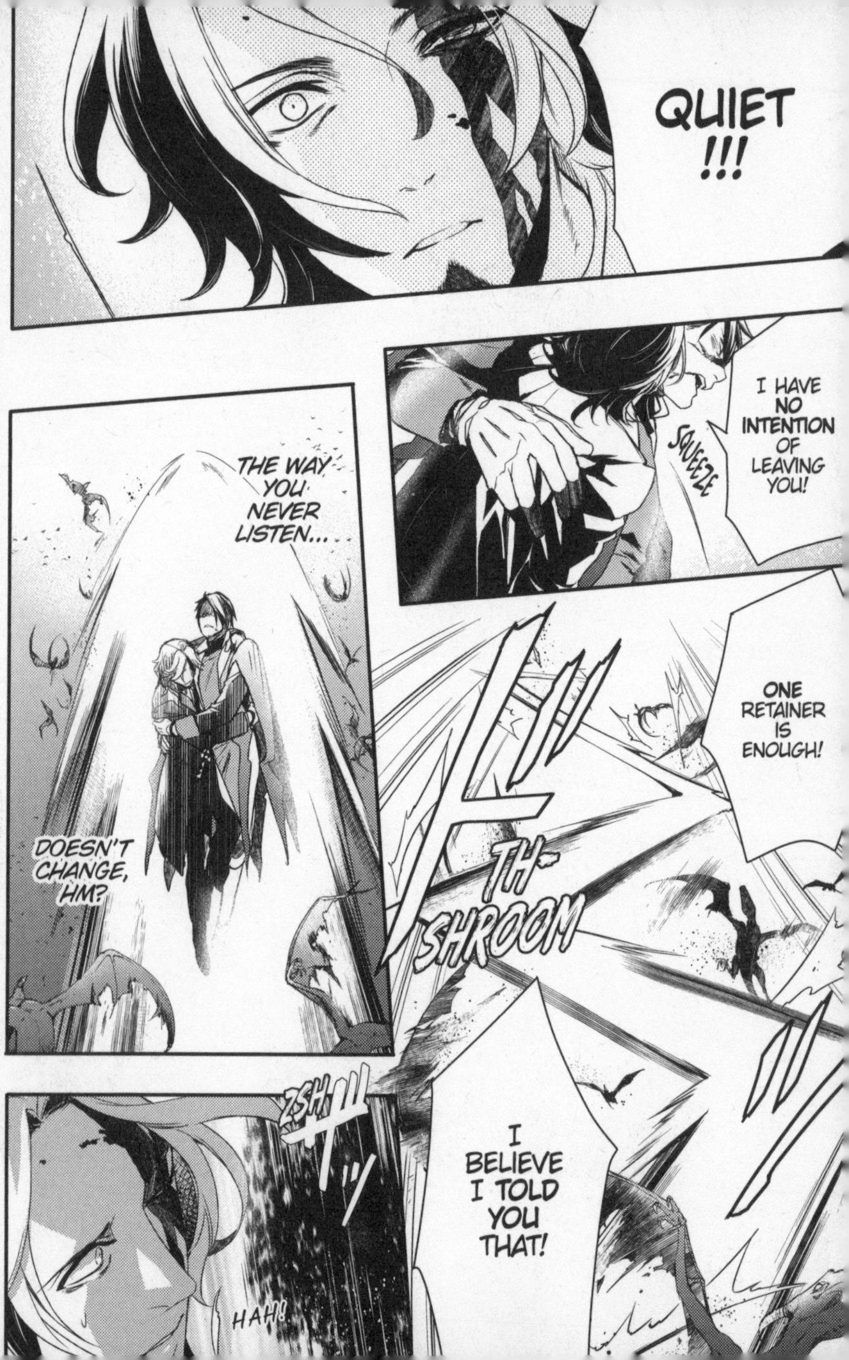
QUIET !!!
I HAVE NO INTENTION OF LEAVING YOU!
SQUEEZE
ONE RETAINER IS ENOUGH!
TH-SHROOM
I BELIEVE I TOLD YOU THAT!
THE WAY YOU NEVER LISTEN...
DOESN'T CHANGE, HM?
ZSH
HAH!

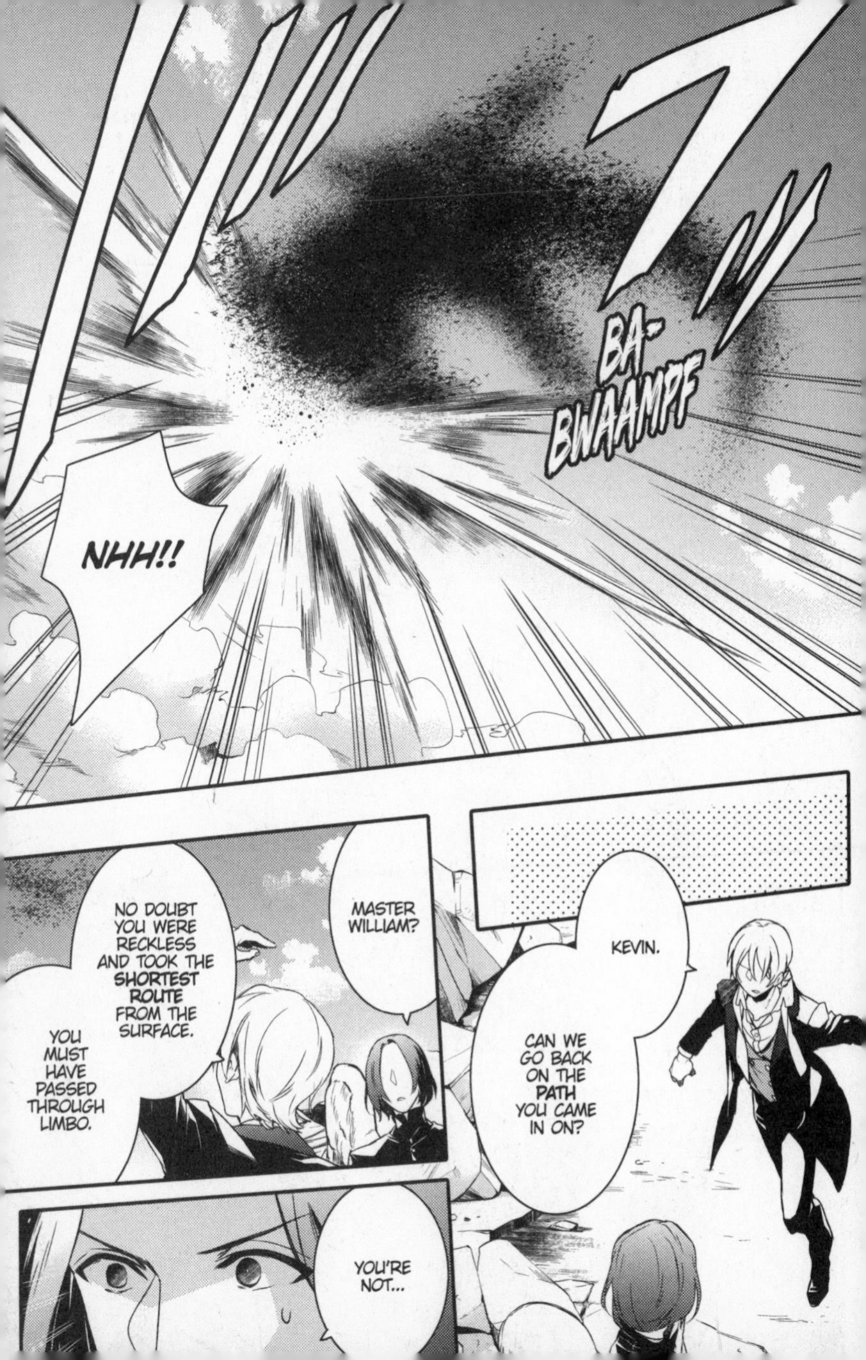
BA-BWAAMPF
NHH!!
KEVIN.
CAN WE GO BACK ON THE PATH YOU CAME IN ON?
MASTER WILLIAM?
NO DOUBT YOU WERE RECKLESS AND TOOK THE SHORTEST ROUTE FROM THE SURFACE.
YOU MUST HAVE PASSED THROUGH LIMBO.
YOU'RE NOT...

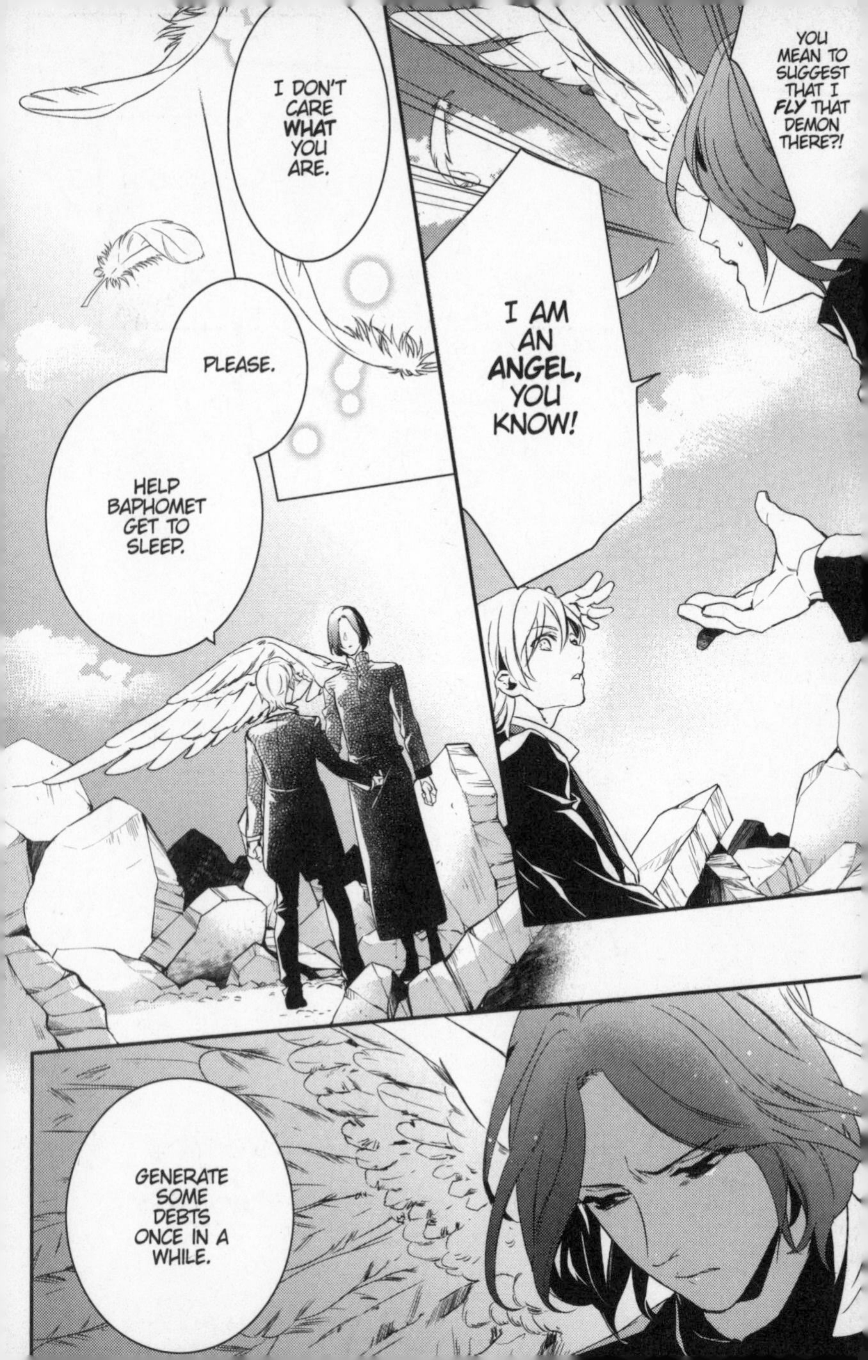
YOU MEAN TO SUGGEST THAT I FLY THAT DEMON THERE?!
I AM AN ANGEL, YOU KNOW!
I DON'T CARE WHAT YOU ARE.
PLEASE.
HELP BAPHOMET GET TO SLEEP.
GENERATE SOME DEBTS ONCE IN A WHILE.

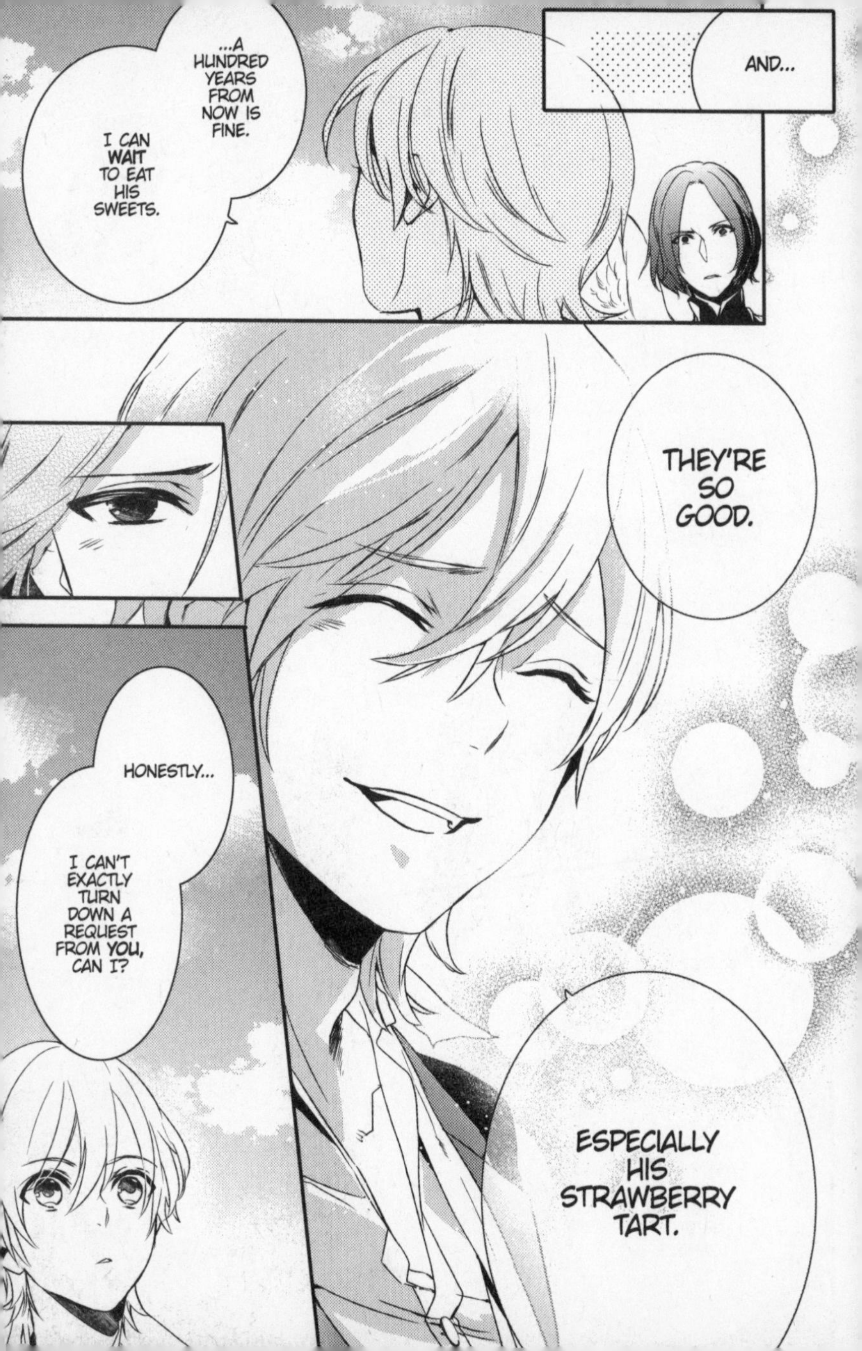
AND...
...A HUNDRED YEARS FROM NOW IS FINE.
I CAN WAIT TO EAT HIS SWEETS.
THEY'RE SO GOOD.
ESPECIALLY HIS STRAWBERRY TART.
HONESTLY...
I CAN'T EXACTLY TURN DOWN A REQUEST FROM YOU, CAN I?

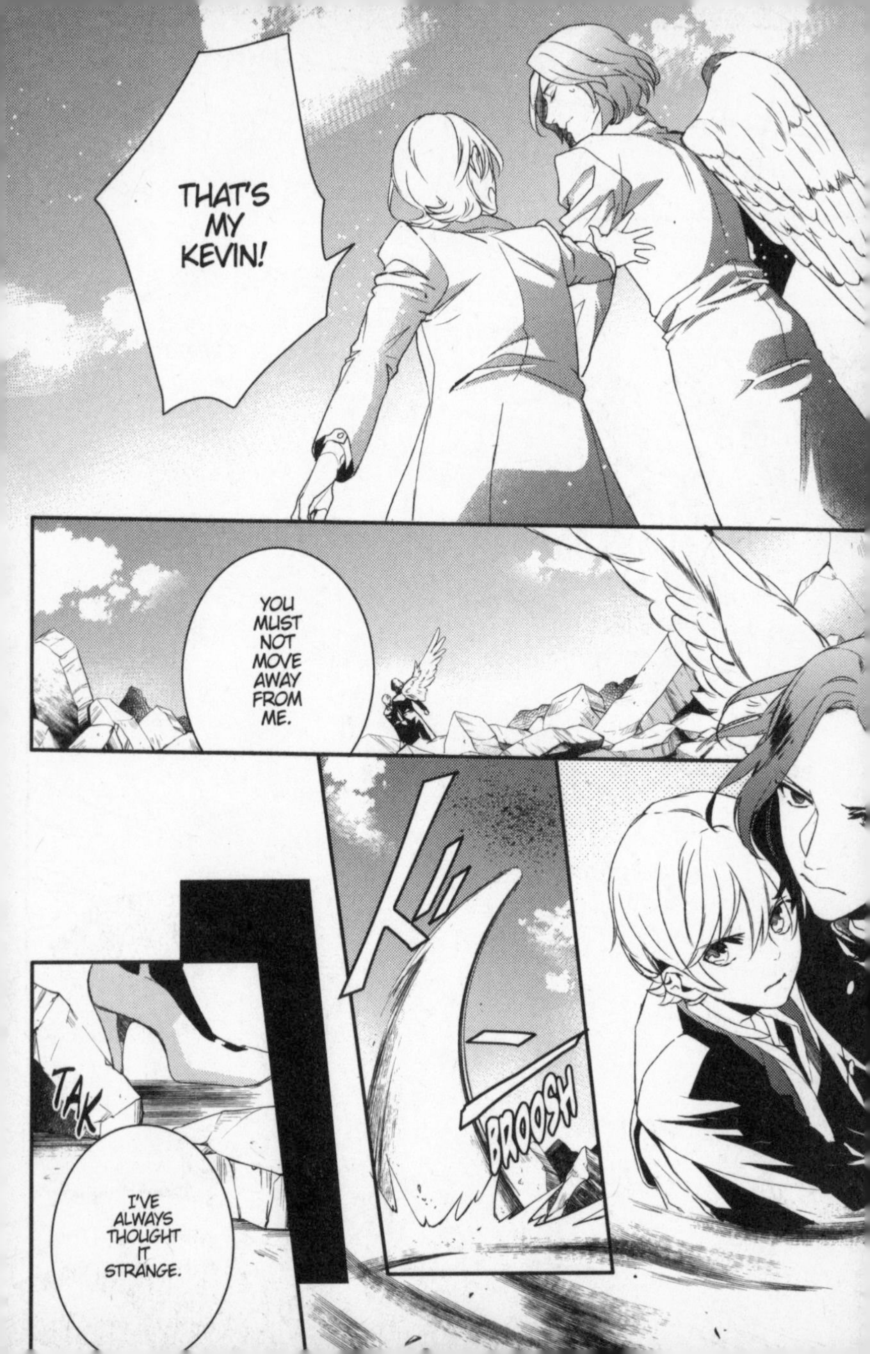
THAT'S MY KEVIN!
YOU MUST NOT MOVE AWAY FROM ME.
KI
BROOSH
TAK
I'VE ALWAYS THOUGHT IT STRANGE.

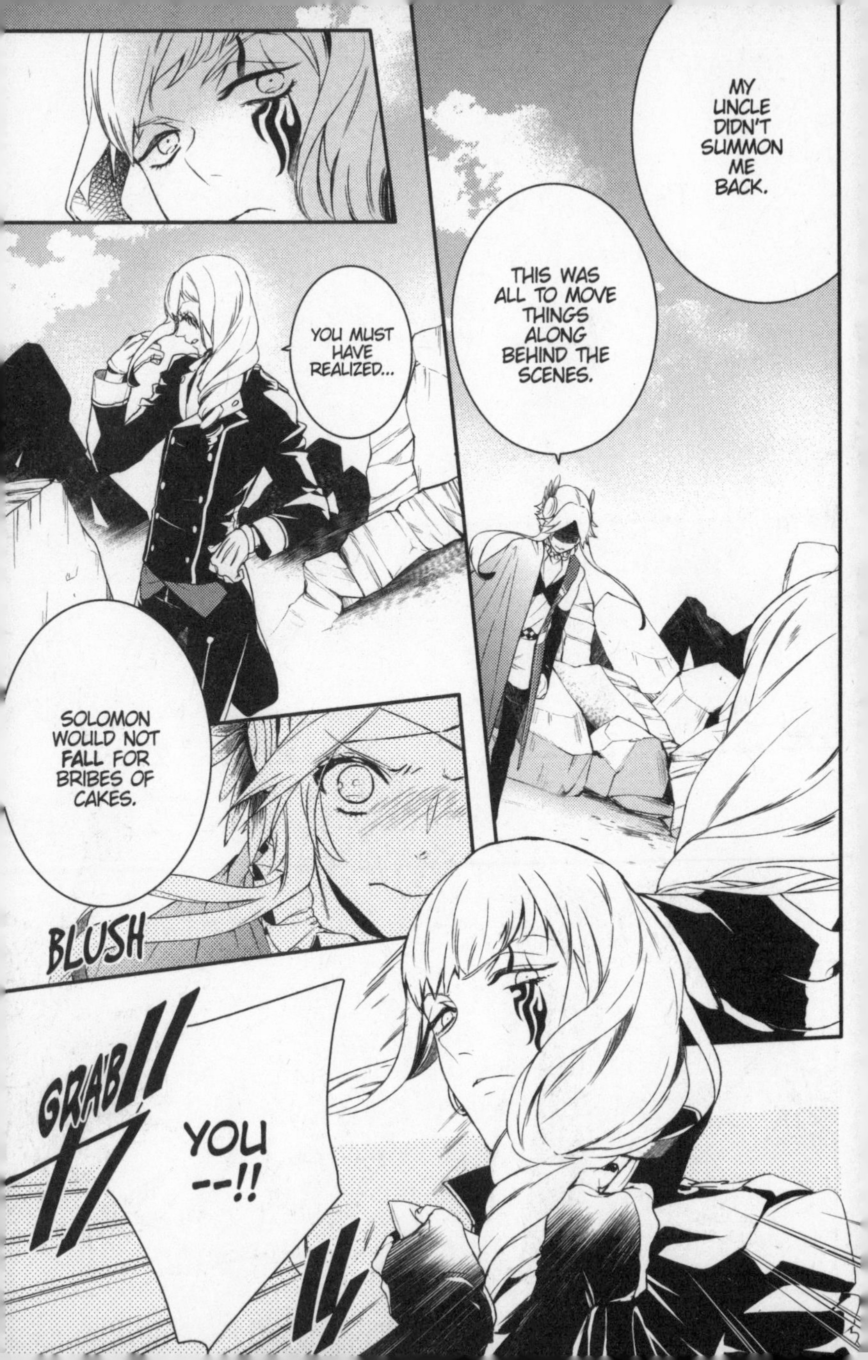
MY UNCLE DIDN'T SUMMON ME BACK.
THIS WAS ALL TO MOVE THINGS ALONG BEHIND THE SCENES.
YOU MUST HAVE REALIZED...
SOLOMON WOULD NOT FALL FOR BRIBES OF CAKES.
BLUSH
GRAB!!
YOU --!!

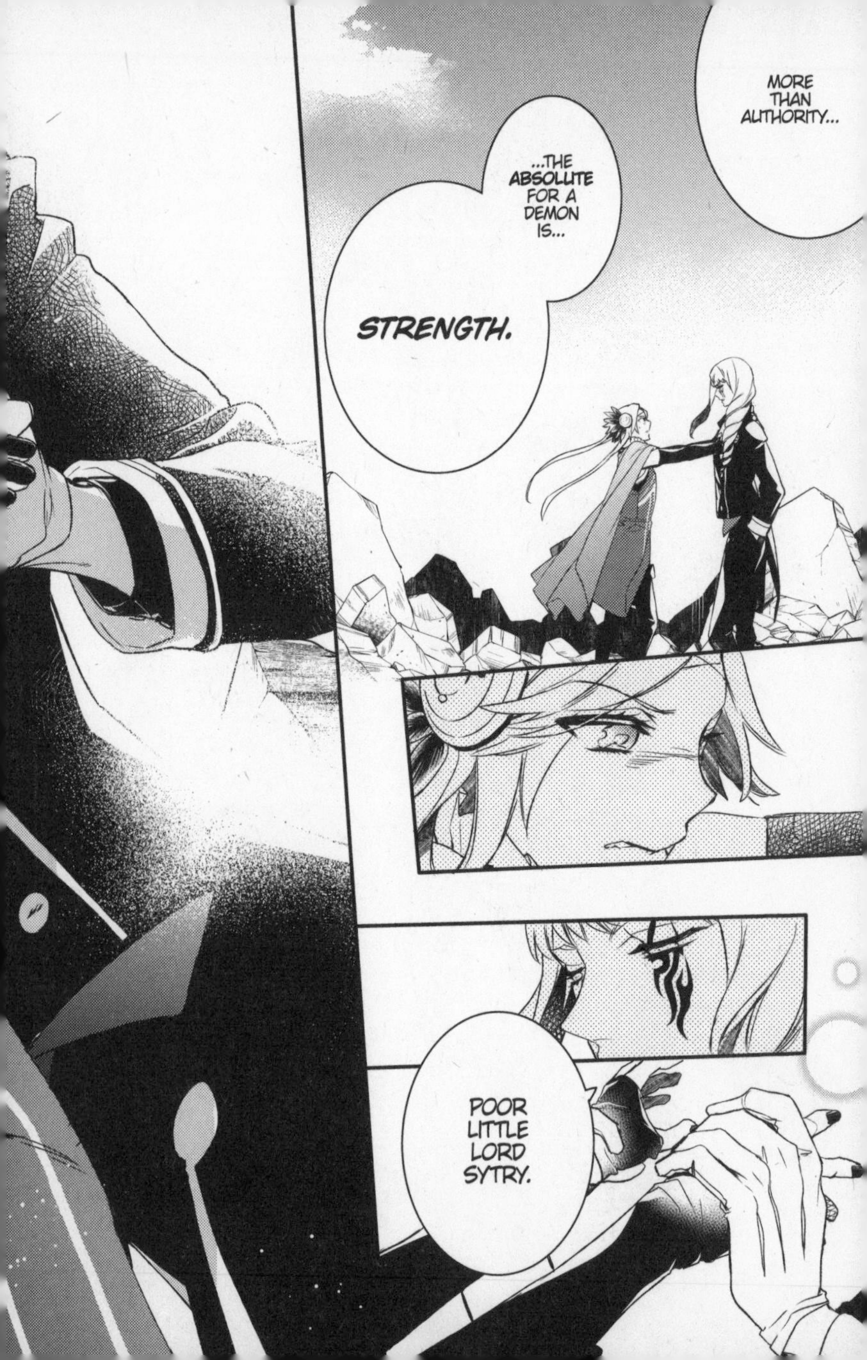
MORE THAN AUTHORITY...
...THE ABSOLUTE FOR A DEMON IS...
STRENGTH.
POOR LITTLE LORD SYTRY.

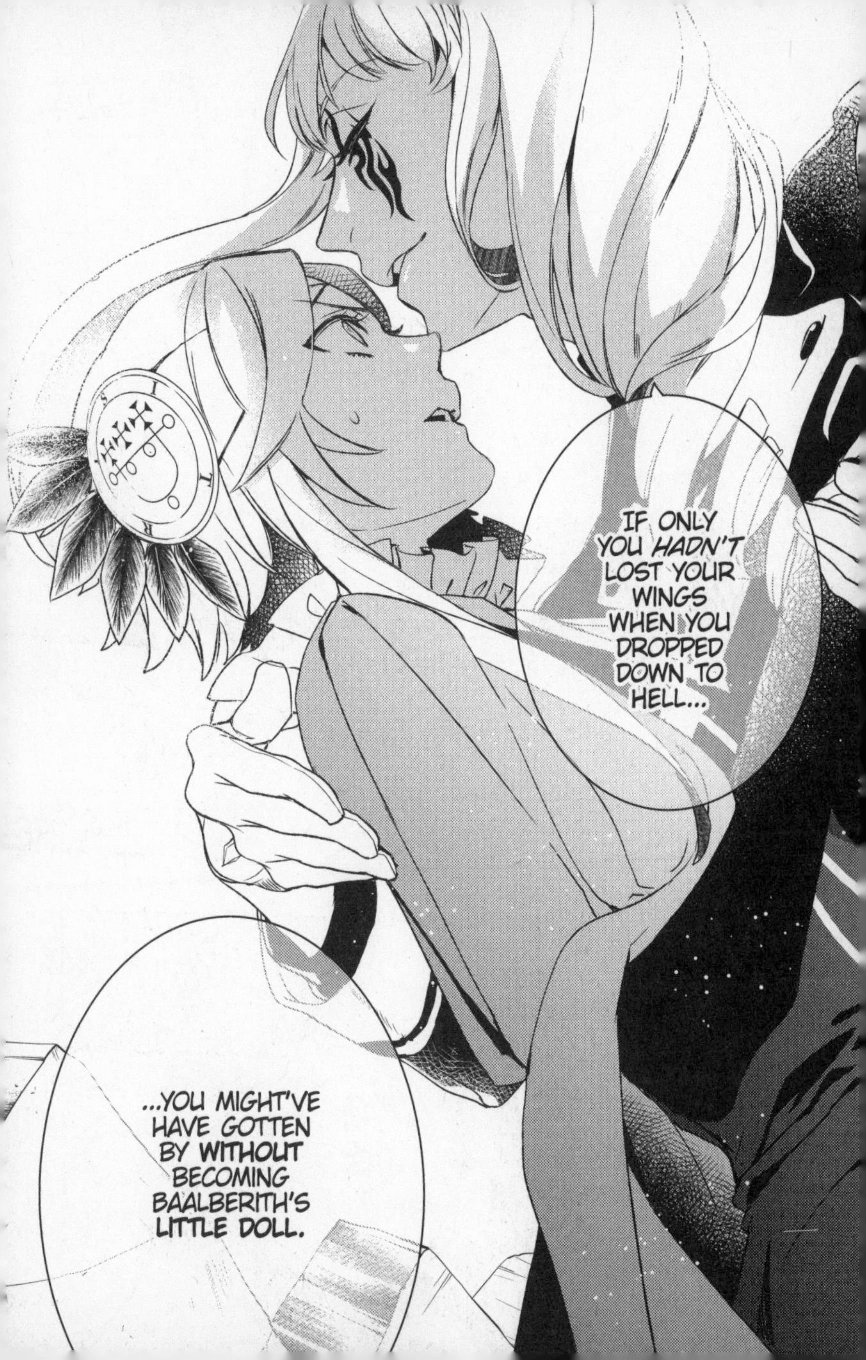
IF ONLY YOU *HADN'T* LOST YOUR WINGS WHEN YOU DROPPED DOWN TO HELL...
...YOU MIGHT'VE HAVE GOTTEN BY WITHOUT BECOMING BAALBERITH'S LITTLE DOLL.

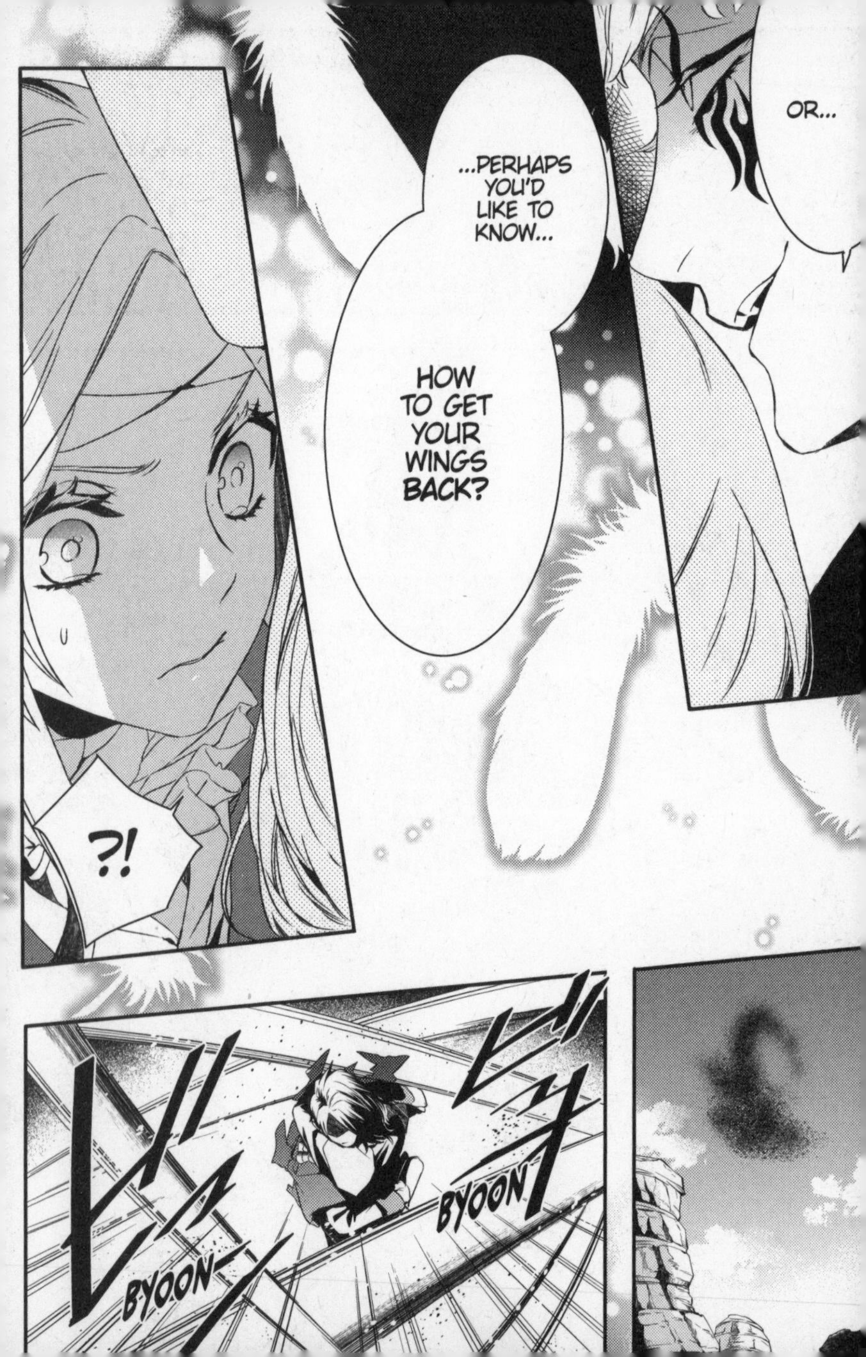
OR...
...PERHAPS YOU'D LIKE TO KNOW...
HOW TO GET YOUR WINGS BACK?
?!
BYOON
BYOON

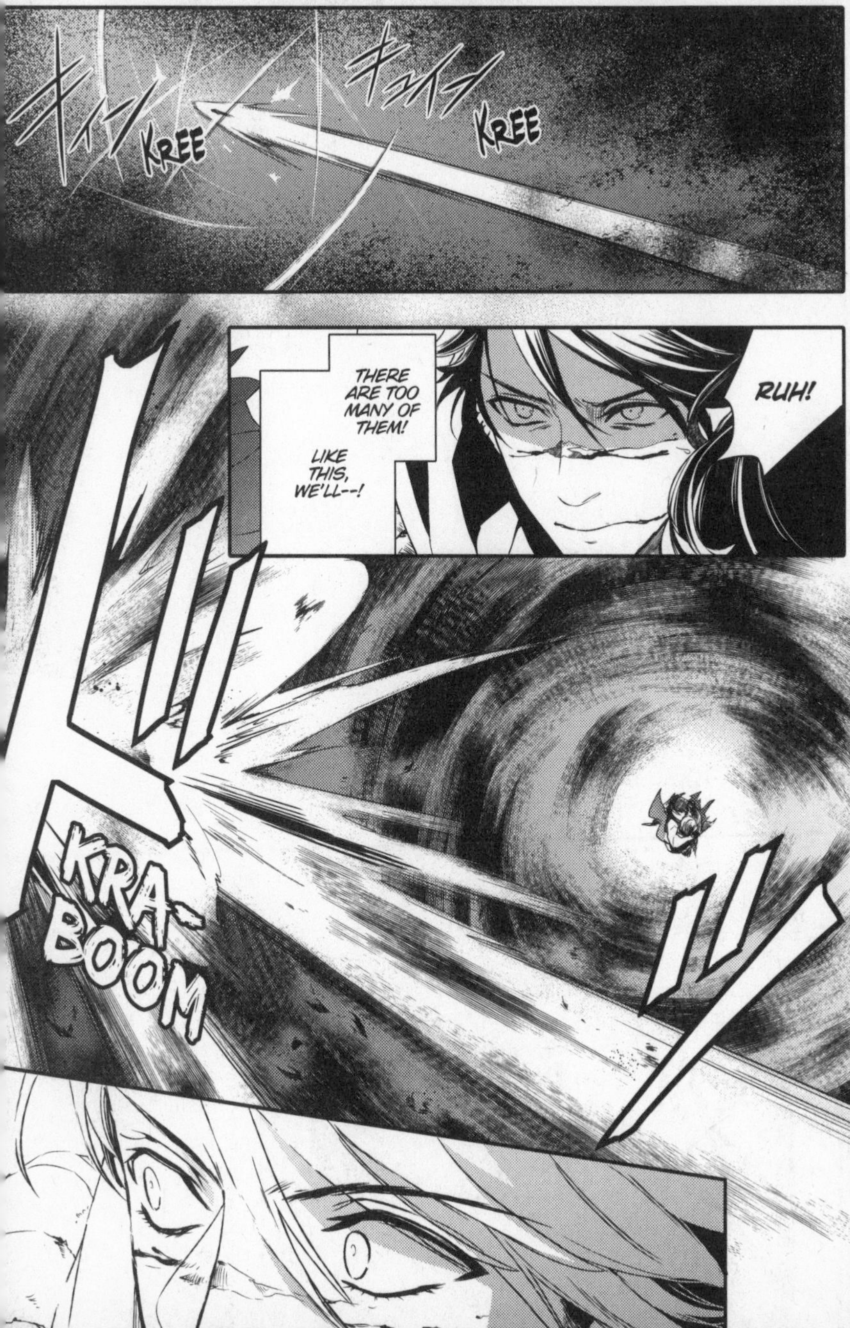
KREE
KREE
RUH!
THERE ARE TOO MANY OF THEM!
LIKE THIS, WE'LL--!
KRA-BOOM

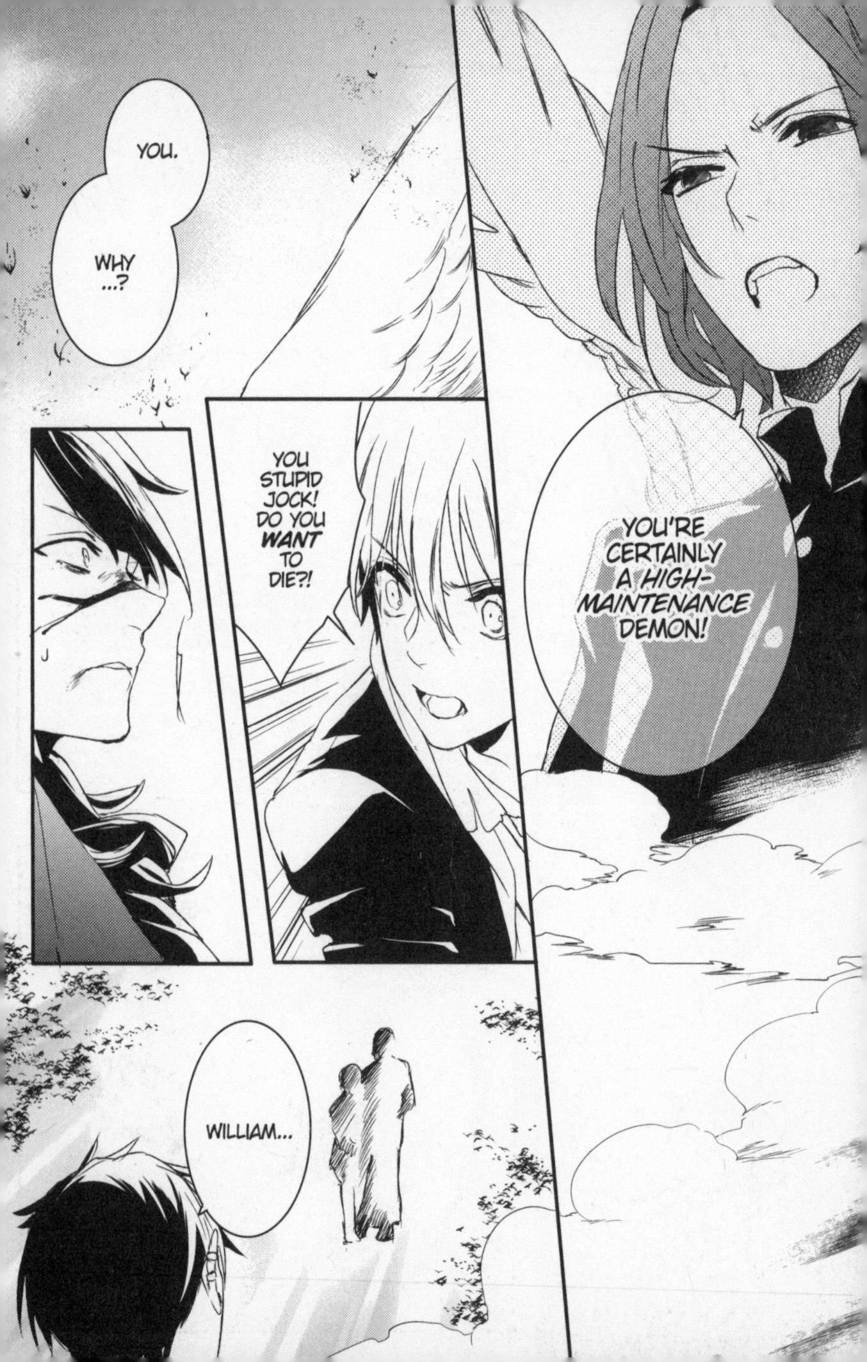
YOU'RE CERTAINLY A HIGH-MAINTENANCE DEMON!
YOU.
WHY ...?
YOU STUPID JOCK! DO YOU WANT TO DIE?!
WILLIAM...

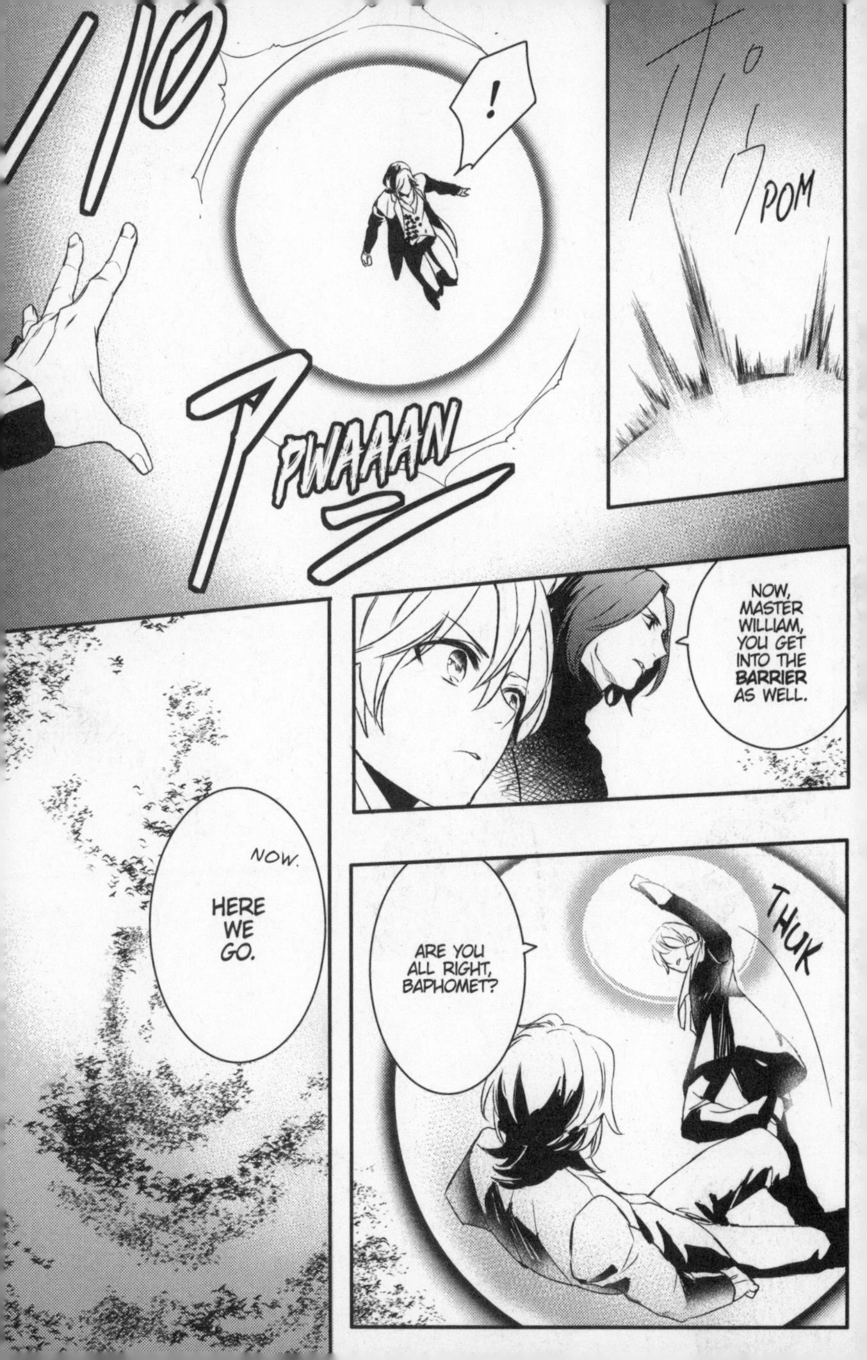
POM
!
PWAAAN
NOW, MASTER WILLIAM, YOU GET INTO THE BARRIER AS WELL.
THUK
ARE YOU ALL RIGHT, BAPHOMET?
NOW.
HERE WE GO.

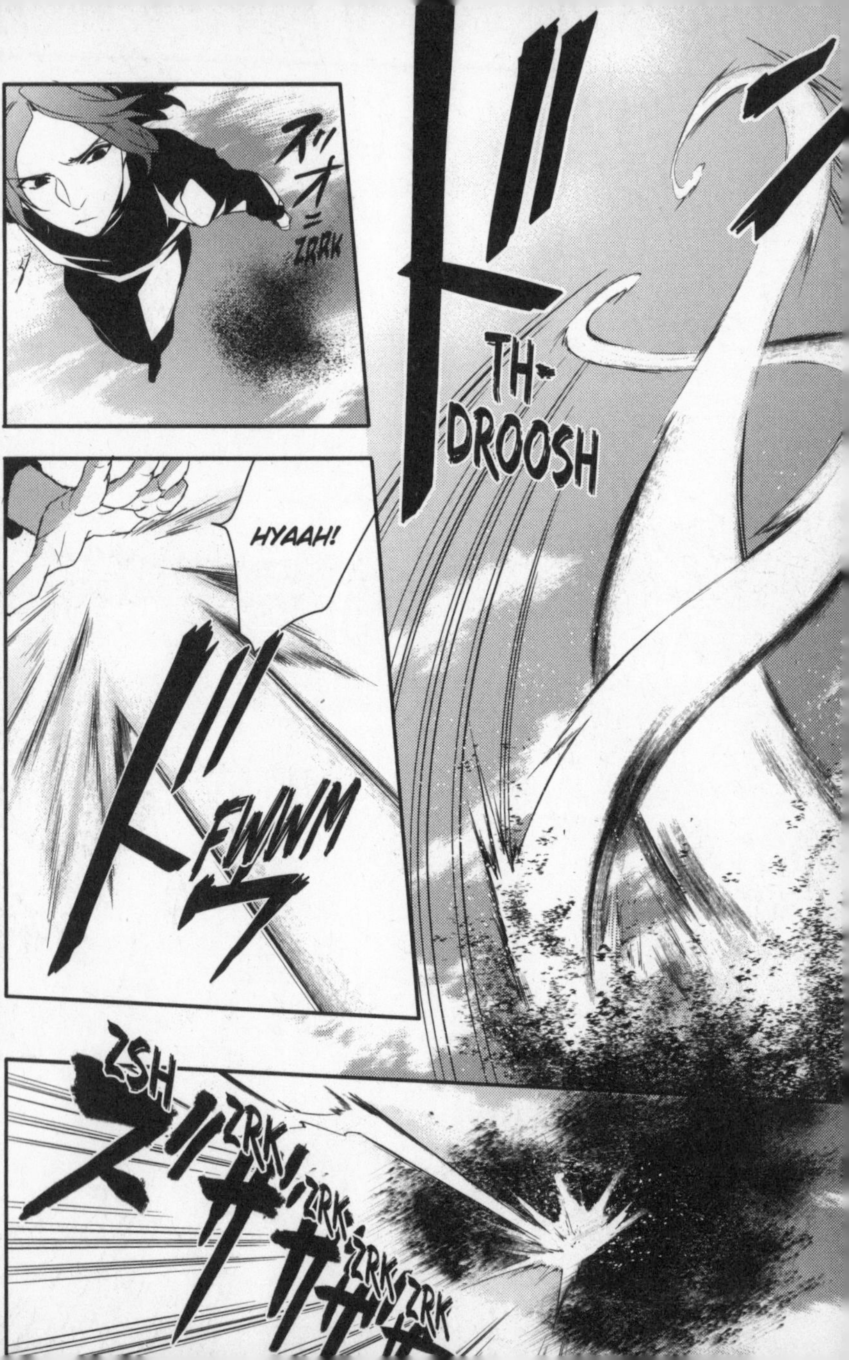
TH-DROOSH
ZRRK
HYAAH!
FWUM
ZSH
ZRK
ZRK
ZRK
ZRK

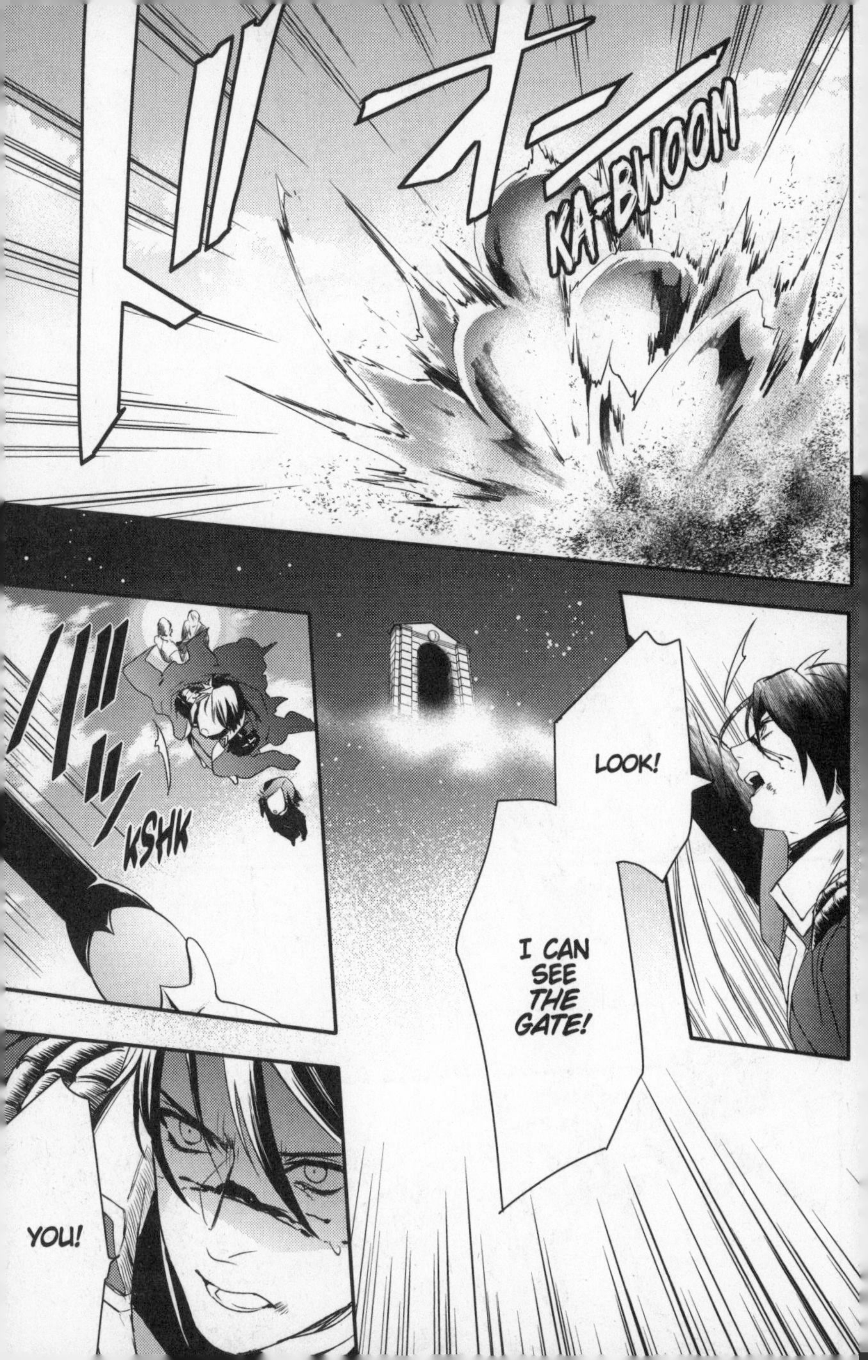
KA-BWOOM
LOOK!
I CAN SEE THE GATE!
KSHK
YOU!

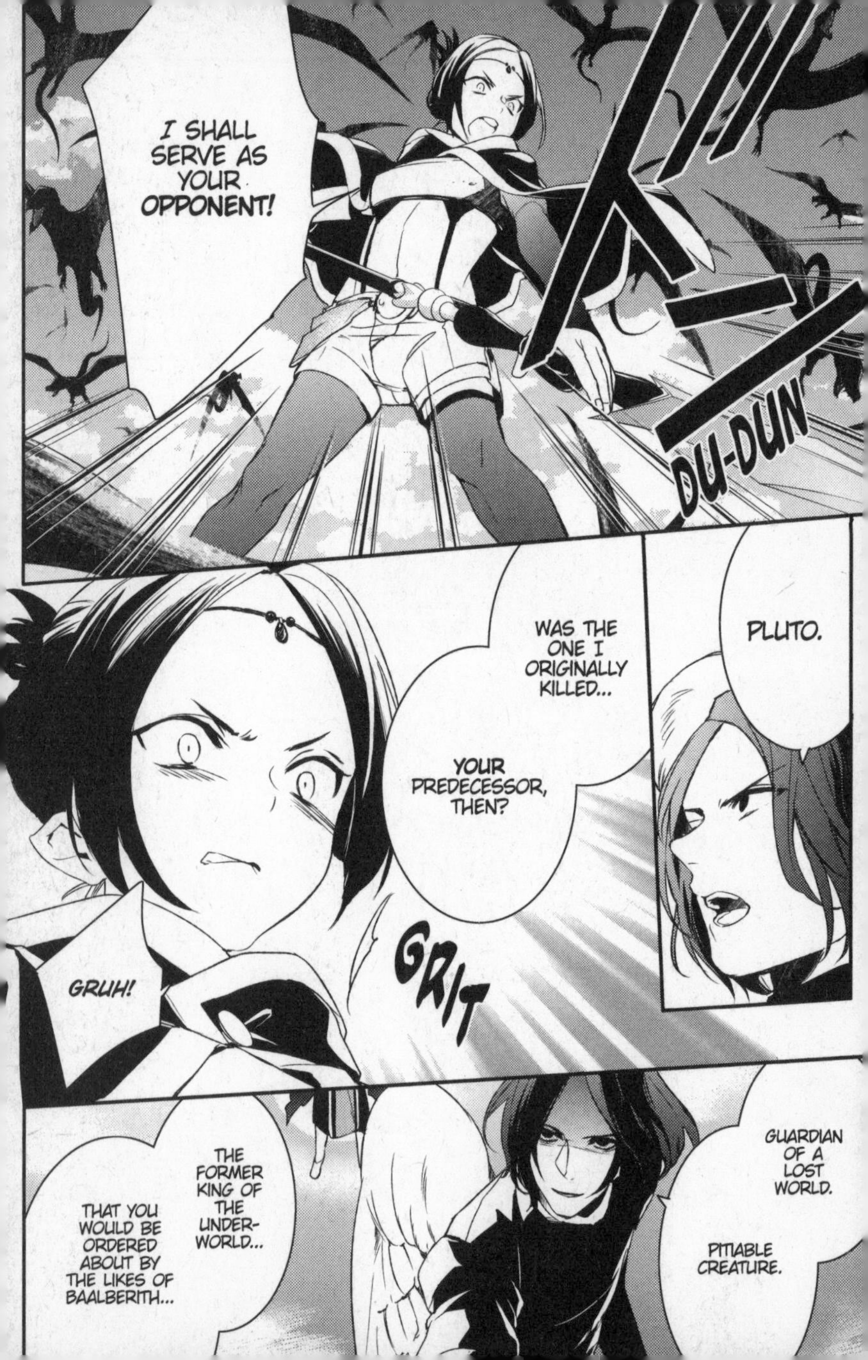
I SHALL SERVE AS YOUR OPPONENT!
DU-DUN
PLUTO.
WAS THE ONE I ORIGINALLY KILLED...
YOUR PREDECESSOR, THEN?
GRIT
GRUH!
GUARDIAN OF A LOST WORLD.
PITIABLE CREATURE.
THE FORMER KING OF THE UNDER-WORLD...
THAT YOU WOULD BE ORDERED ABOUT BY THE LIKES OF BAALBERITH...

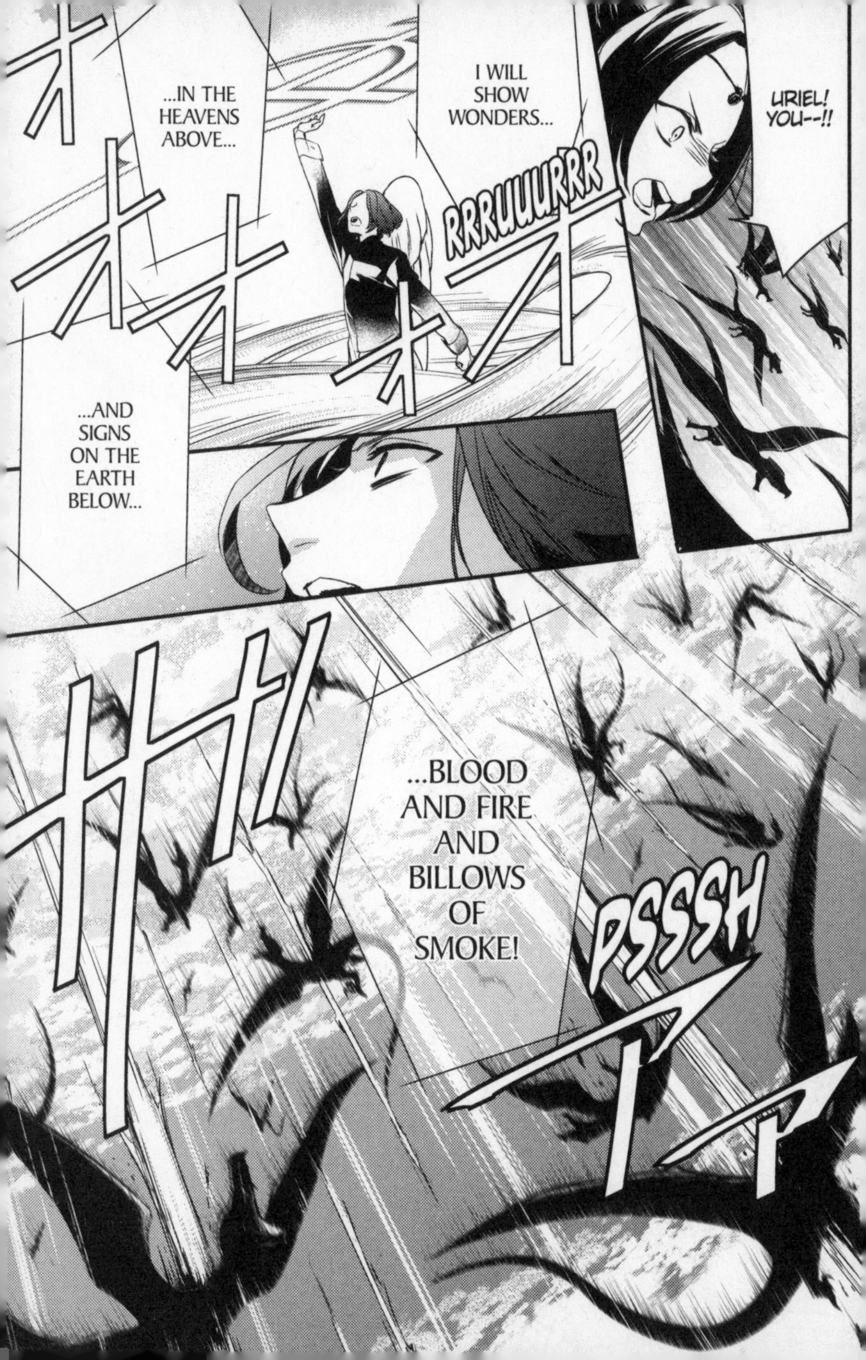
URIEL! YOU--!!
I WILL SHOW WONDERS...
...IN THE HEAVENS ABOVE...
RRRUUUURRR
...AND SIGNS ON THE EARTH BELOW...
...BLOOD AND FIRE AND BILLOWS OF SMOKE!
PSSSH

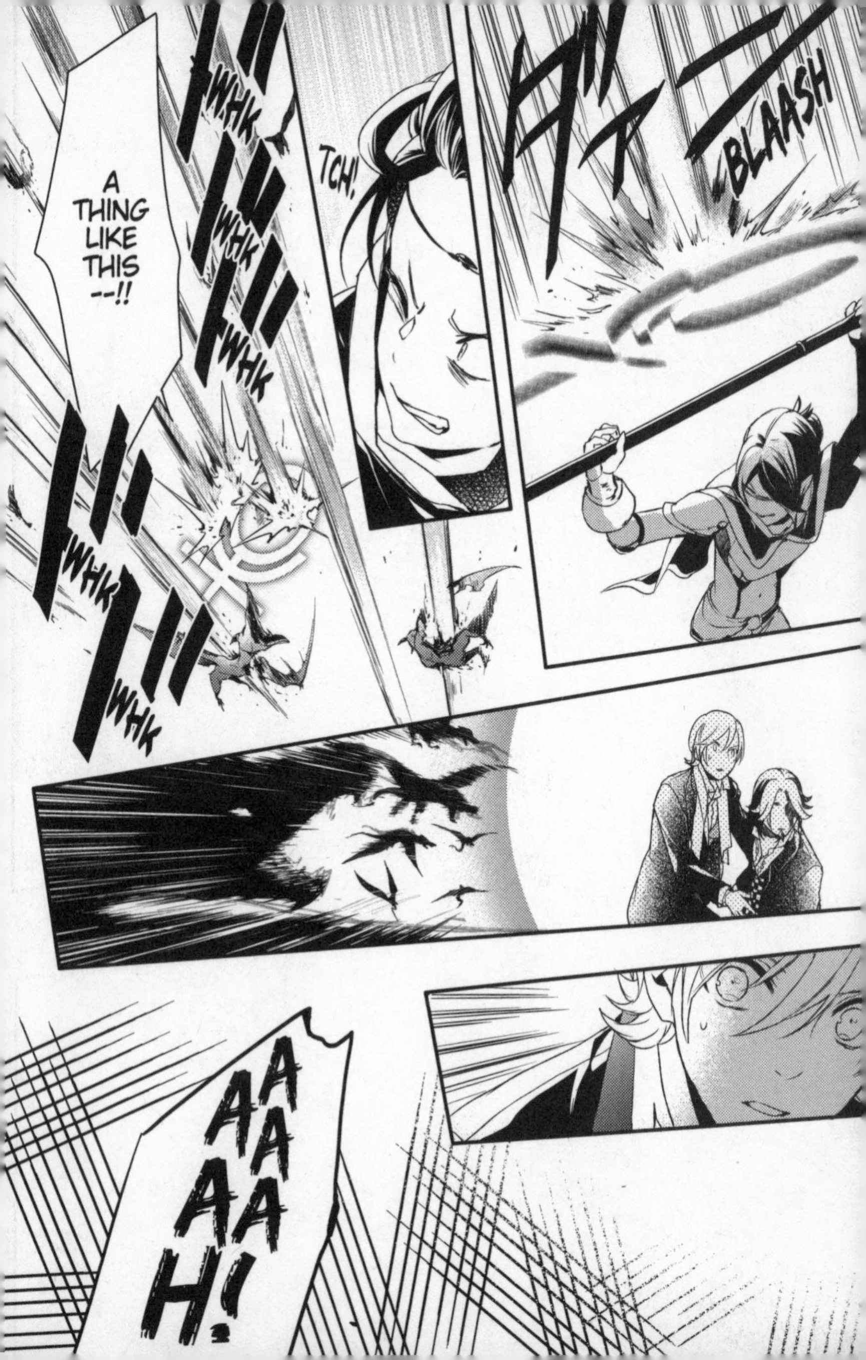
BLAASH
TCH!
A THING LIKE THIS --!!
WHK
WHK
WHK
WHK
WHK
AAAAAH!

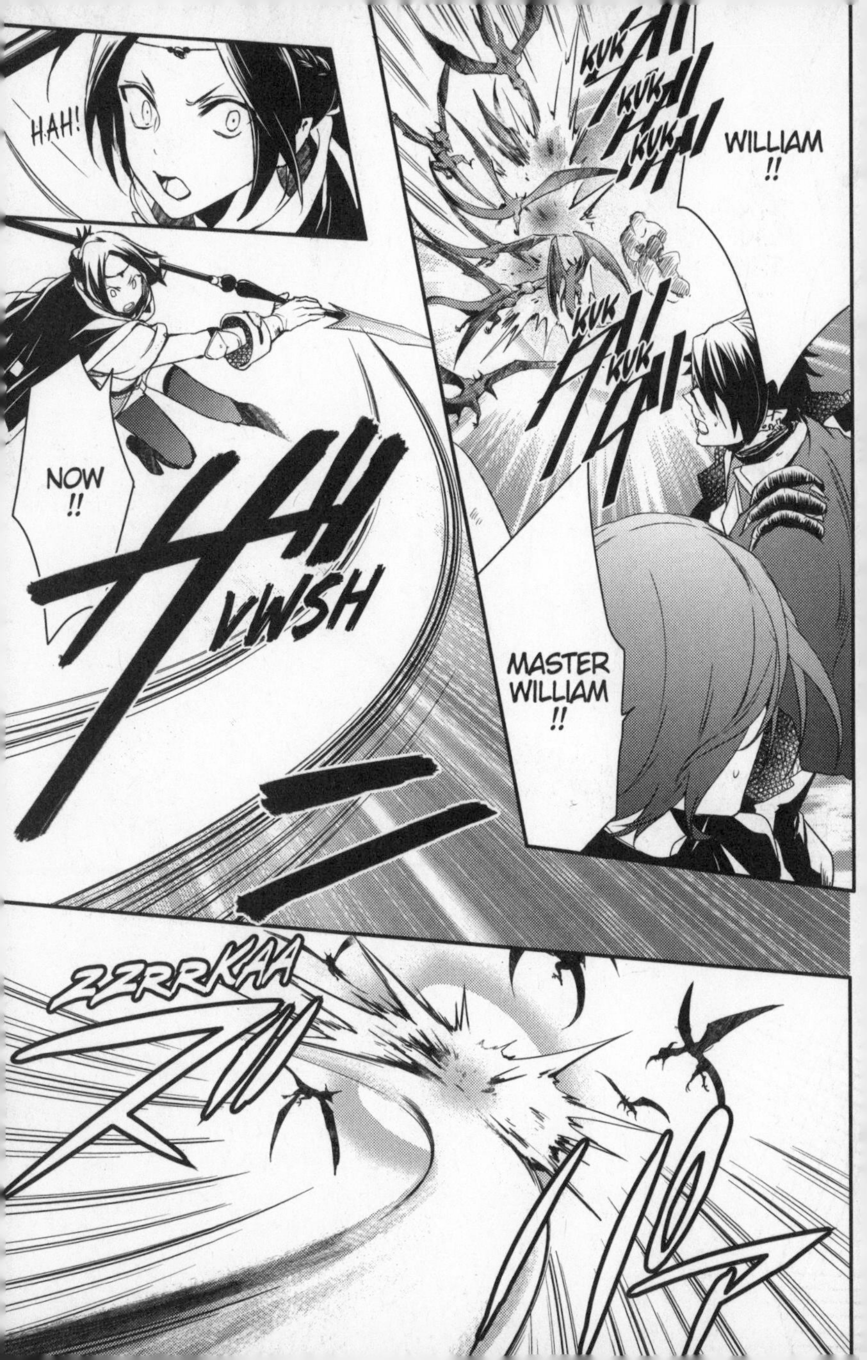
KUK
KUK
KUK
WILLIAM !!
KUK
KUK
MASTER WILLIAM !!
HAH!
NOW !!
VWSH
ZZRRKAA

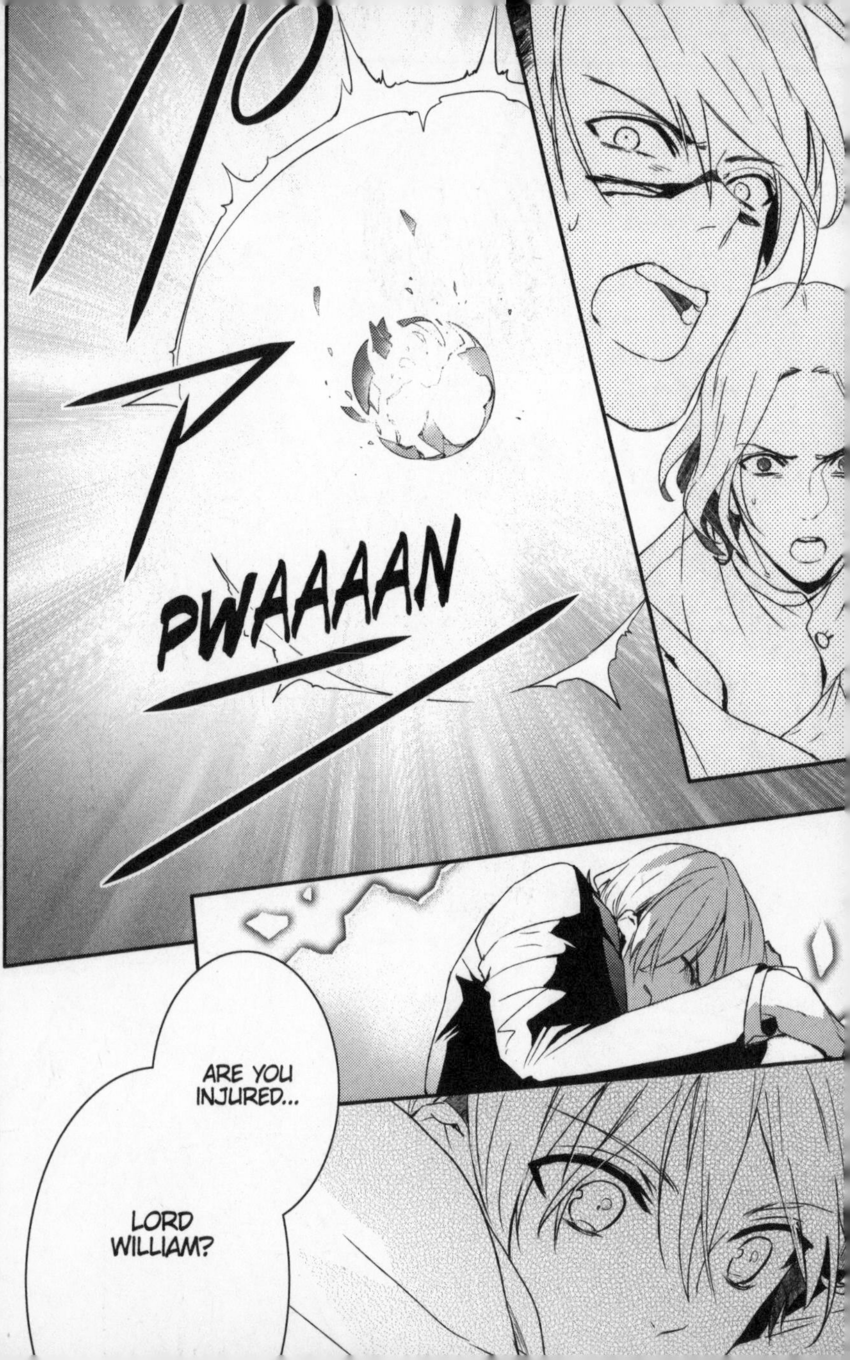
PWAAAAN
ARE YOU INJURED...
LORD WILLIAM?

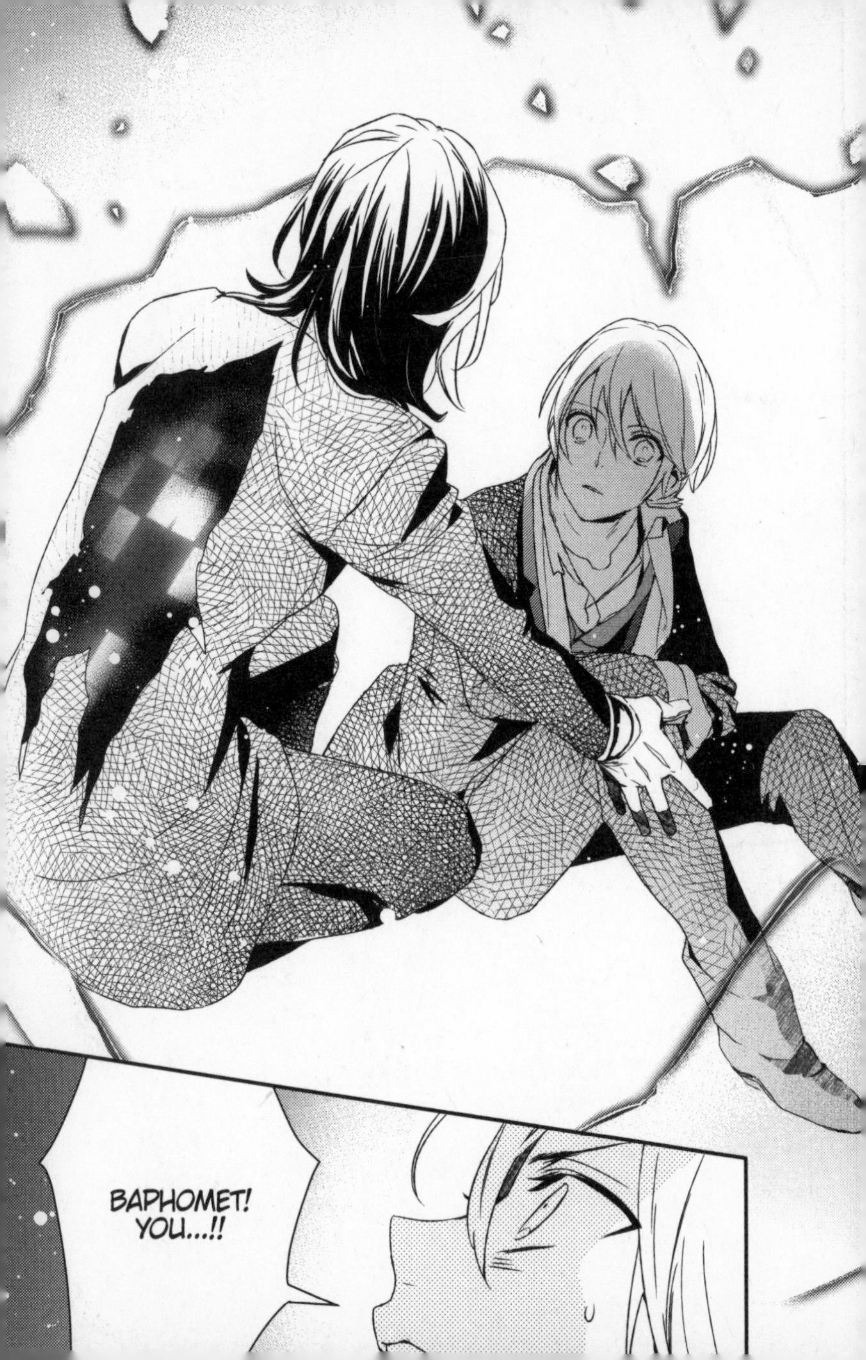
BAPHOMET!
YOU...!!

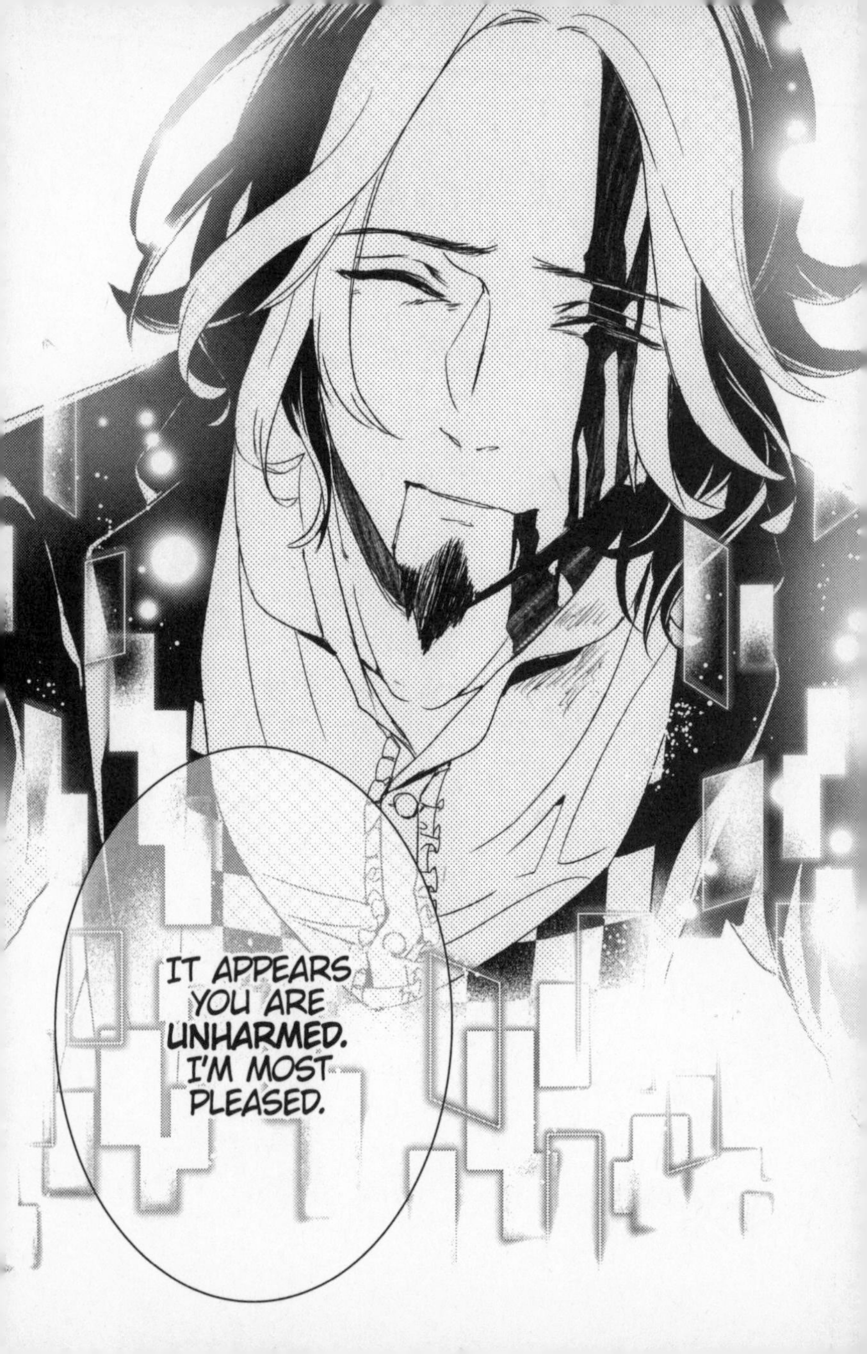
IT APPEARS YOU ARE UNHARMED. I'M MOST PLEASED.

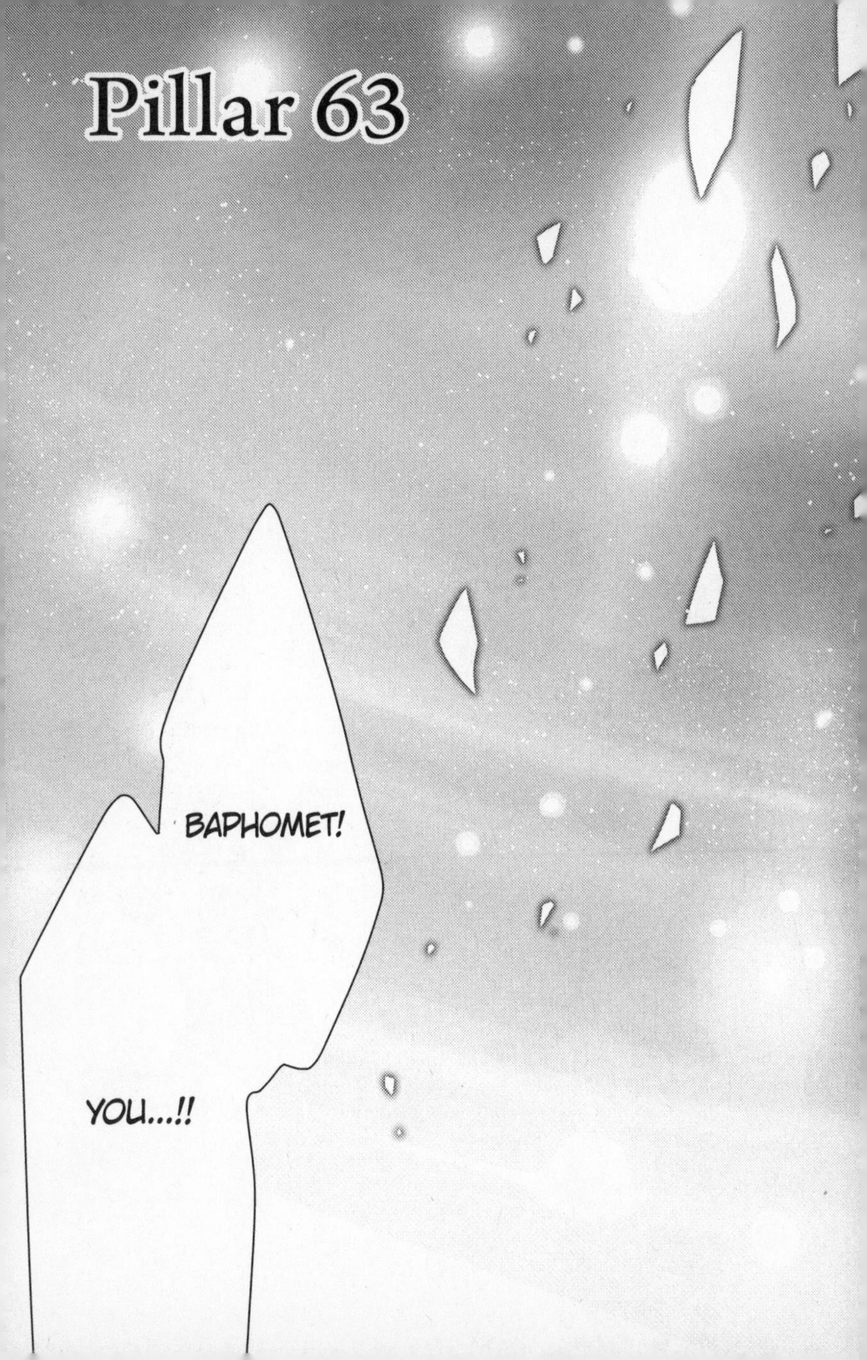
Pillar 63
BAPHOMET!
YOU...!!

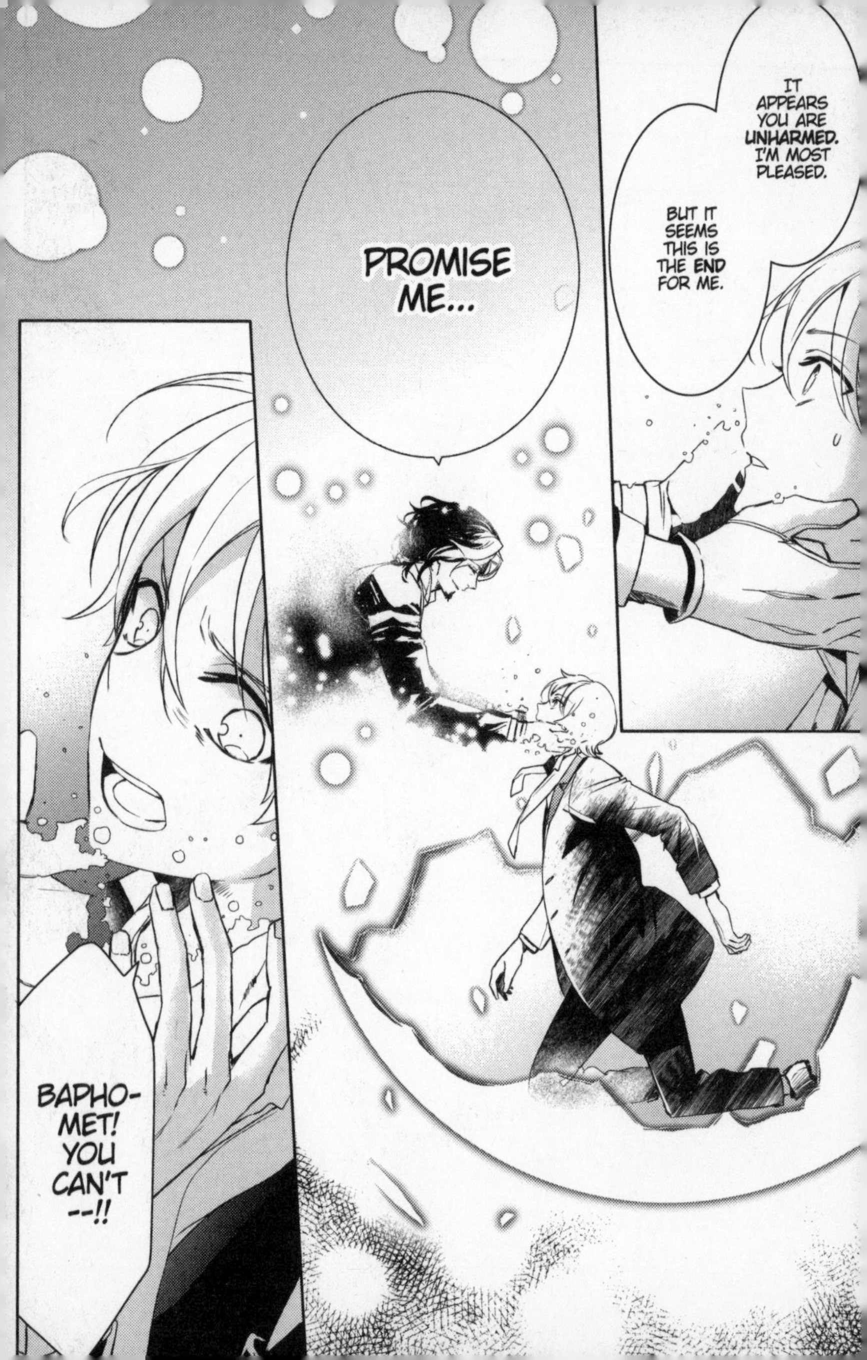
IT APPEARS YOU ARE UNHARMED. I'M MOST PLEASED.
BUT IT SEEMS THIS IS THE END FOR ME.
PROMISE ME...
BAPHO-MET! YOU CAN'T--!!

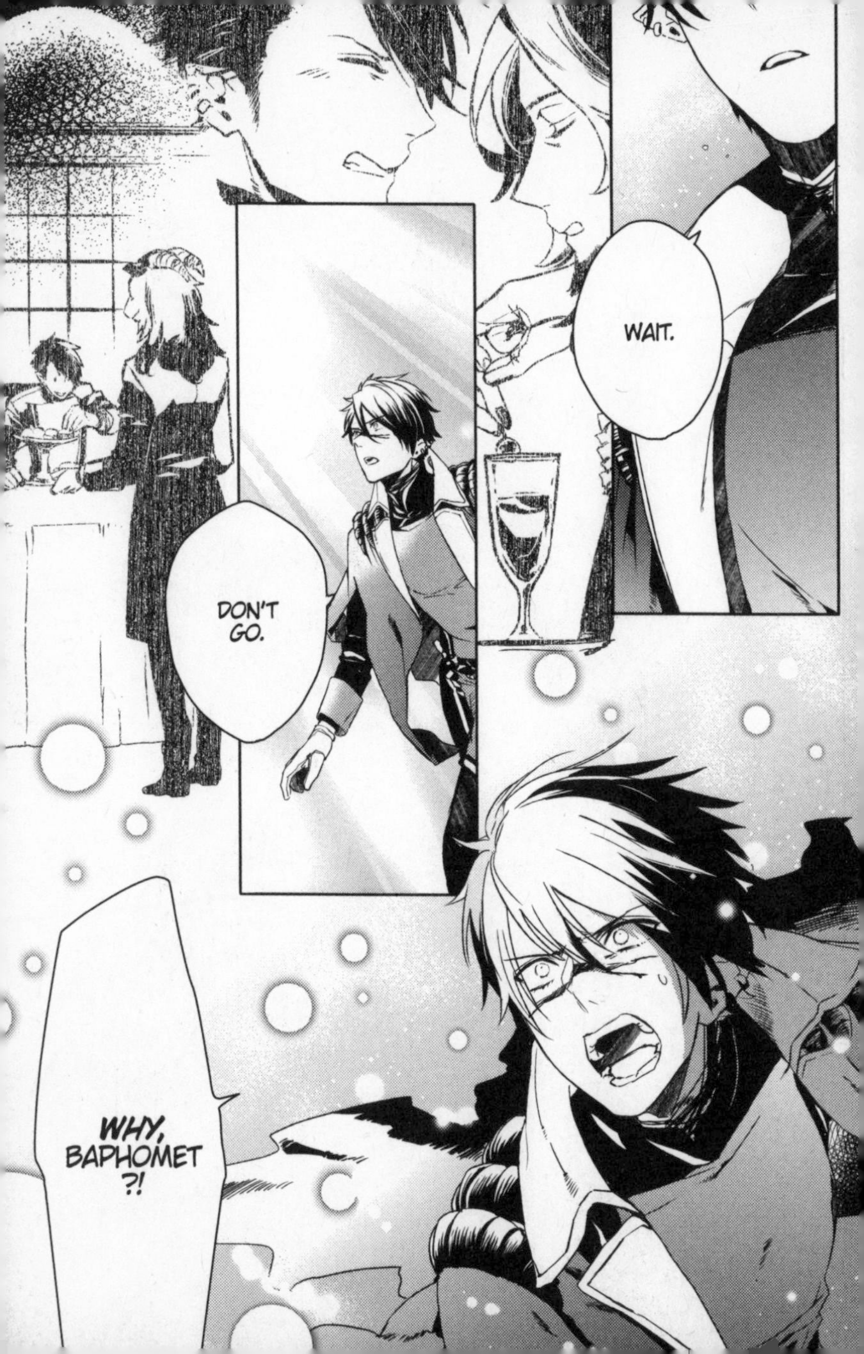
WAIT.
DON'T GO.
WHY, BAPHOMET?!

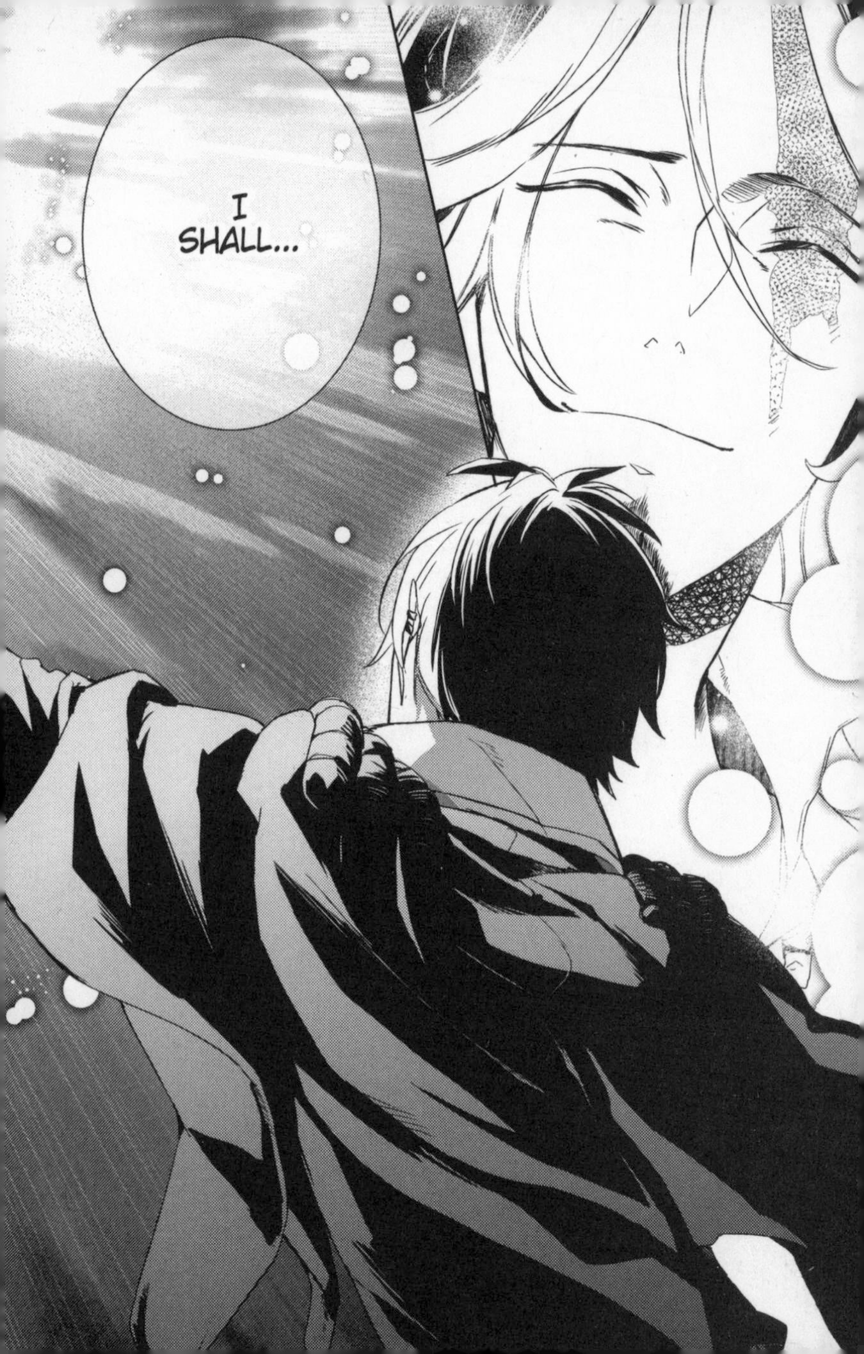
I SHALL...

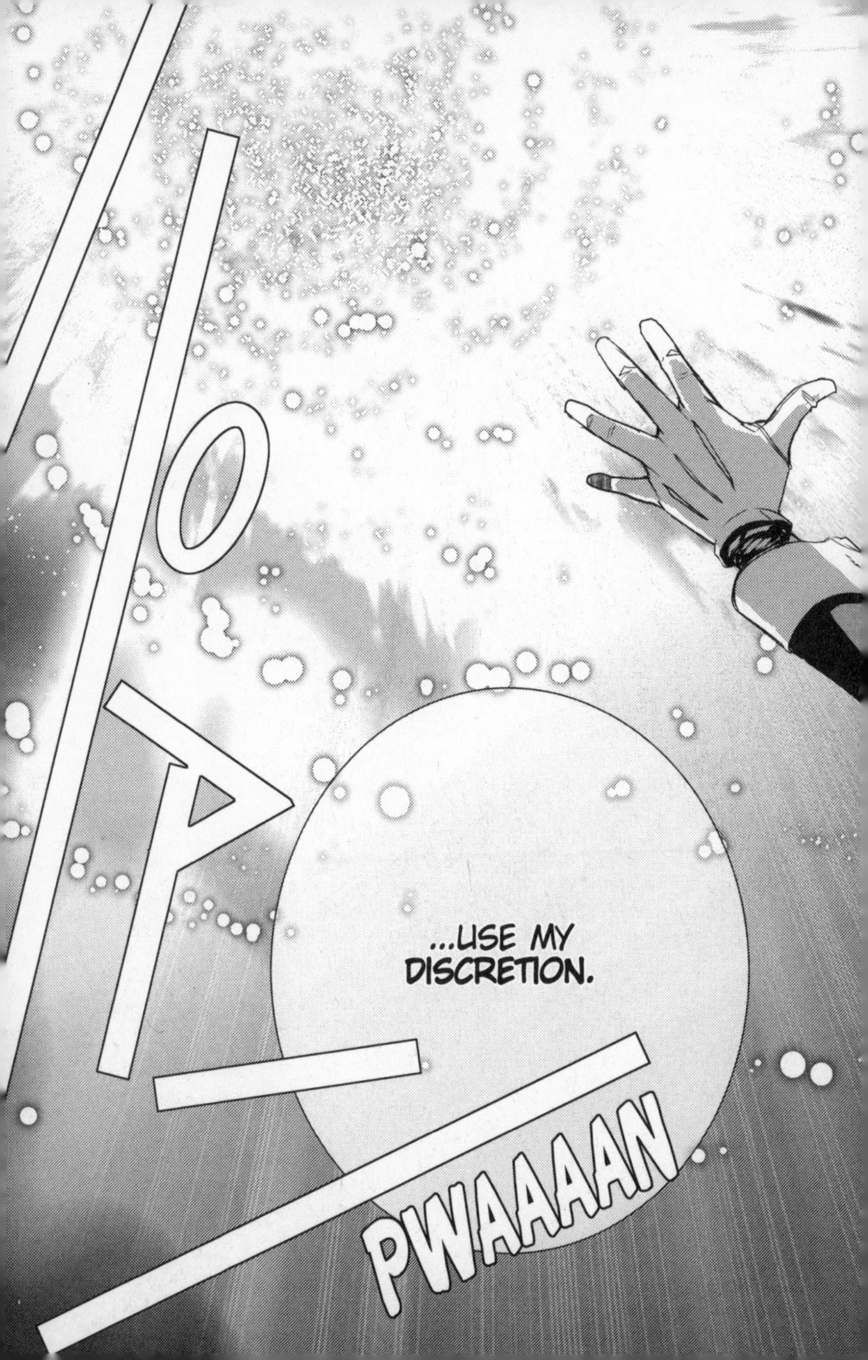
...USE MY DISCRETION.
PWAAAAN

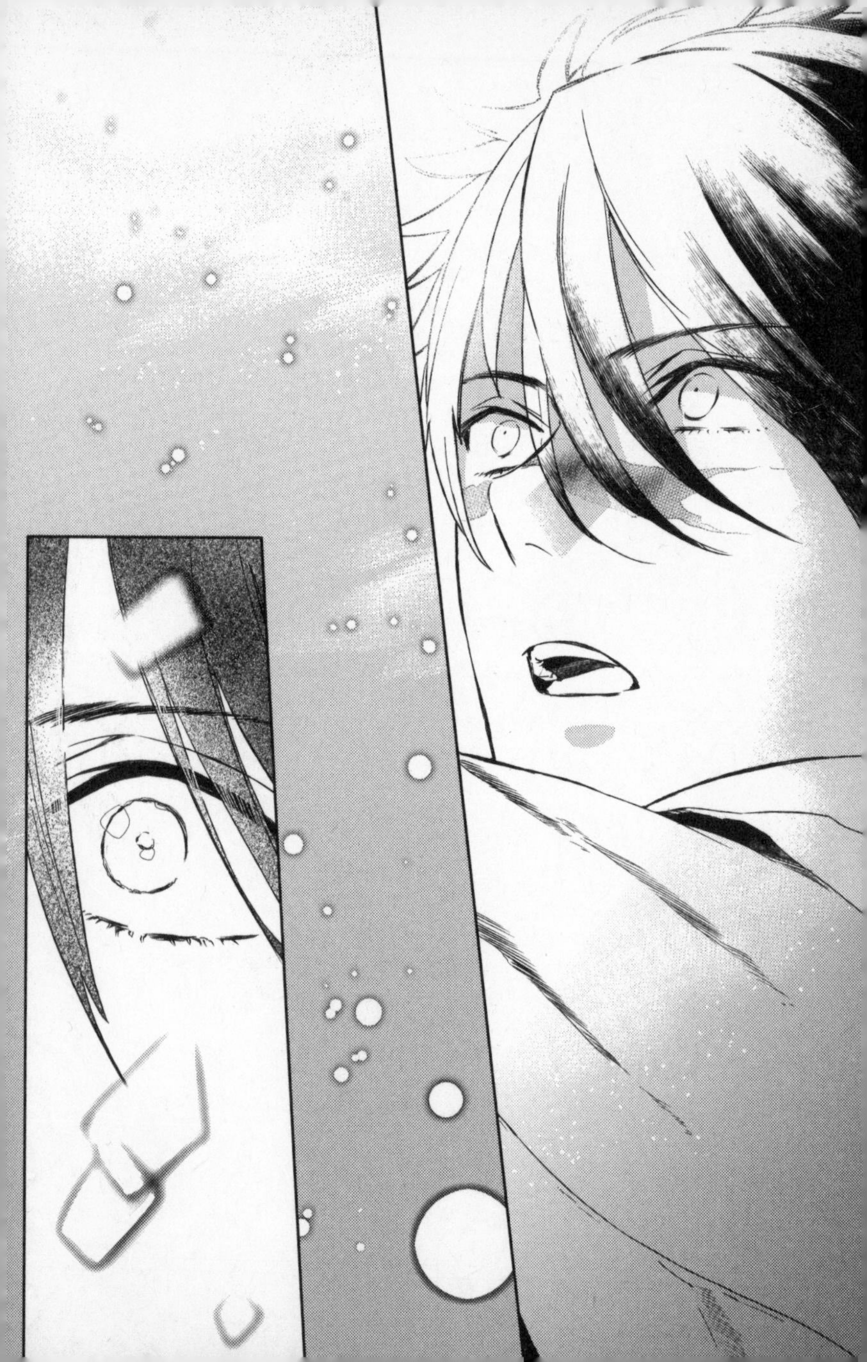

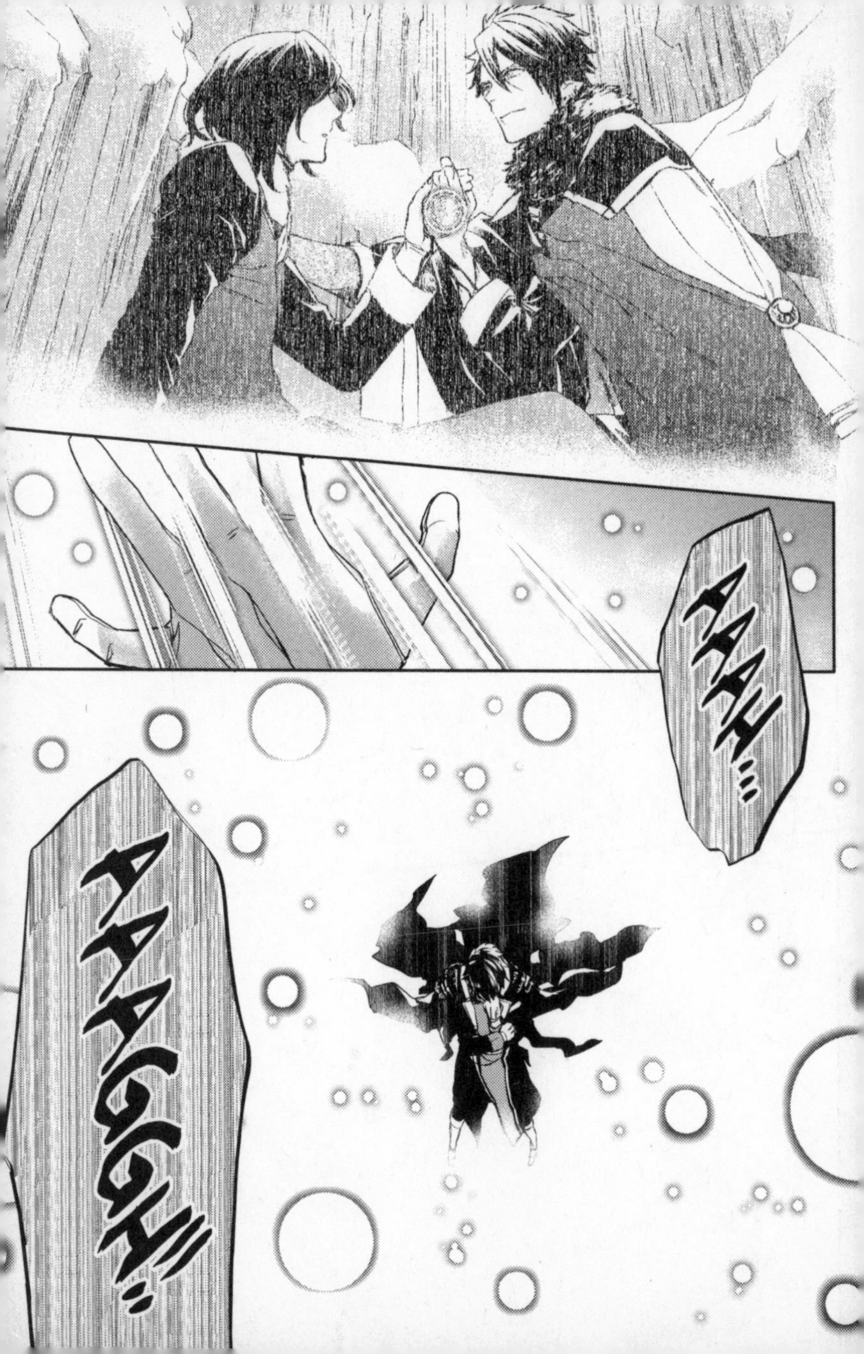
AAAH...
AAAAGGH!!

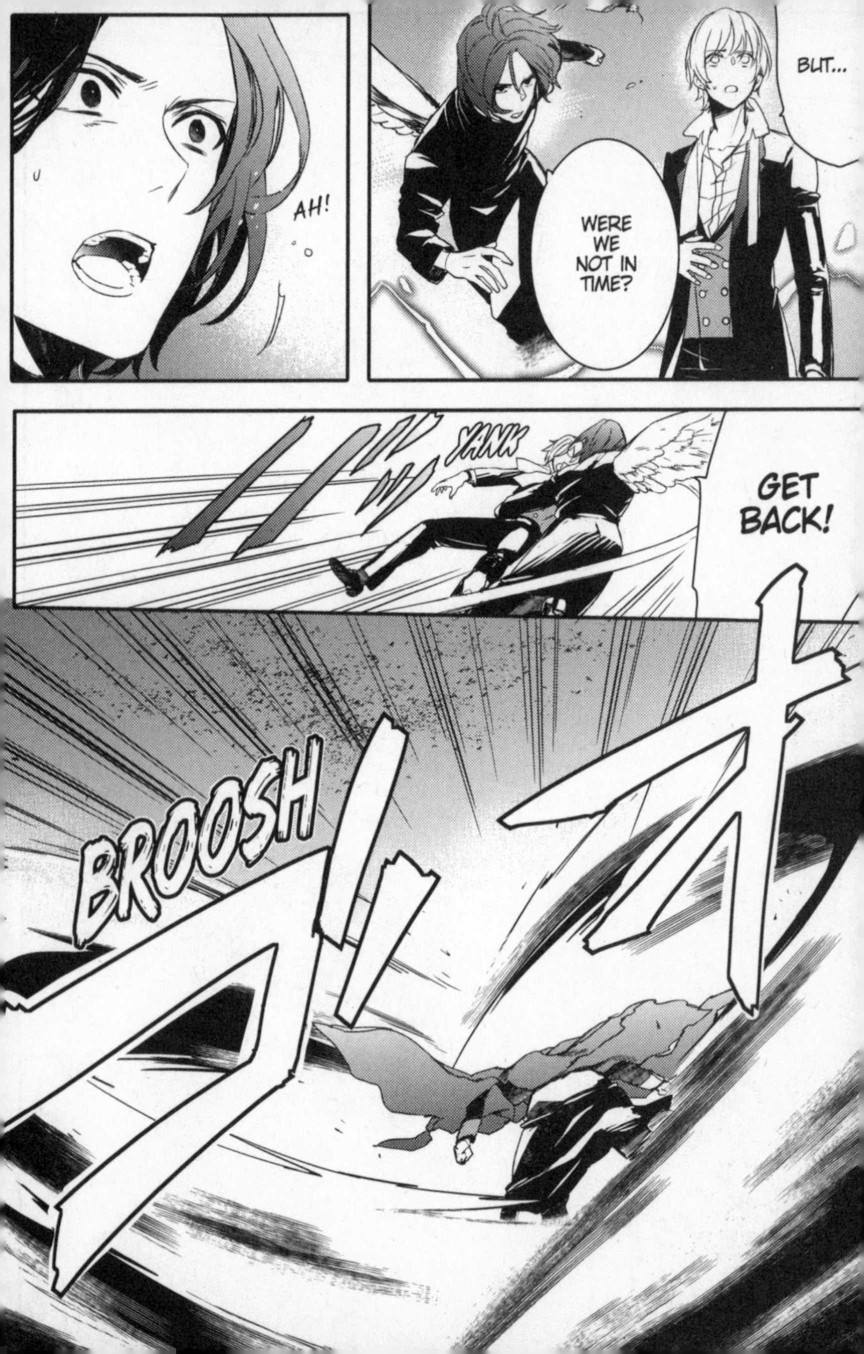
BUT...
WERE WE NOT IN TIME?
AH!
GET BACK!
YANK
BROOSH

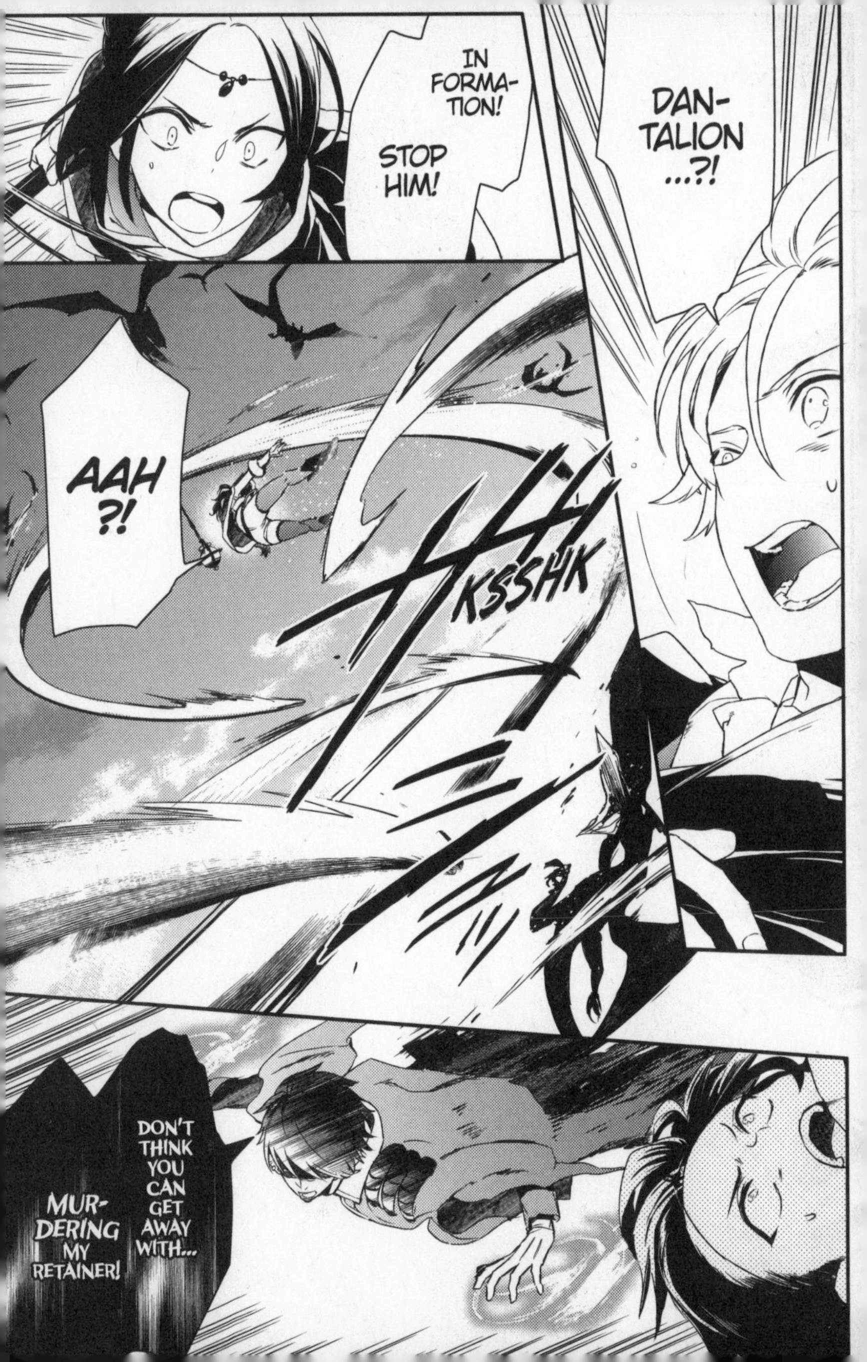
DAN-TALION ...?!
IN FORMA-TION!
STOP HIM!
AAH ?!
KSSHK
DON'T THINK YOU CAN GET AWAY WITH...
MUR-DERING MY RETAINER!

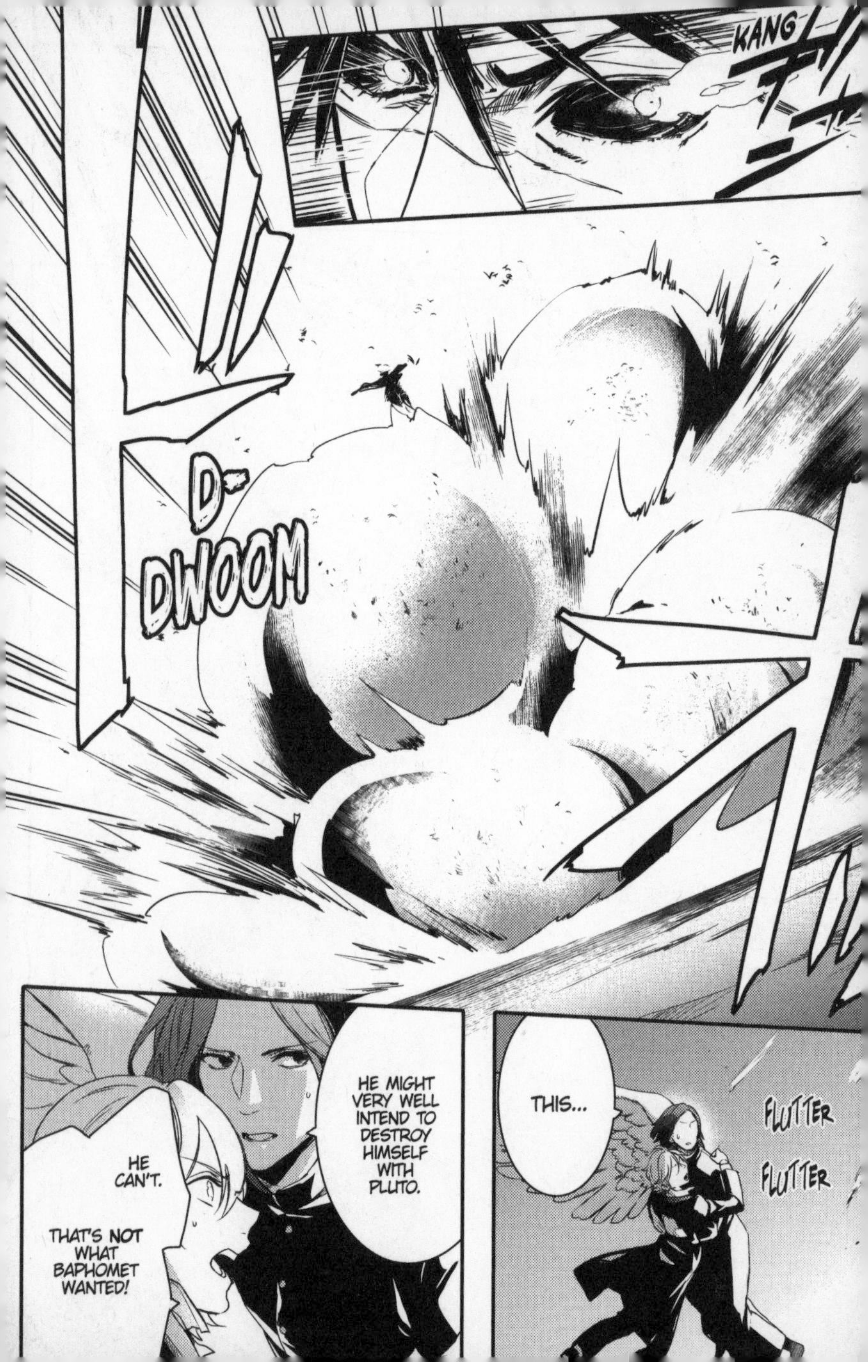
KANG
D-DWOOM
THIS...
FLUTTER
FLUTTER
HE MIGHT VERY WELL INTEND TO DESTROY HIMSELF WITH PLUTO.
HE CAN'T.
THAT'S NOT WHAT BAPHOMET WANTED!

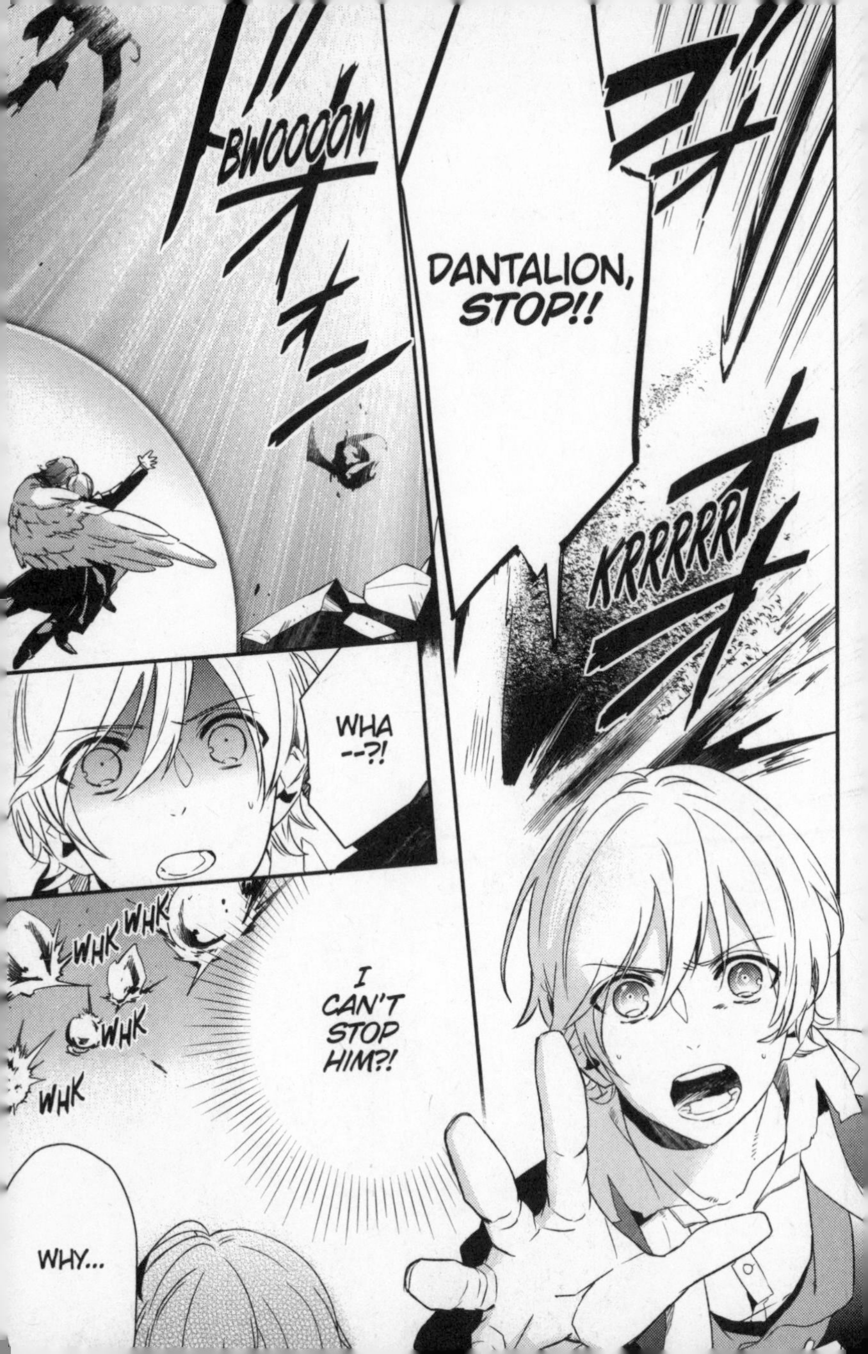
DANTALION, STOP!!
KRRRRR
BWOOOOM
WHA--?!
WHK WHK
WHK
WHK
WHK
I CAN'T STOP HIM?!
WHY...

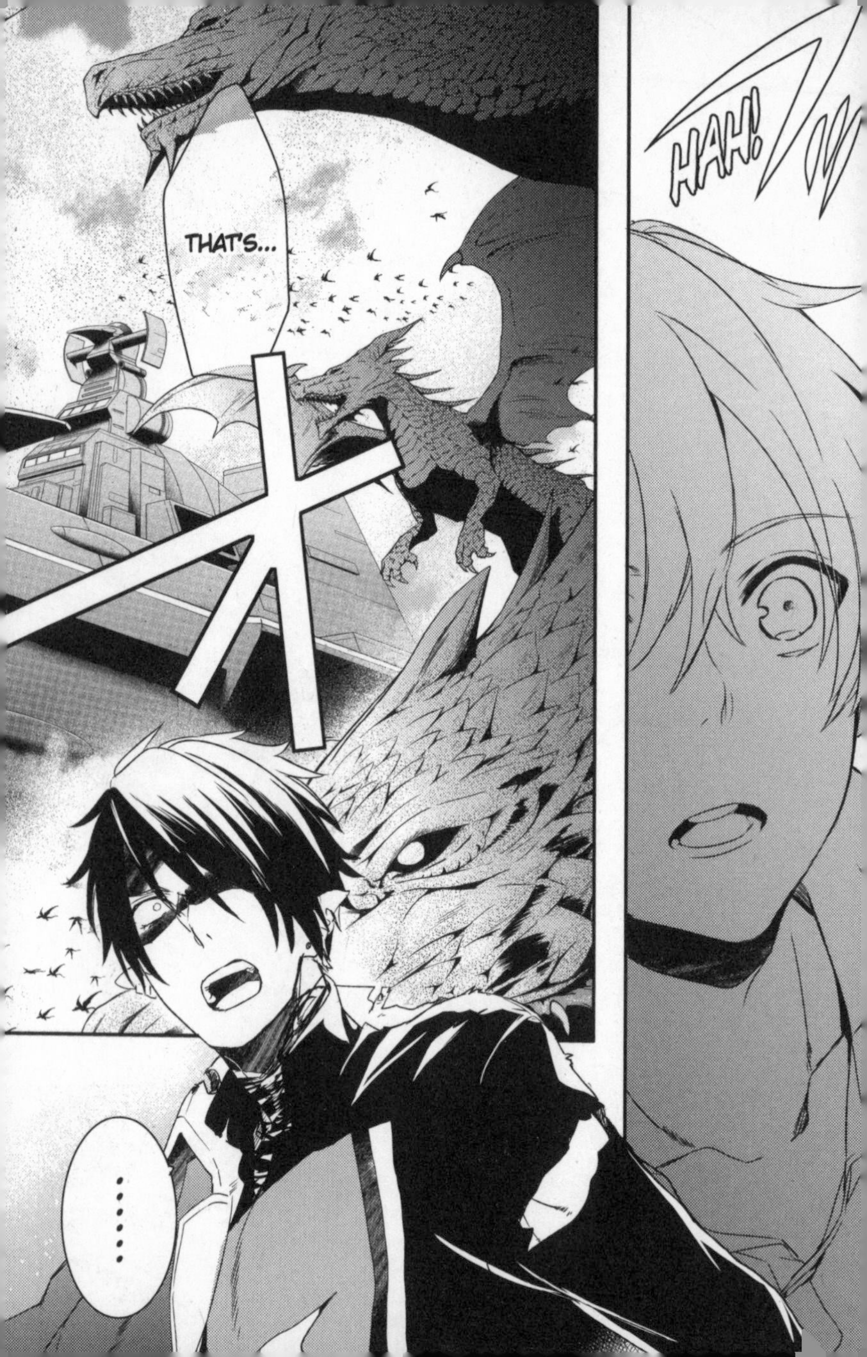
HAH!
THAT'S...
......

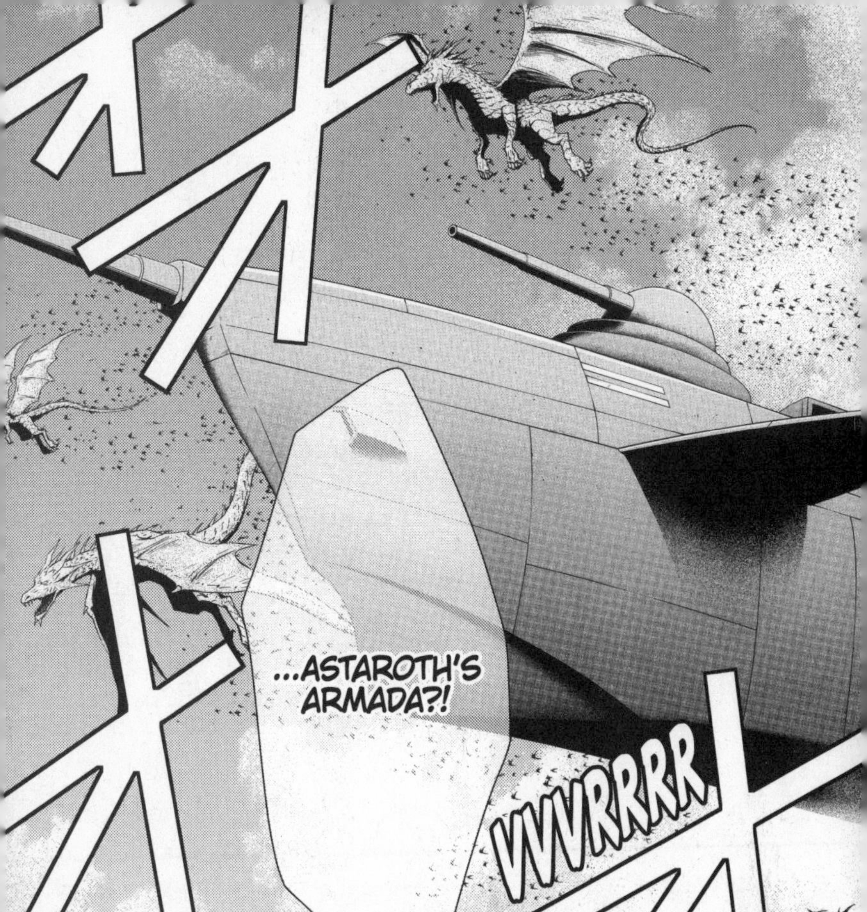
...ASTAROTH'S ARMADA?!
VVVRRRR
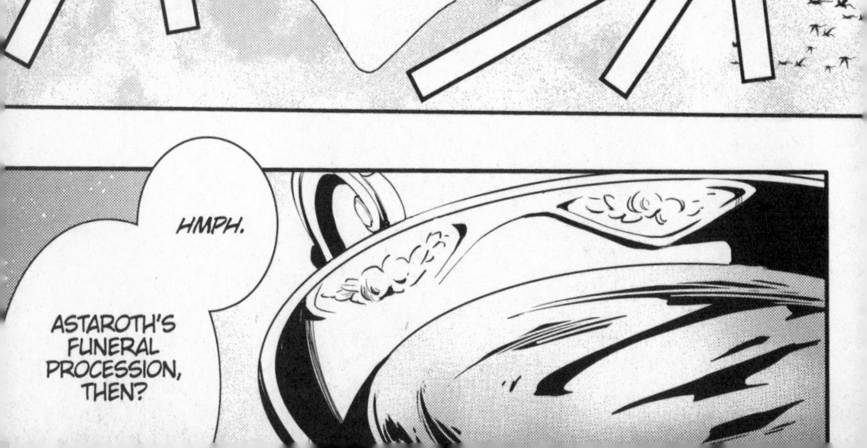
HMPH.
ASTAROTH'S FUNERAL PROCESSION, THEN?

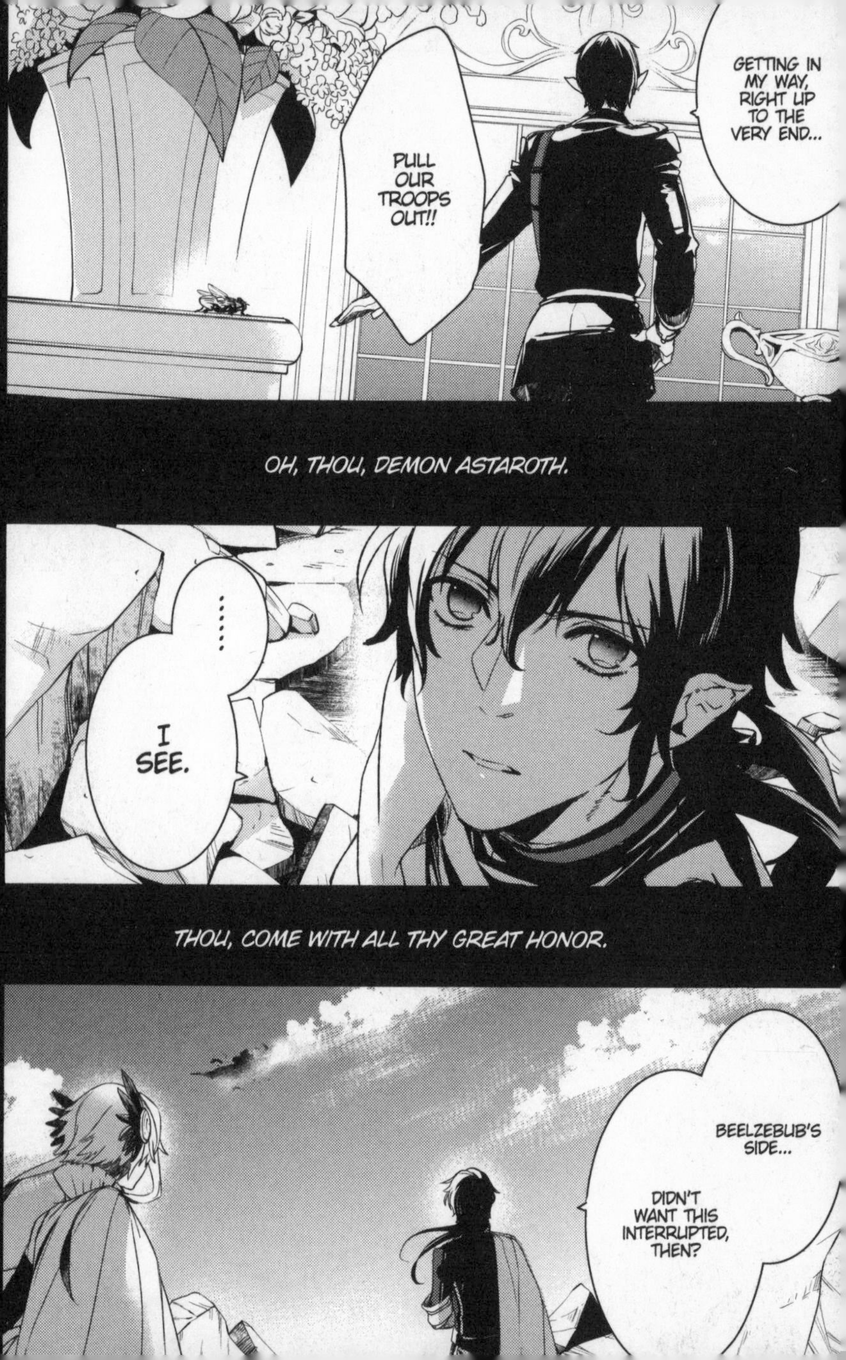
GETTING IN MY WAY, RIGHT UP TO THE VERY END...
PULL OUR TROOPS OUT!!
OH, THOU, DEMON ASTAROTH.
......
I SEE.
THOU, COME WITH ALL THY GREAT HONOR.
BEELZEBUB'S SIDE...
DIDN'T WANT THIS INTERRUPTED, THEN?

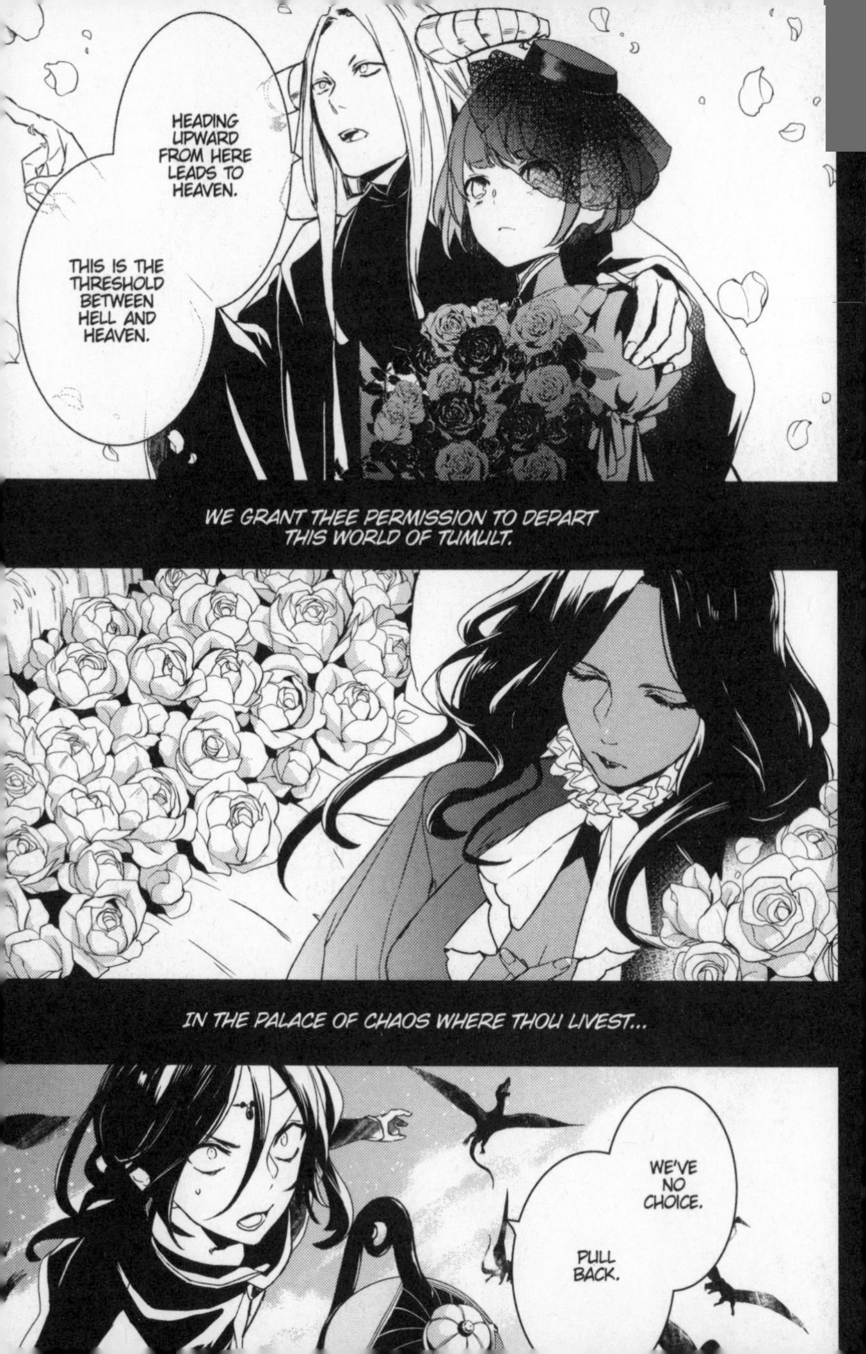
HEADING UPWARD FROM HERE LEADS TO HEAVEN.
THIS IS THE THRESHOLD BETWEEN HELL AND HEAVEN.
WE GRANT THEE PERMISSION TO DEPART THIS WORLD OF TUMULT.
IN THE PALACE OF CHAOS WHERE THOU LIVEST...
WE'VE NO CHOICE.
PULL BACK.

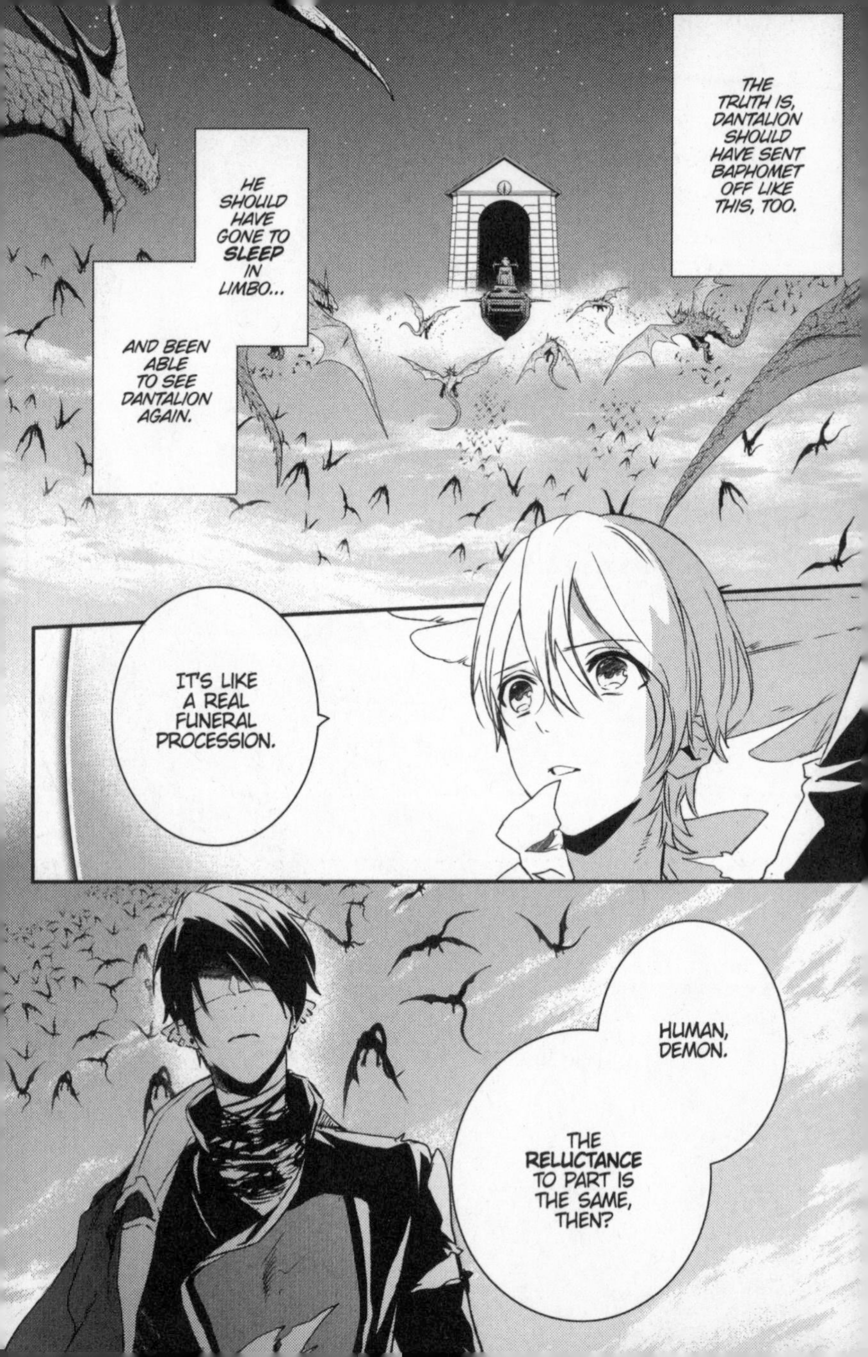
THE TRUTH IS, DANTALION SHOULD HAVE SENT BAPHOMET OFF LIKE THIS, TOO.
HE SHOULD HAVE GONE TO SLEEP IN LIMBO...
AND BEEN ABLE TO SEE DANTALION AGAIN.
IT'S LIKE A REAL FUNERAL PROCESSION.
HUMAN, DEMON.
THE RELUCTANCE TO PART IS THE SAME, THEN?

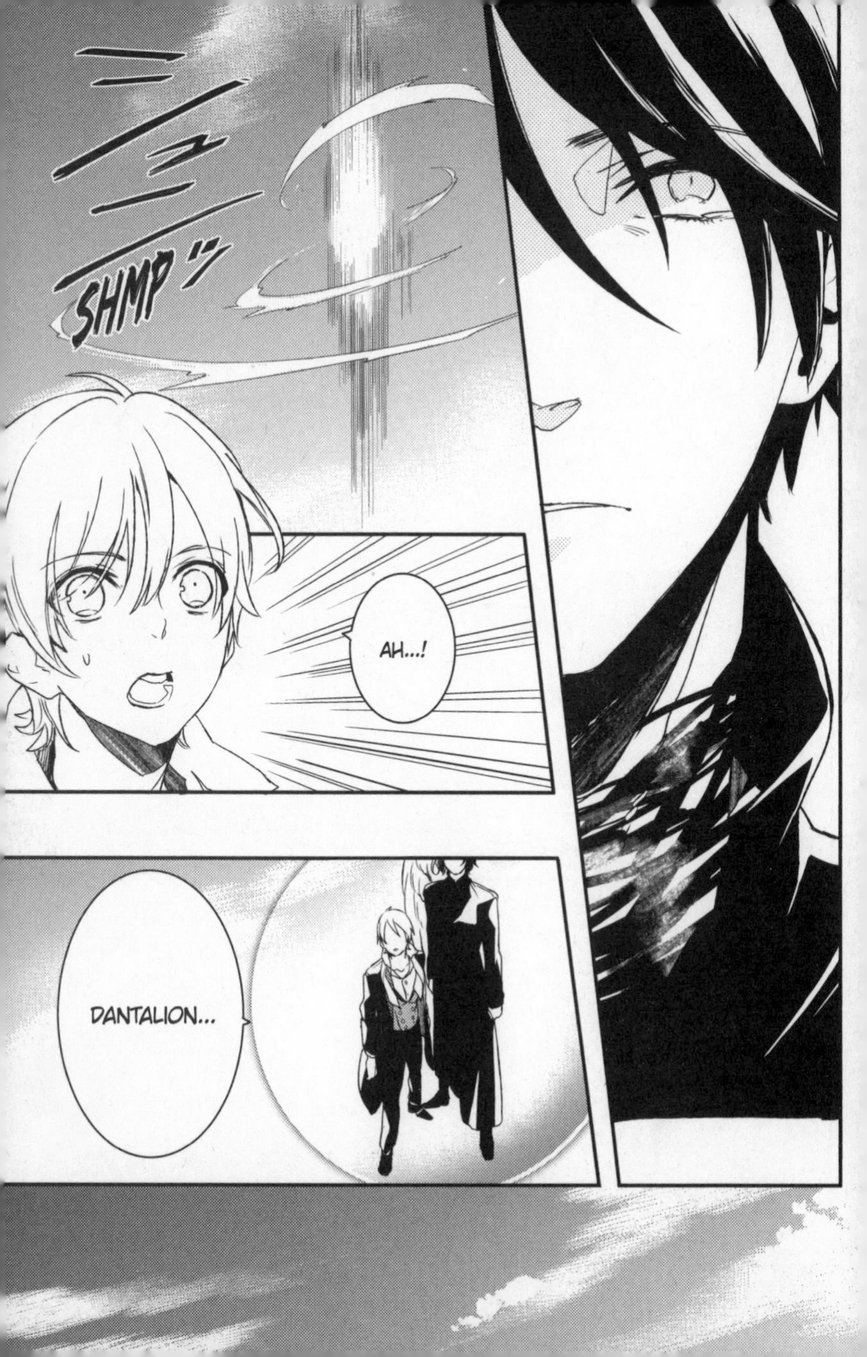
SHMP
AH...!
DANTALION...

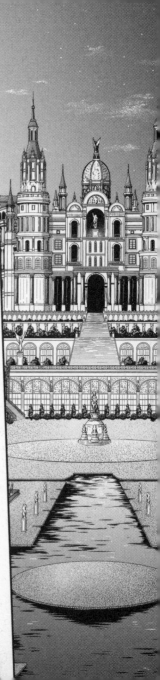

DID YOU HEAR?

SO UNSIGHTLY.

ARE WE ALREADY SEEING A STAIN ON BAALBERITH'S INFLUENCE?

THIS REWRITES THE POWER STRUCTURE OF THE CANDIDATES FOR REPRESENTATIVE KING.

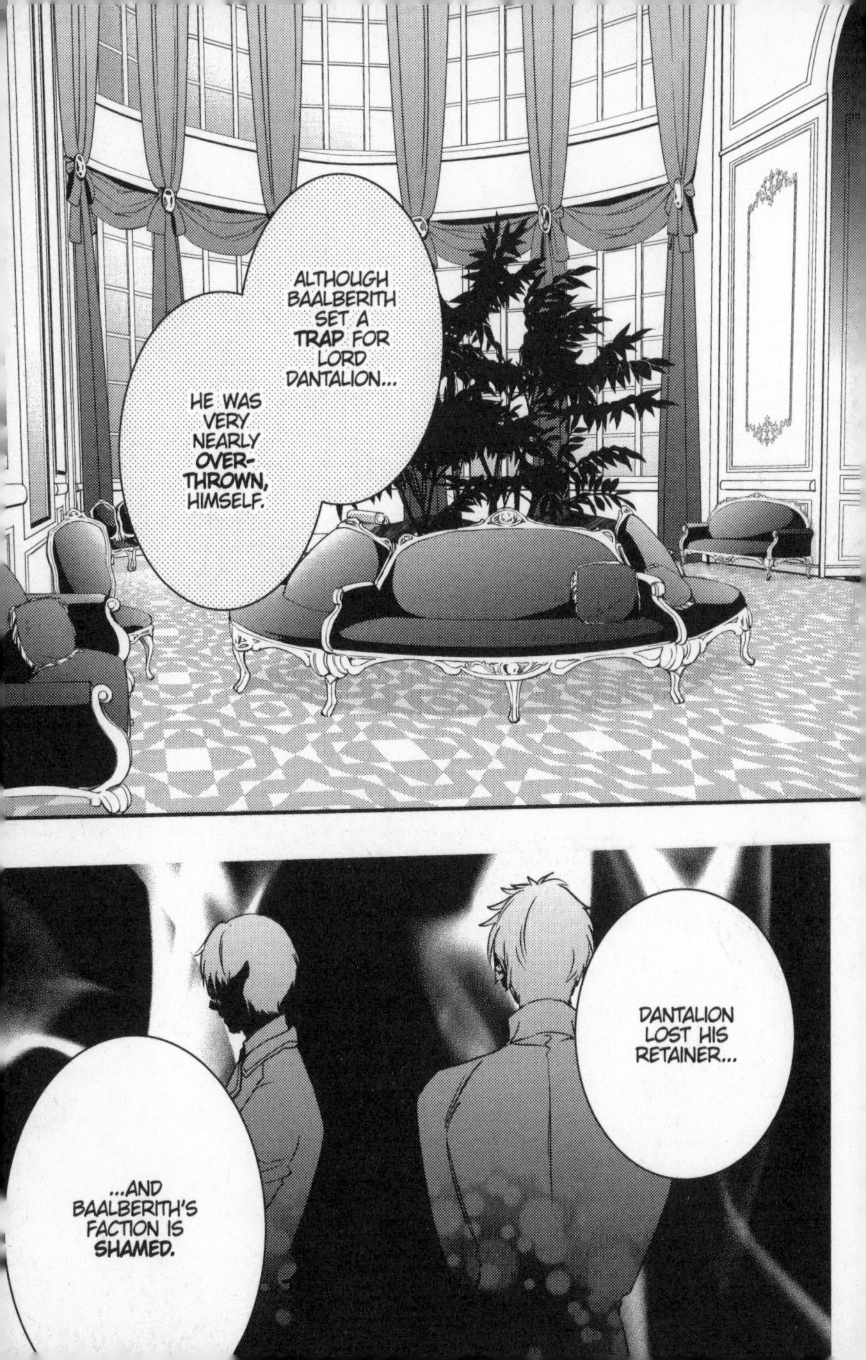
ALTHOUGH BAALBERITH SET A TRAP FOR LORD DANTALION...
HE WAS VERY NEARLY OVER-THROWN, HIMSELF.
DANTALION LOST HIS RETAINER...
...AND BAALBERITH'S FACTION IS SHAMED.

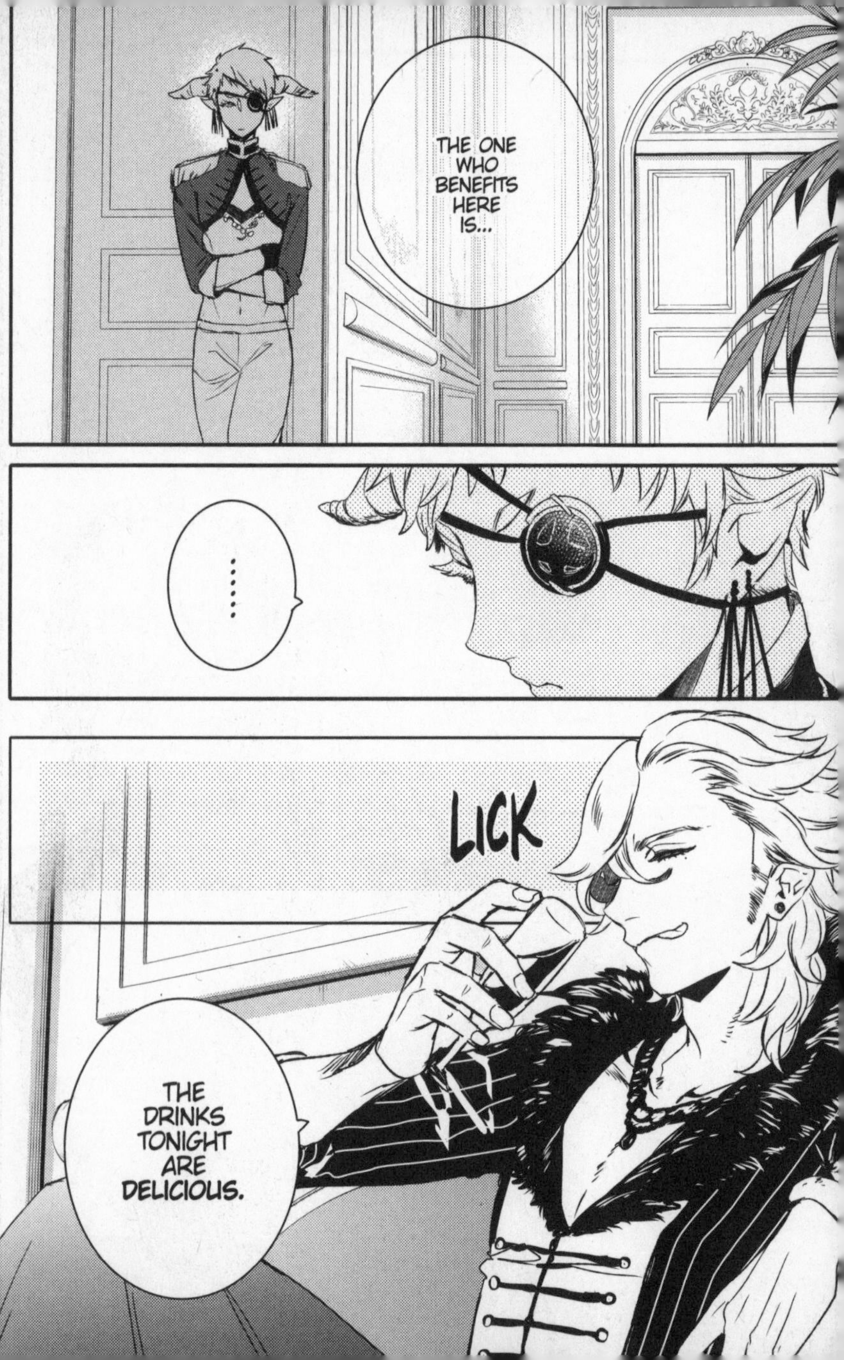
THE ONE WHO BENEFITS HERE IS...
......
LICK
THE DRINKS TONIGHT ARE DELICIOUS.

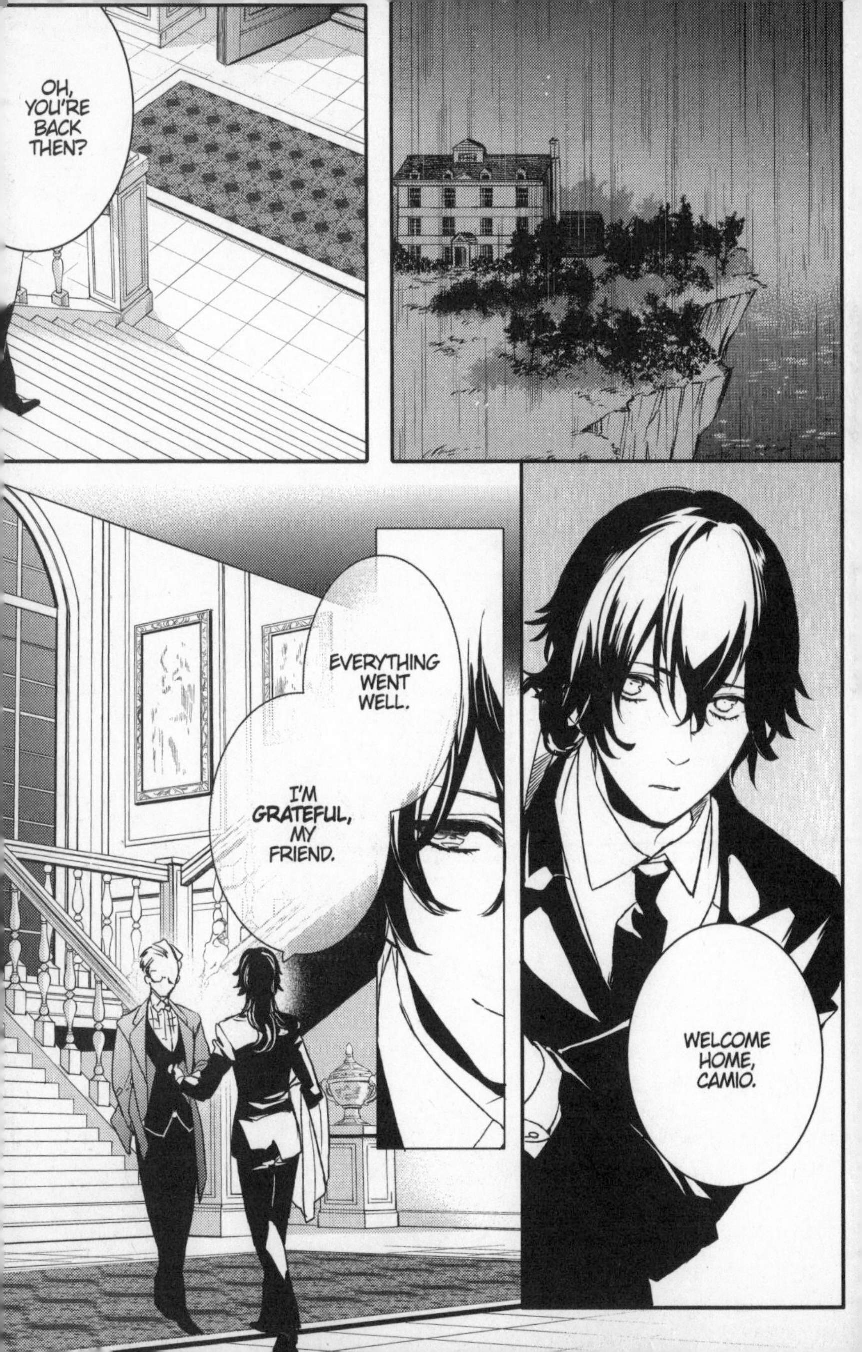
OH, YOU'RE BACK THEN?
WELCOME HOME, CAMIO.
EVERYTHING WENT WELL.
I'M GRATEFUL, MY FRIEND.

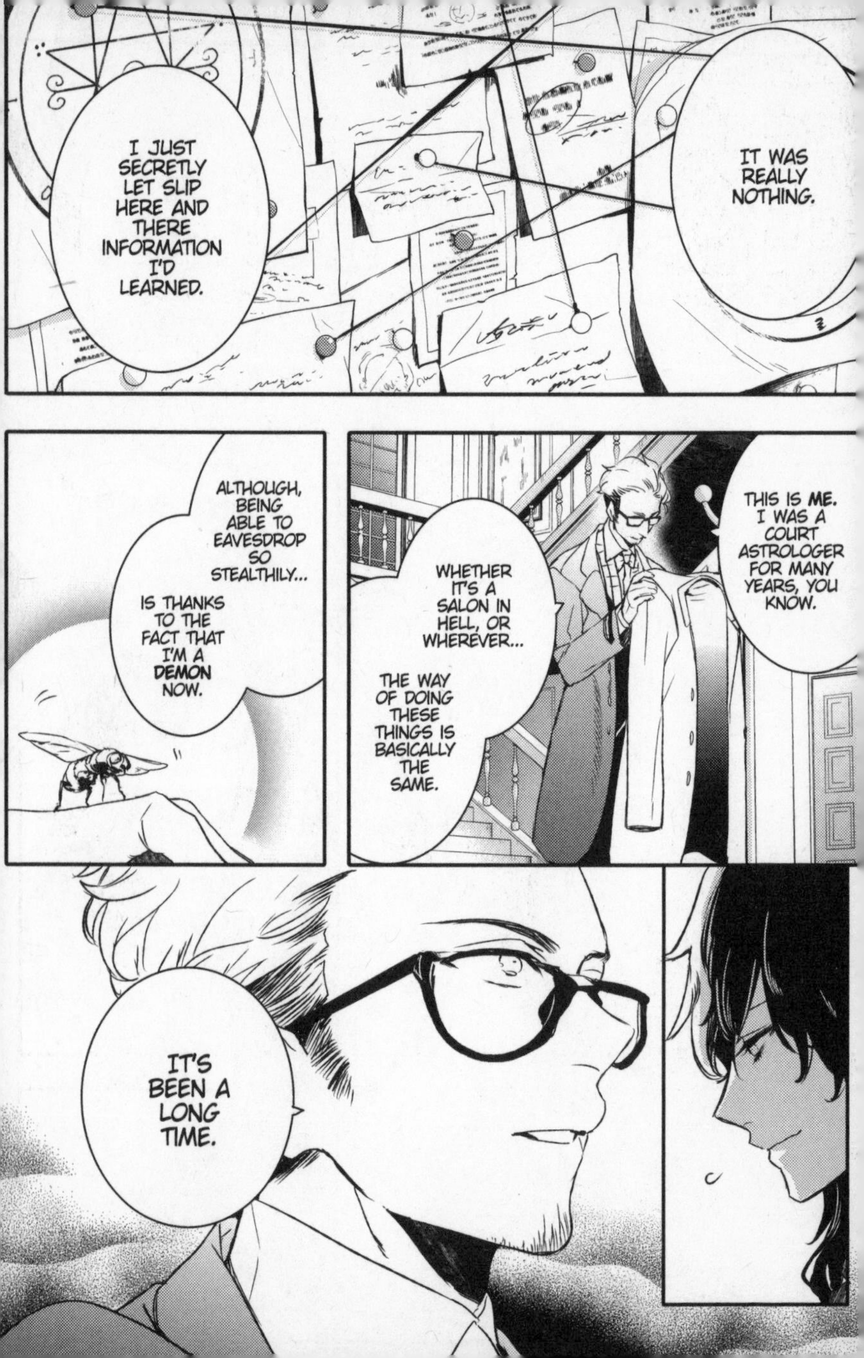
IT WAS REALLY NOTHING.
I JUST SECRETLY LET SLIP HERE AND THERE INFORMATION I'D LEARNED.
THIS IS ME. I WAS A COURT ASTROLOGER FOR MANY YEARS, YOU KNOW.
WHETHER IT'S A SALON IN HELL, OR WHEREVER...
THE WAY OF DOING THESE THINGS IS BASICALLY THE SAME.
ALTHOUGH, BEING ABLE TO EAVESDROP SO STEALTHILY...
IS THANKS TO THE FACT THAT I'M A DEMON NOW.
IT'S BEEN A LONG TIME.

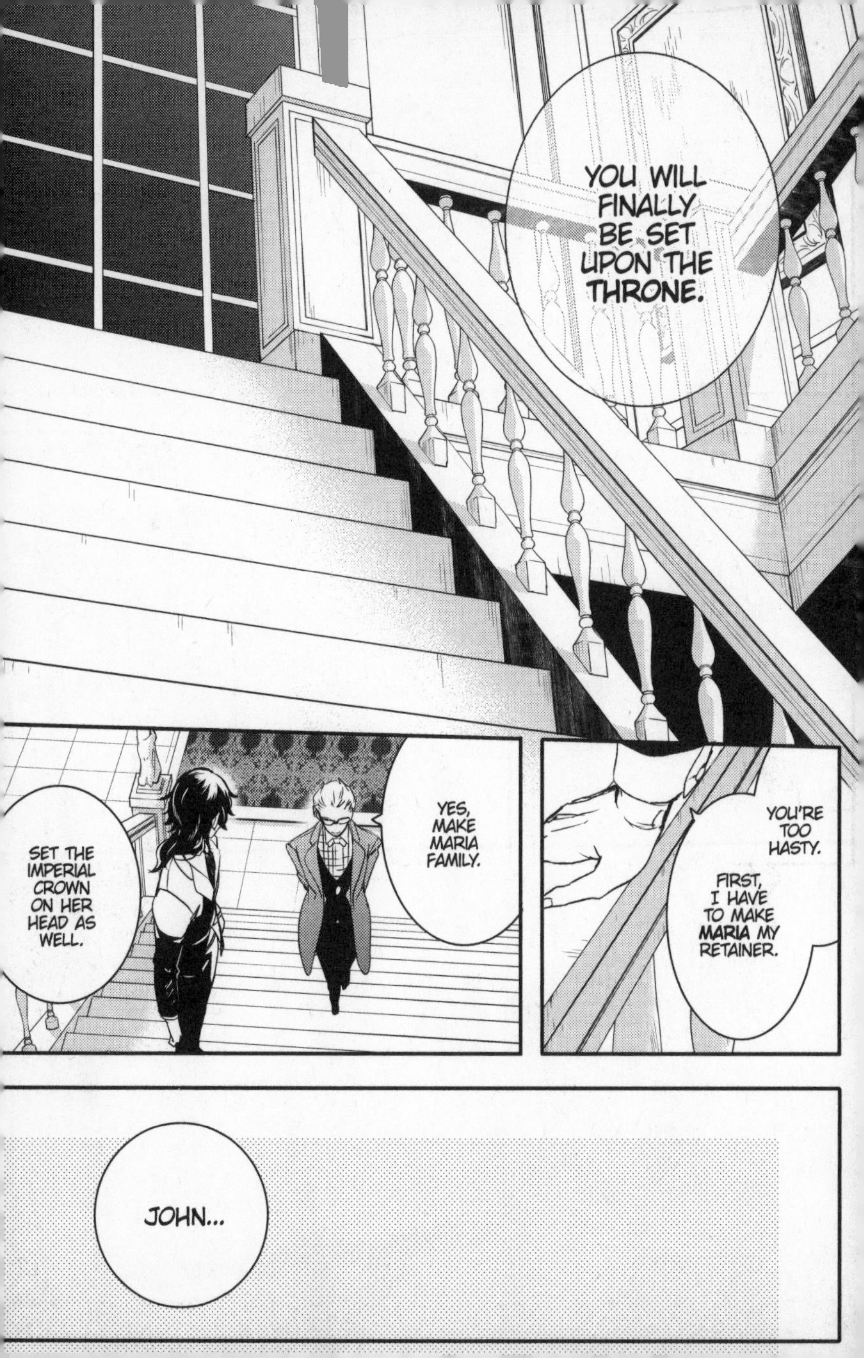
YOU WILL FINALLY BE SET UPON THE THRONE.
YOU'RE TOO HASTY.
FIRST, I HAVE TO MAKE MARIA MY RETAINER.
YES, MAKE MARIA FAMILY.
SET THE IMPERIAL CROWN ON HER HEAD AS WELL.
JOHN...

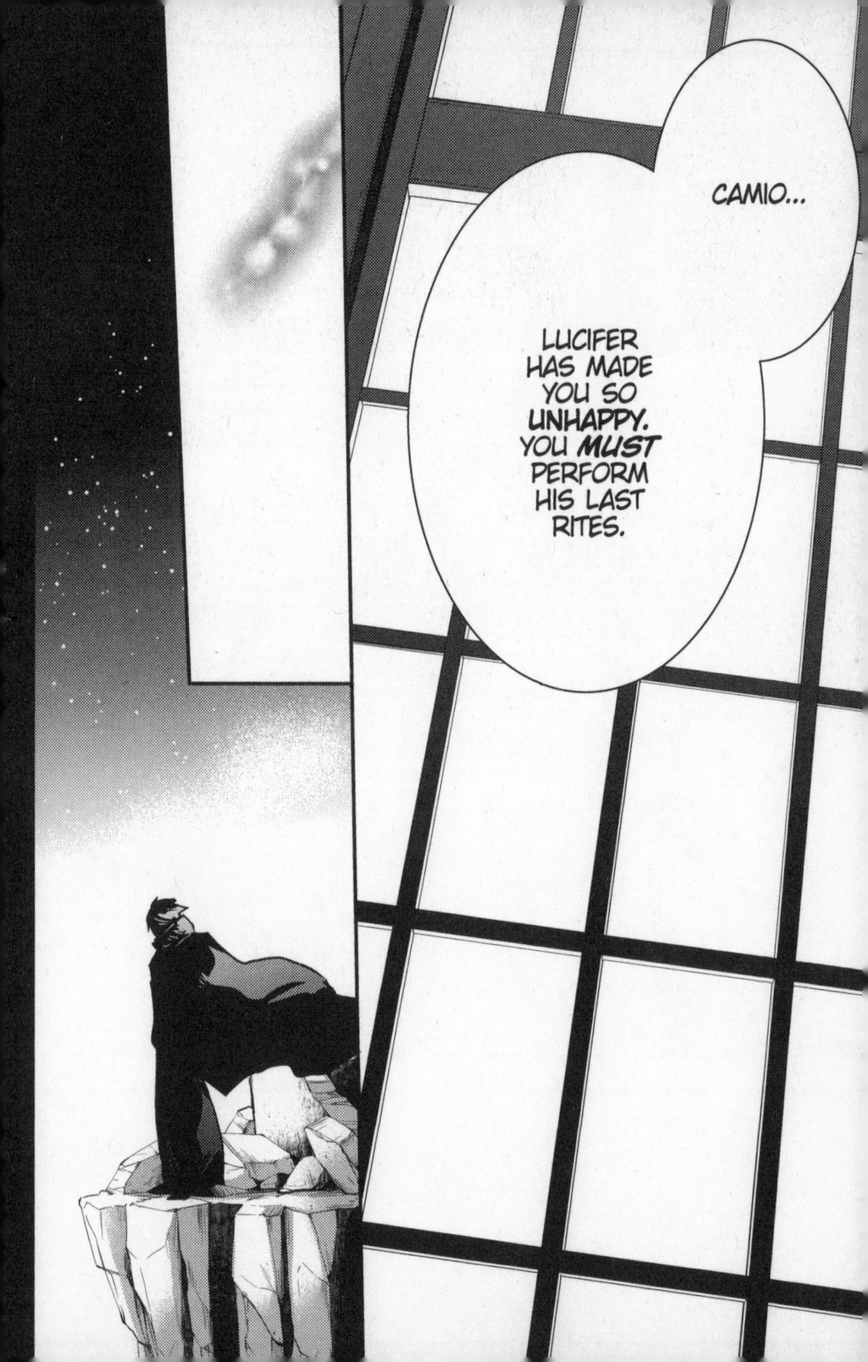
CAMIO...
LUCIFER HAS MADE YOU SO **UNHAPPY.** YOU ***MUST*** PERFORM HIS LAST RITES.

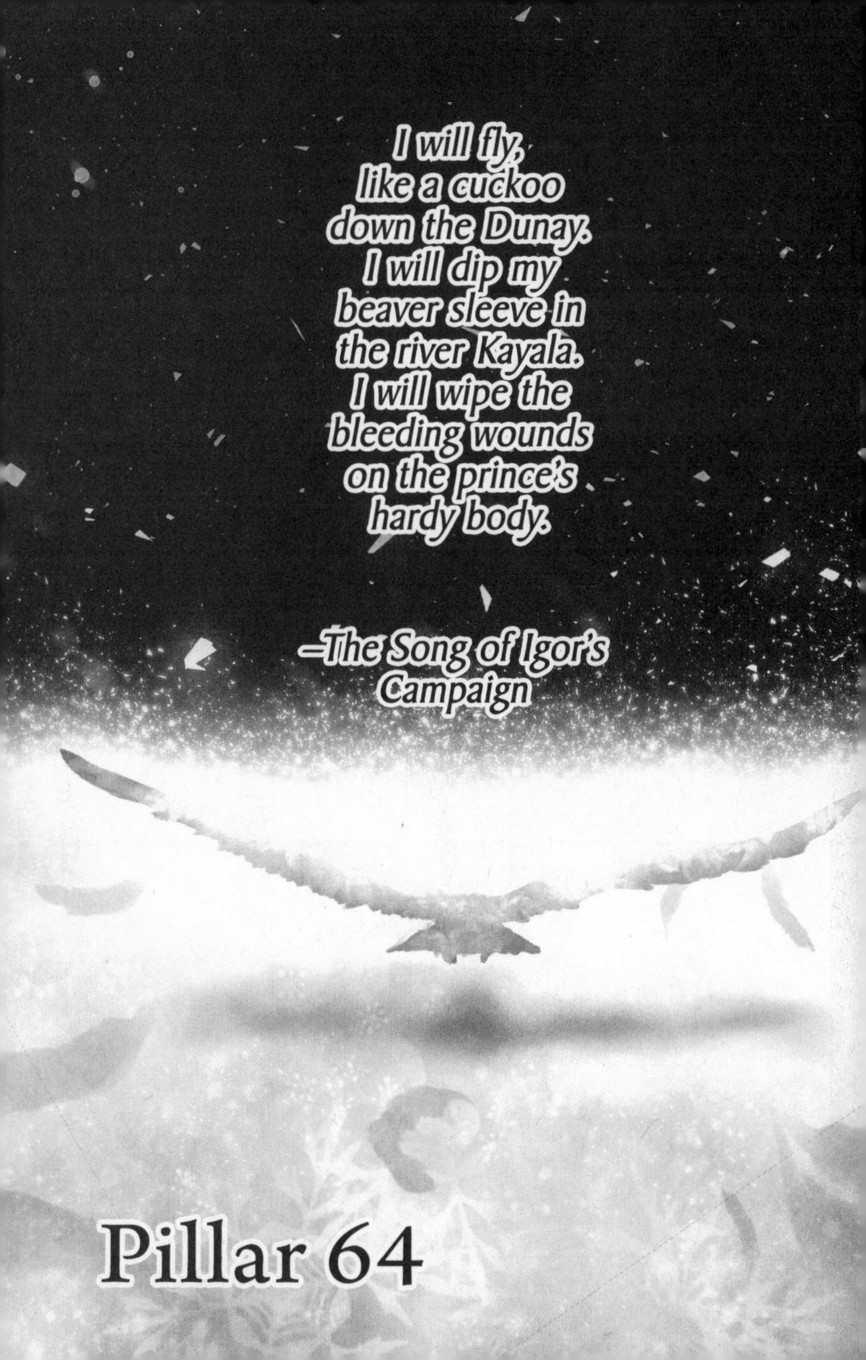
I will fly,
like a cuckoo
down the Dunay.
I will dip my
beaver sleeve in
the river Kayala.
I will wipe the
bleeding wounds
on the prince's
hardy body.
–The Song of Igor's
Campaign

Pillar 64

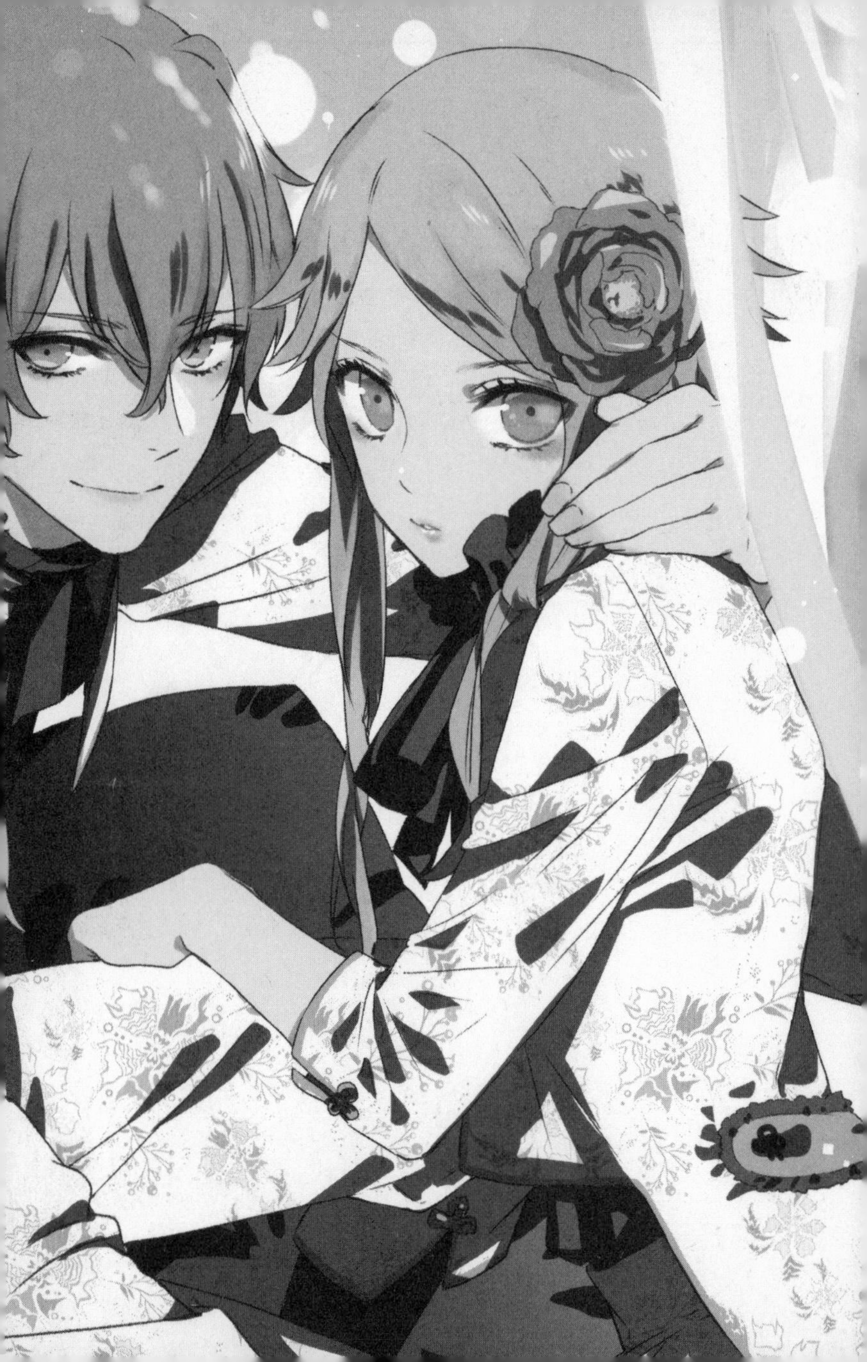

Pillar 64

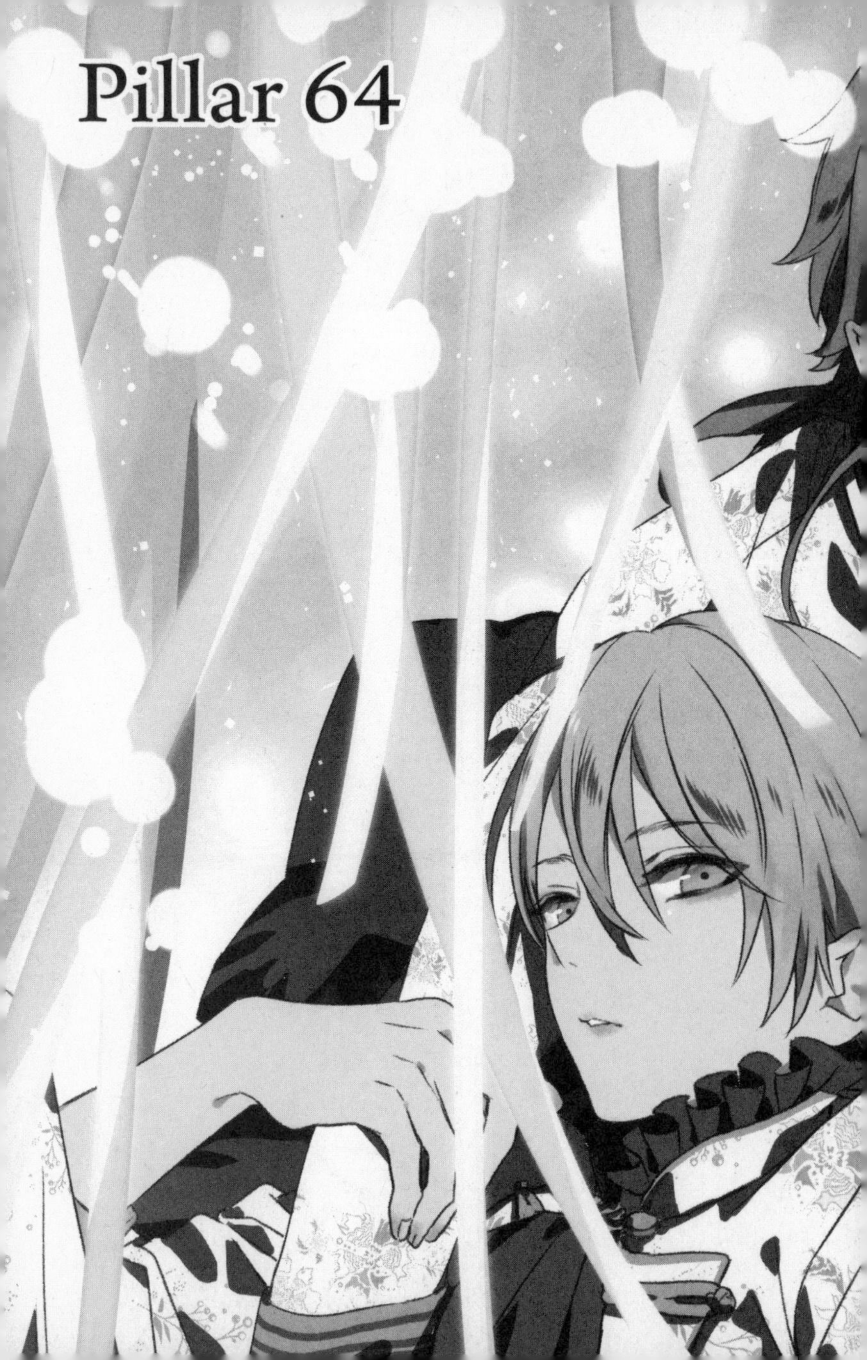

AMEN...

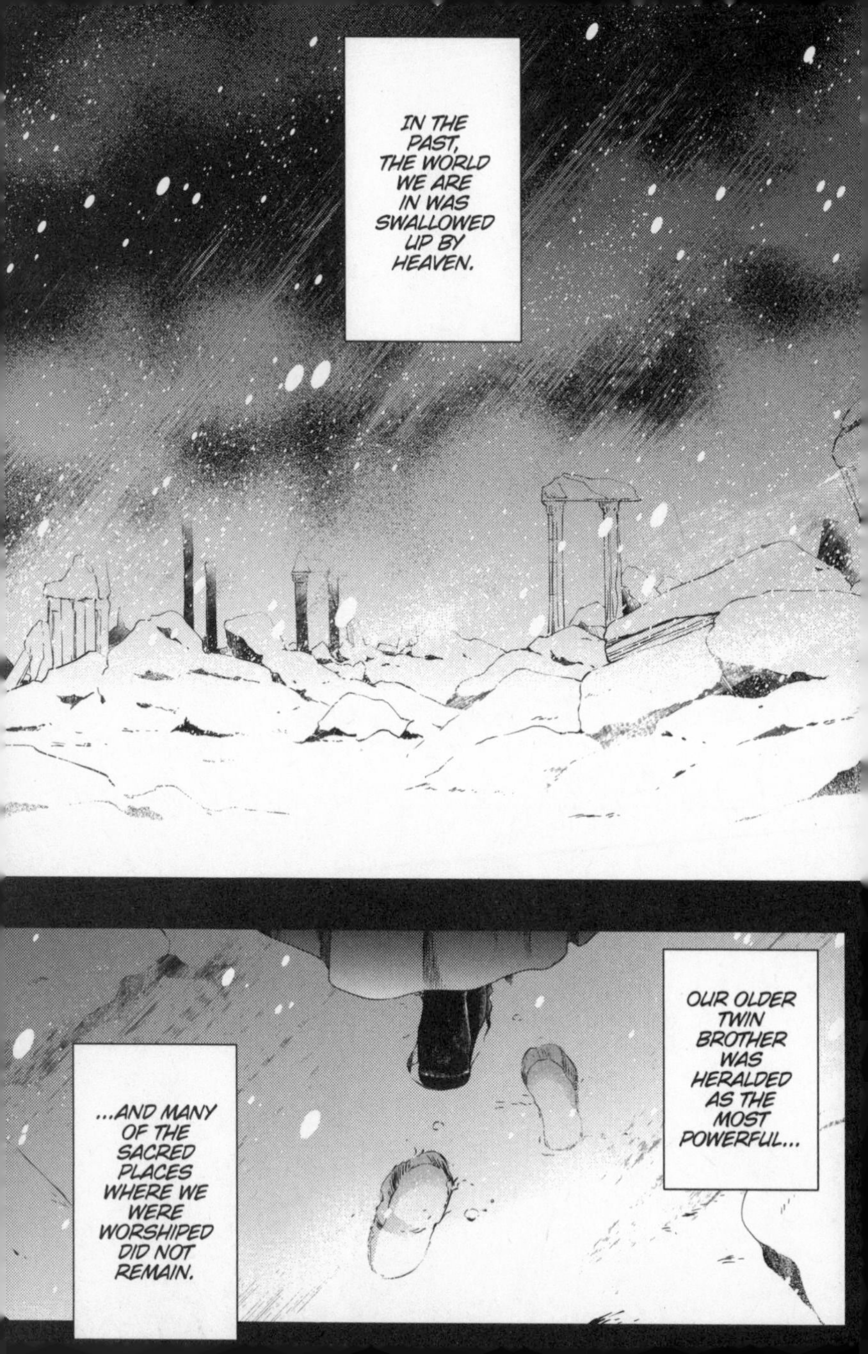
IN THE PAST, THE WORLD WE ARE IN WAS SWALLOWED UP BY HEAVEN.
OUR OLDER TWIN BROTHER WAS HERALDED AS THE MOST POWERFUL...
...AND MANY OF THE SACRED PLACES WHERE WE WERE WORSHIPED DID NOT REMAIN.

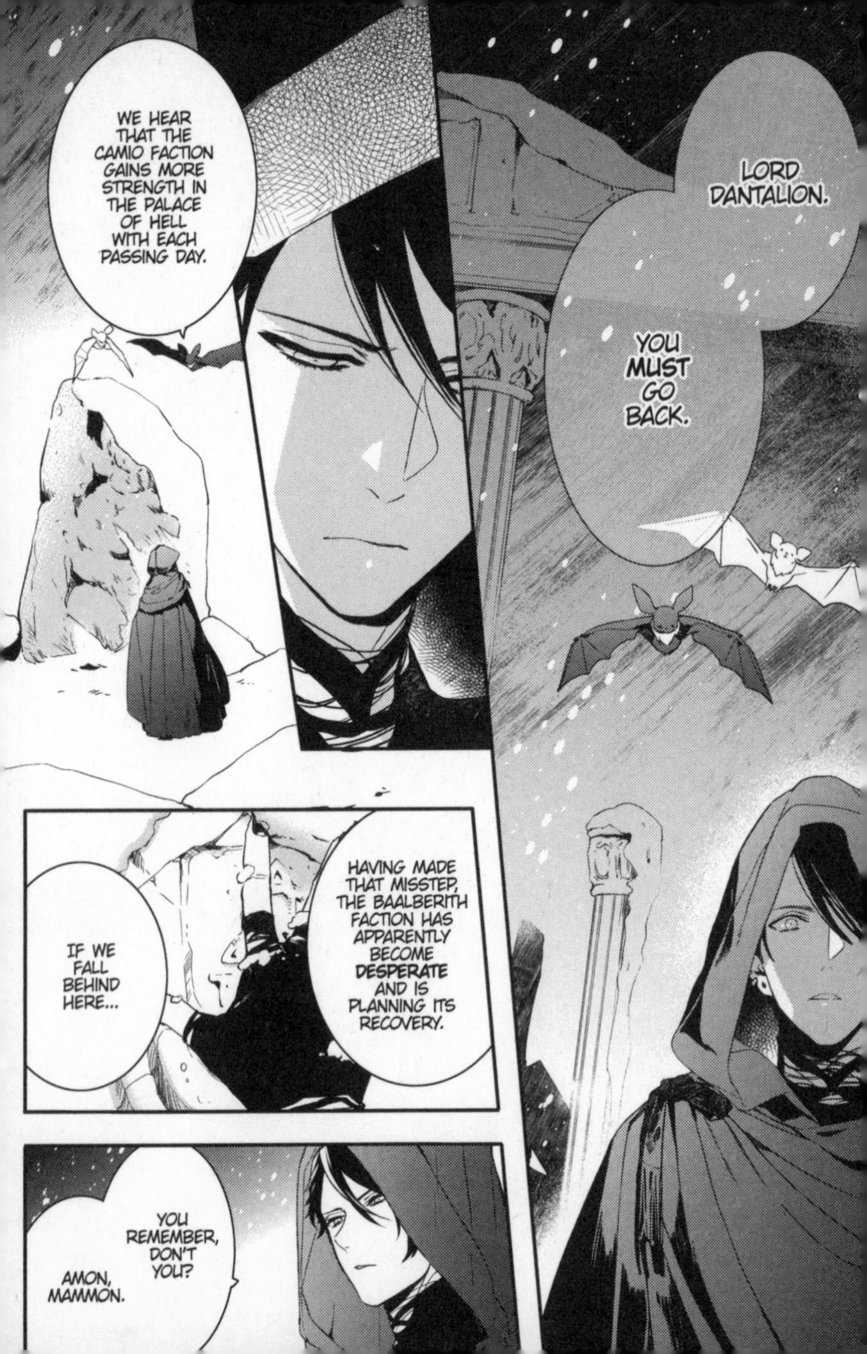
LORD DANTALION.
YOU MUST GO BACK.
WE HEAR THAT THE CAMIO FACTION GAINS MORE STRENGTH IN THE PALACE OF HELL WITH EACH PASSING DAY.
HAVING MADE THAT MISSTEP, THE BAALBERITH FACTION HAS APPARENTLY BECOME DESPERATE AND IS PLANNING ITS RECOVERY.
IF WE FALL BEHIND HERE...
YOU REMEMBER, DON'T YOU?
AMON, MAMMON.

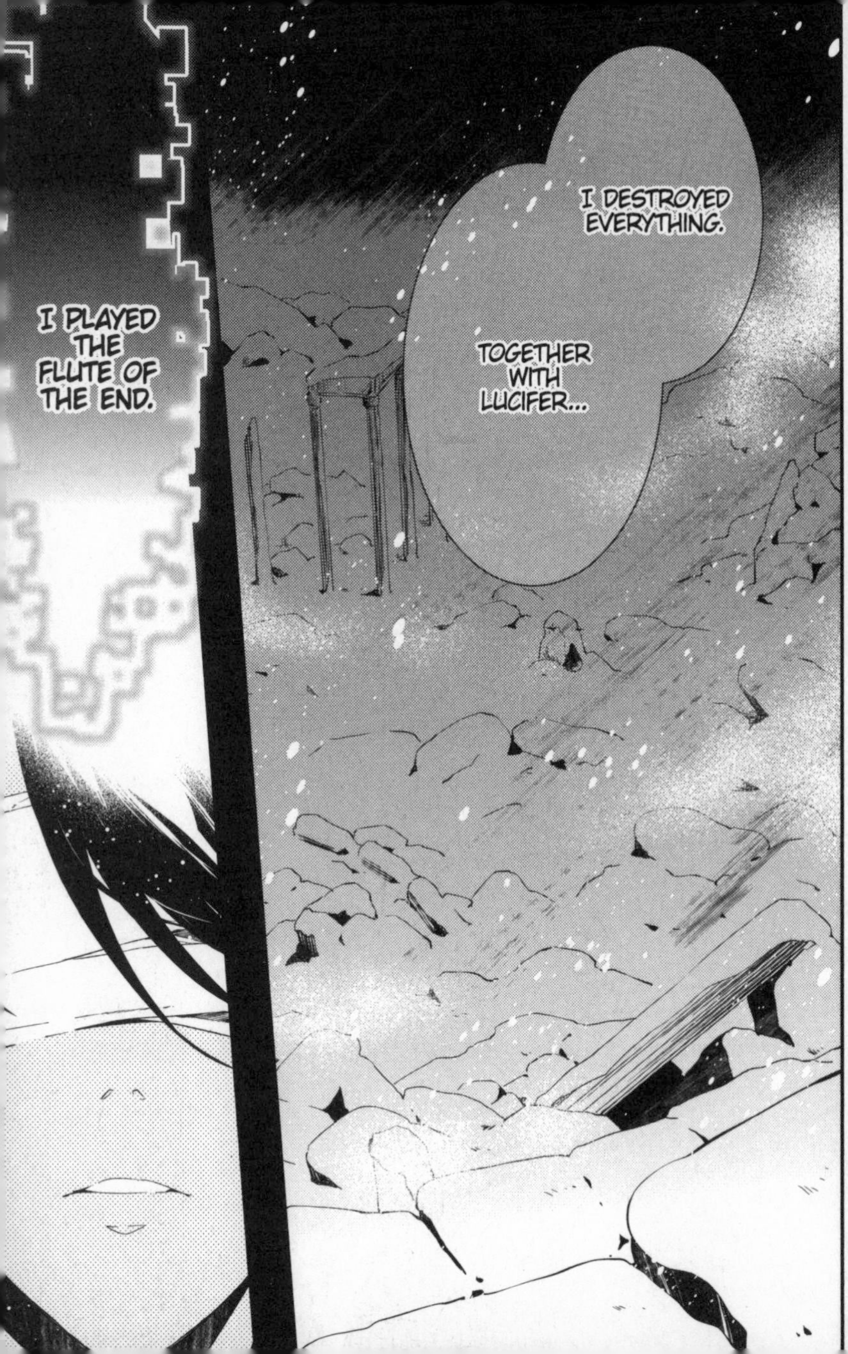
I DESTROYED EVERYTHING.
TOGETHER WITH LUCIFER...
I PLAYED THE FLUTE OF THE END.

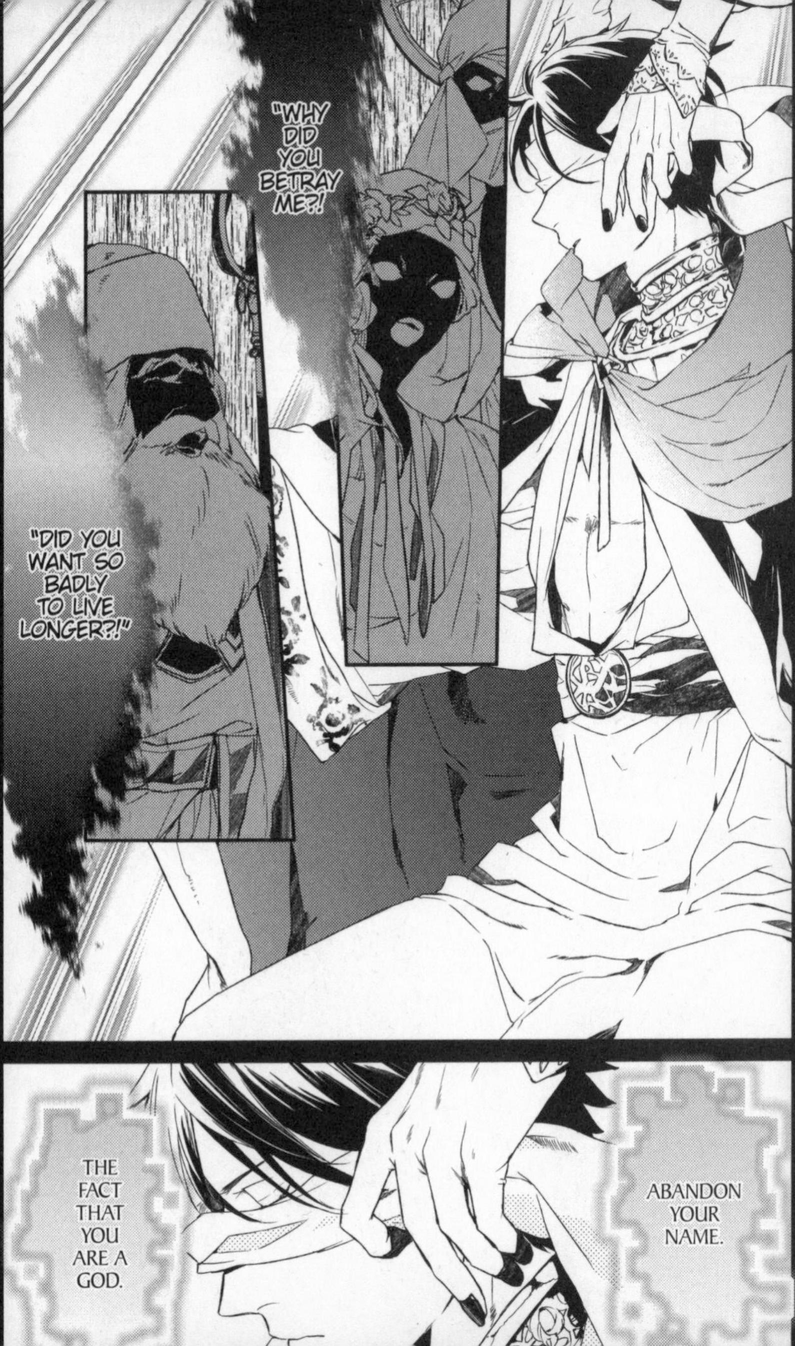
"WHY DID YOU BETRAY ME?!
"DID YOU WANT SO BADLY TO LIVE LONGER?!"
ABANDON YOUR NAME.
THE FACT THAT YOU ARE A GOD.

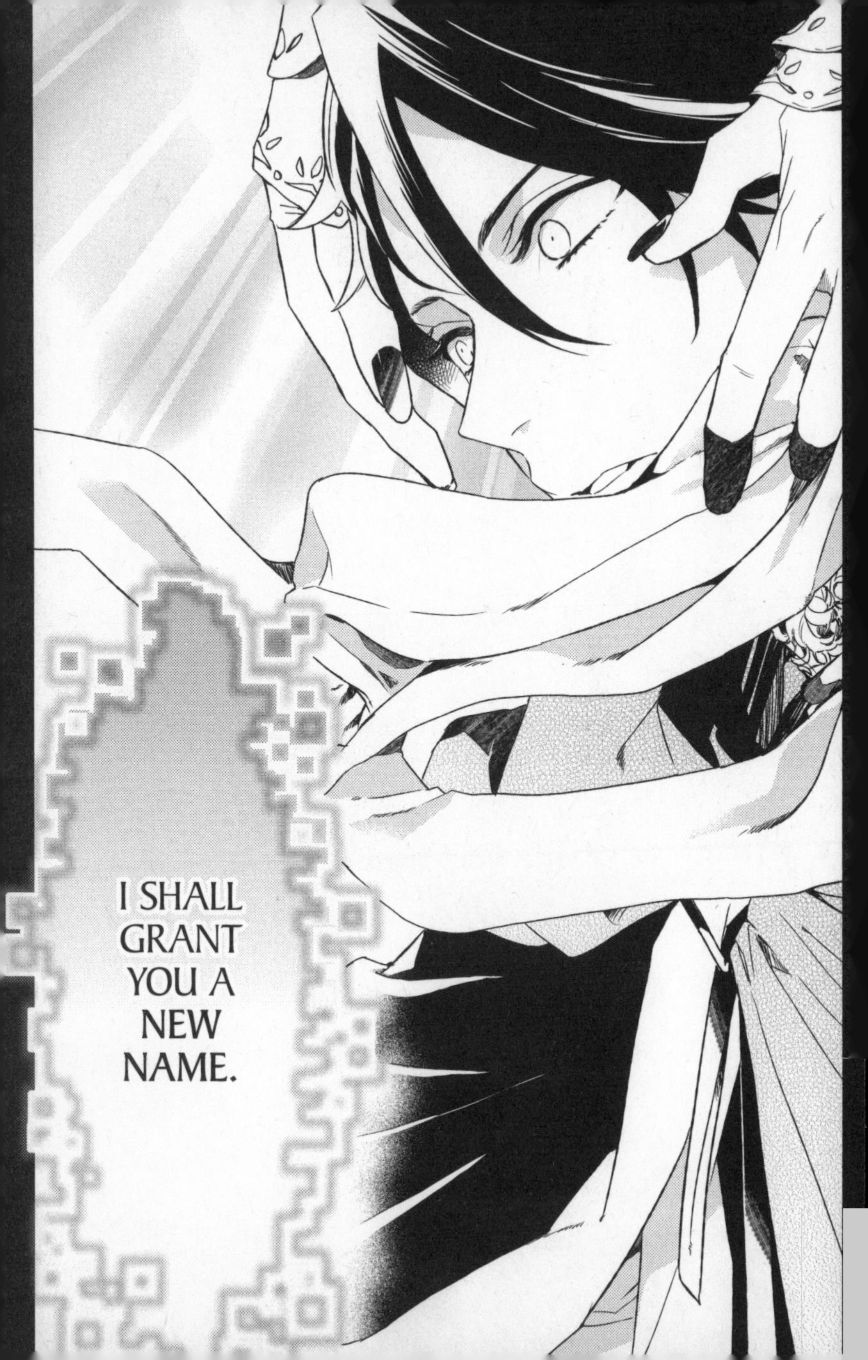
I SHALL GRANT YOU A NEW NAME.

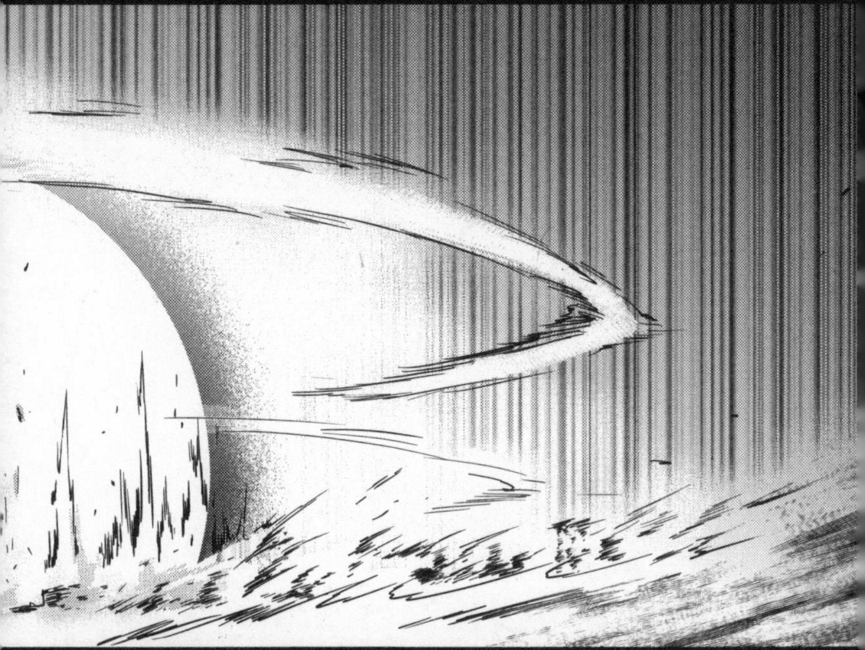
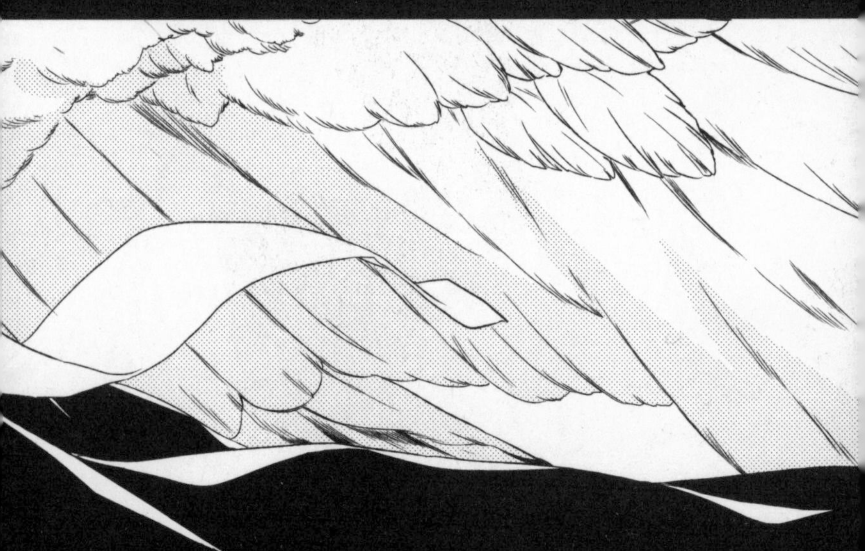

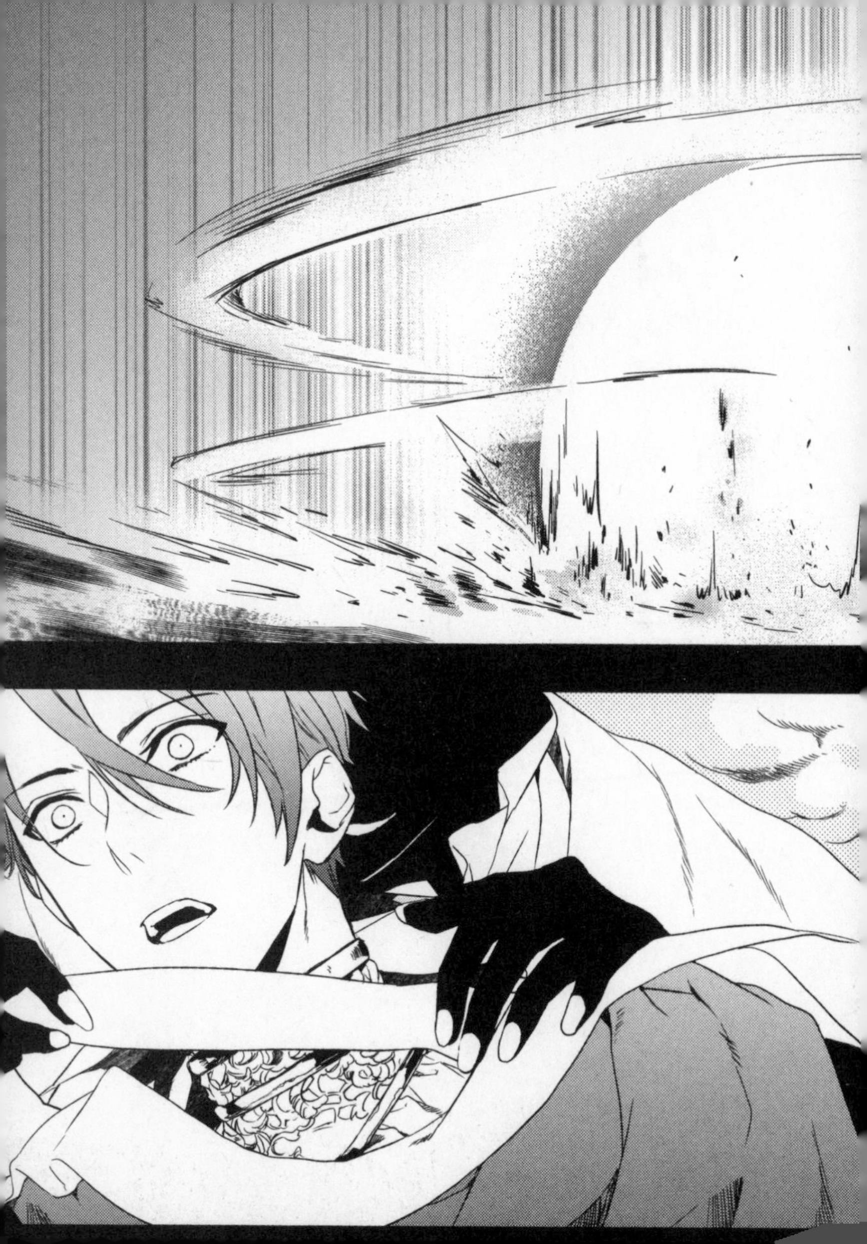

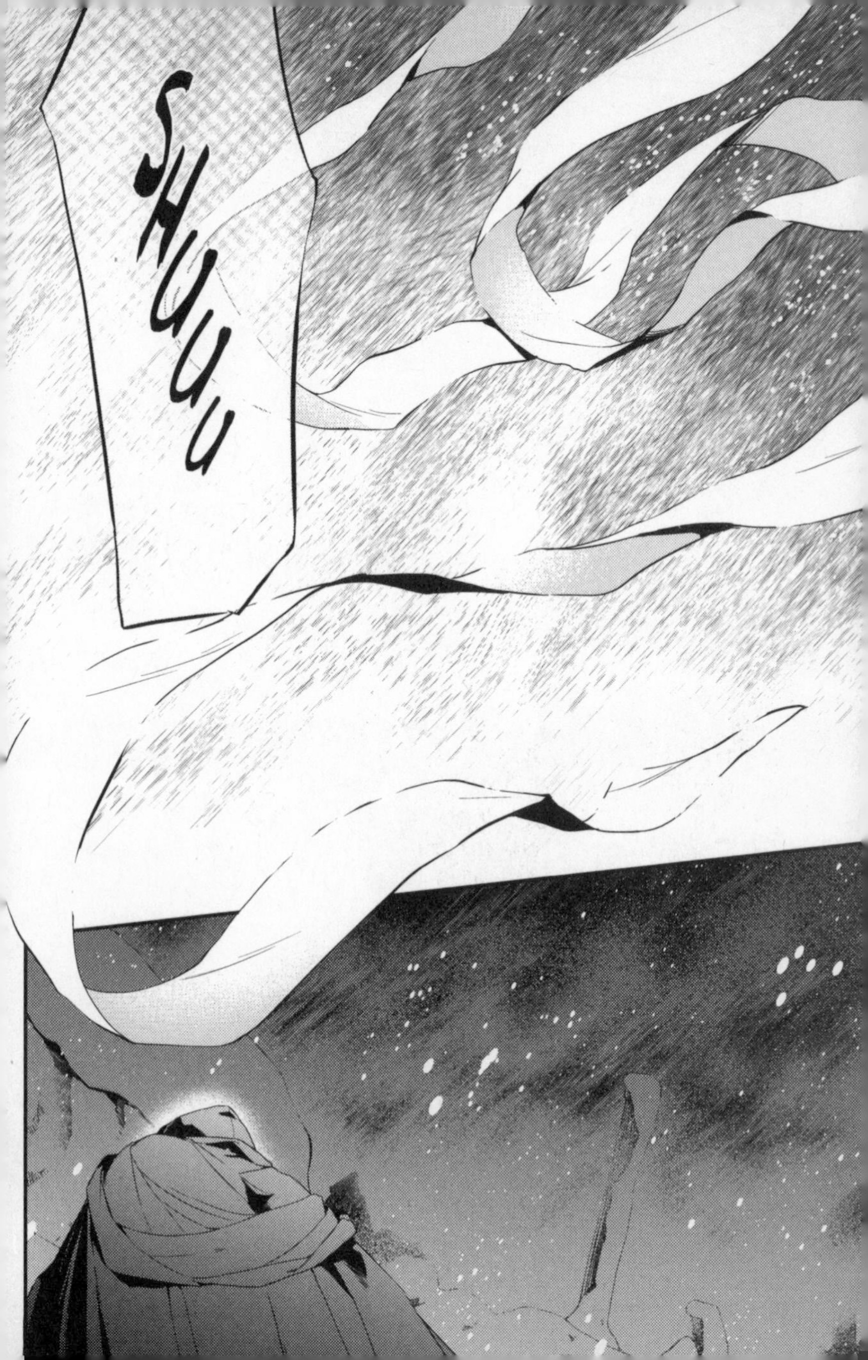
SHUUUU

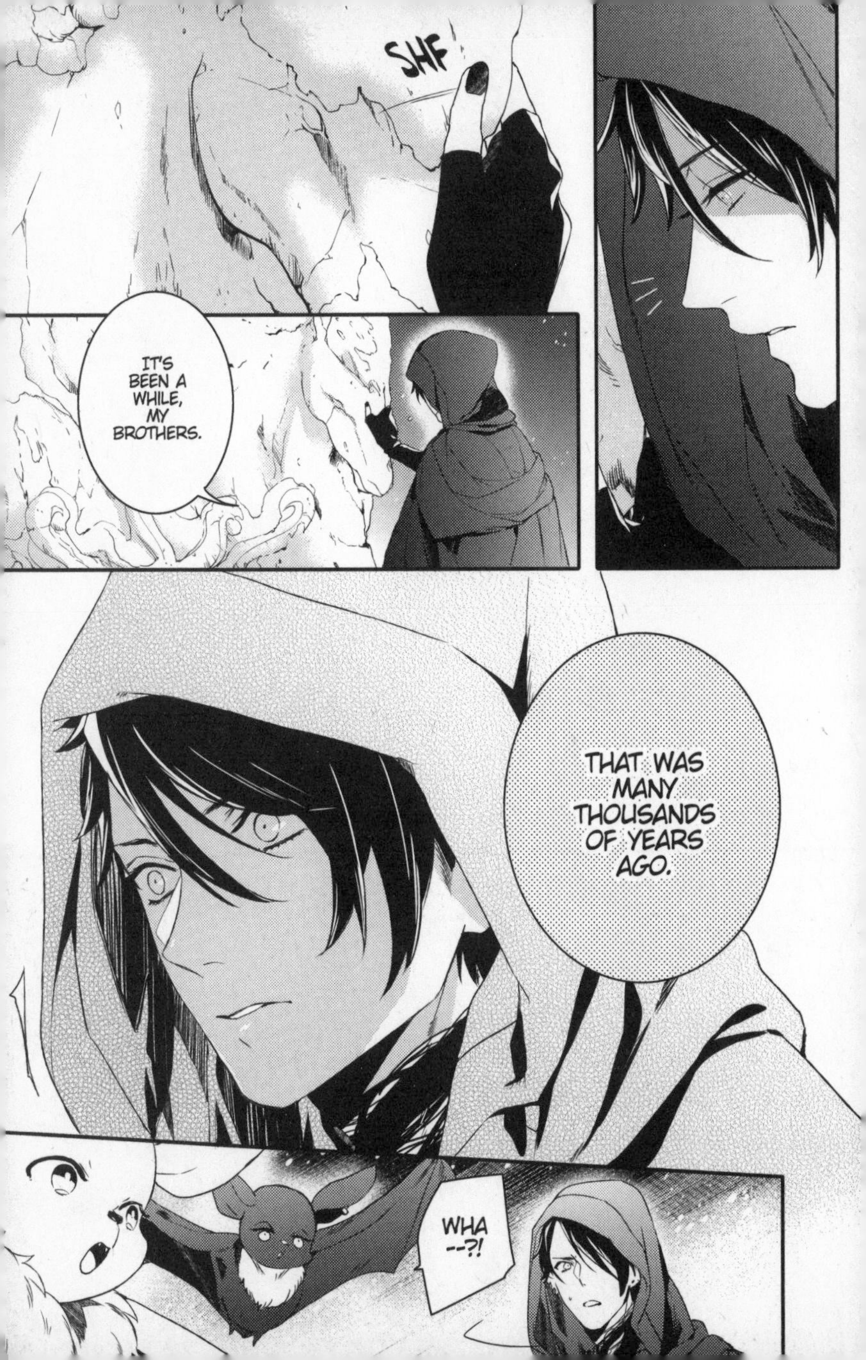
SHF
IT'S BEEN A WHILE, MY BROTHERS.
THAT WAS MANY THOUSANDS OF YEARS AGO.
WHA--?!

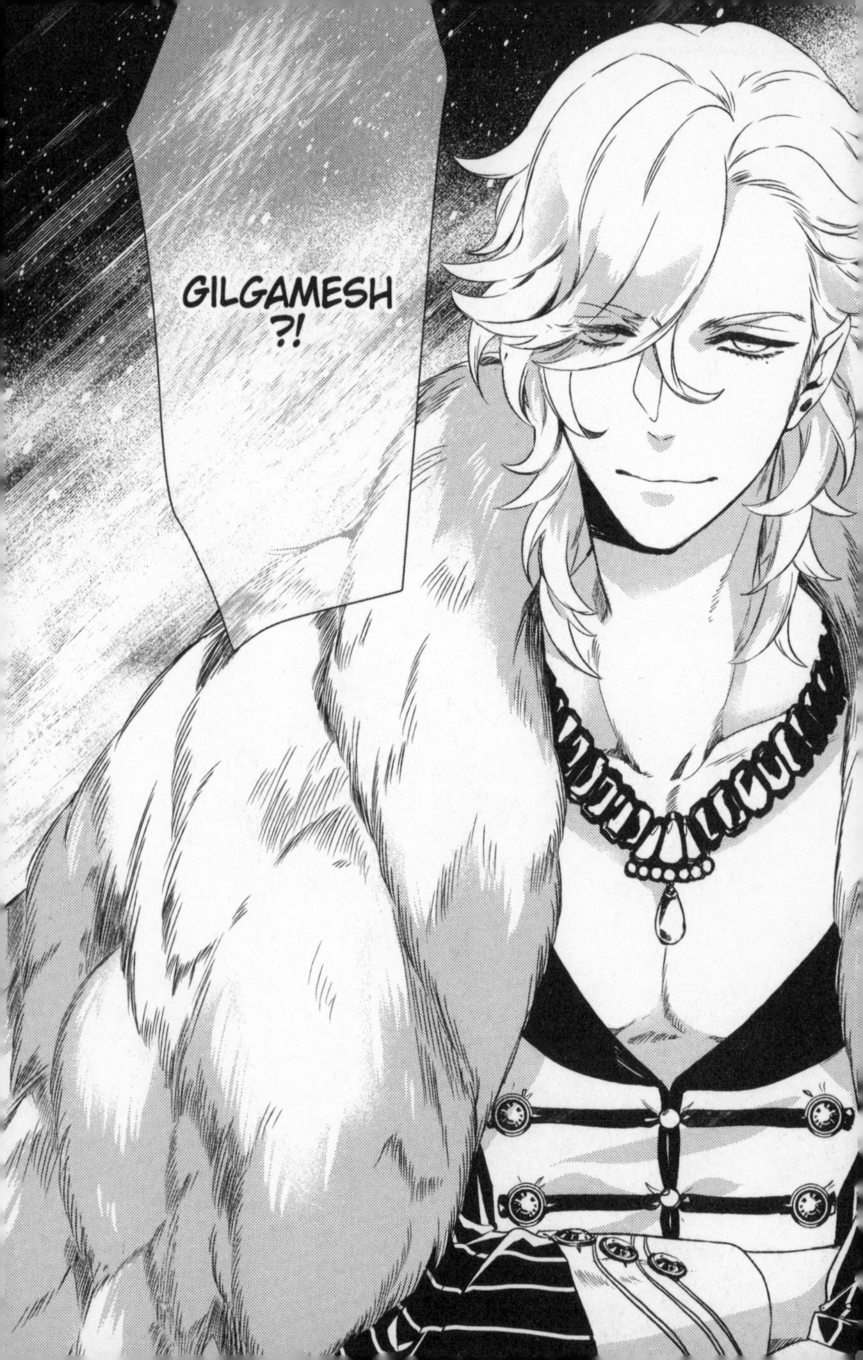
GILGAMESH ?!

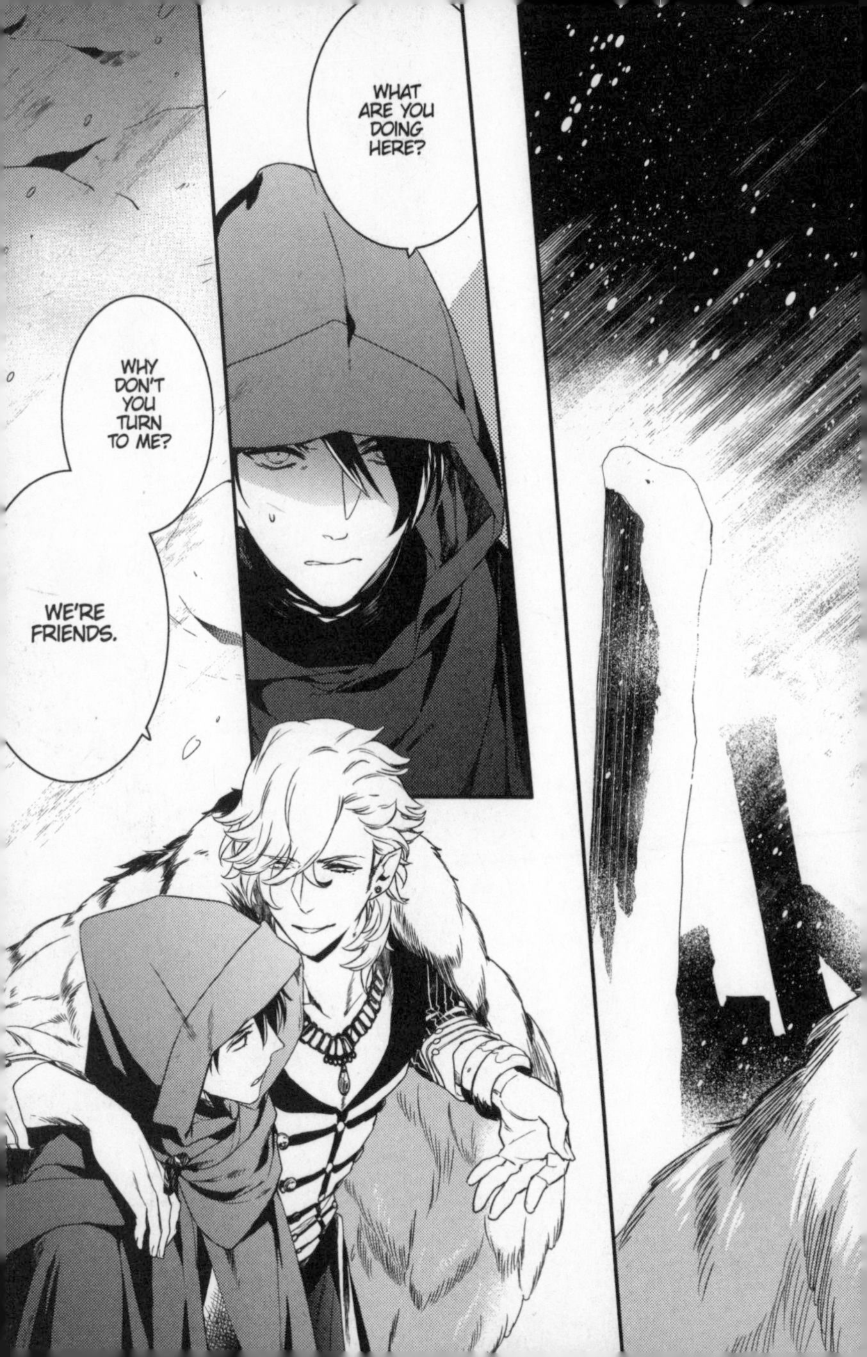
WHAT ARE YOU DOING HERE?
WHY DON'T YOU TURN TO ME?
WE'RE FRIENDS.

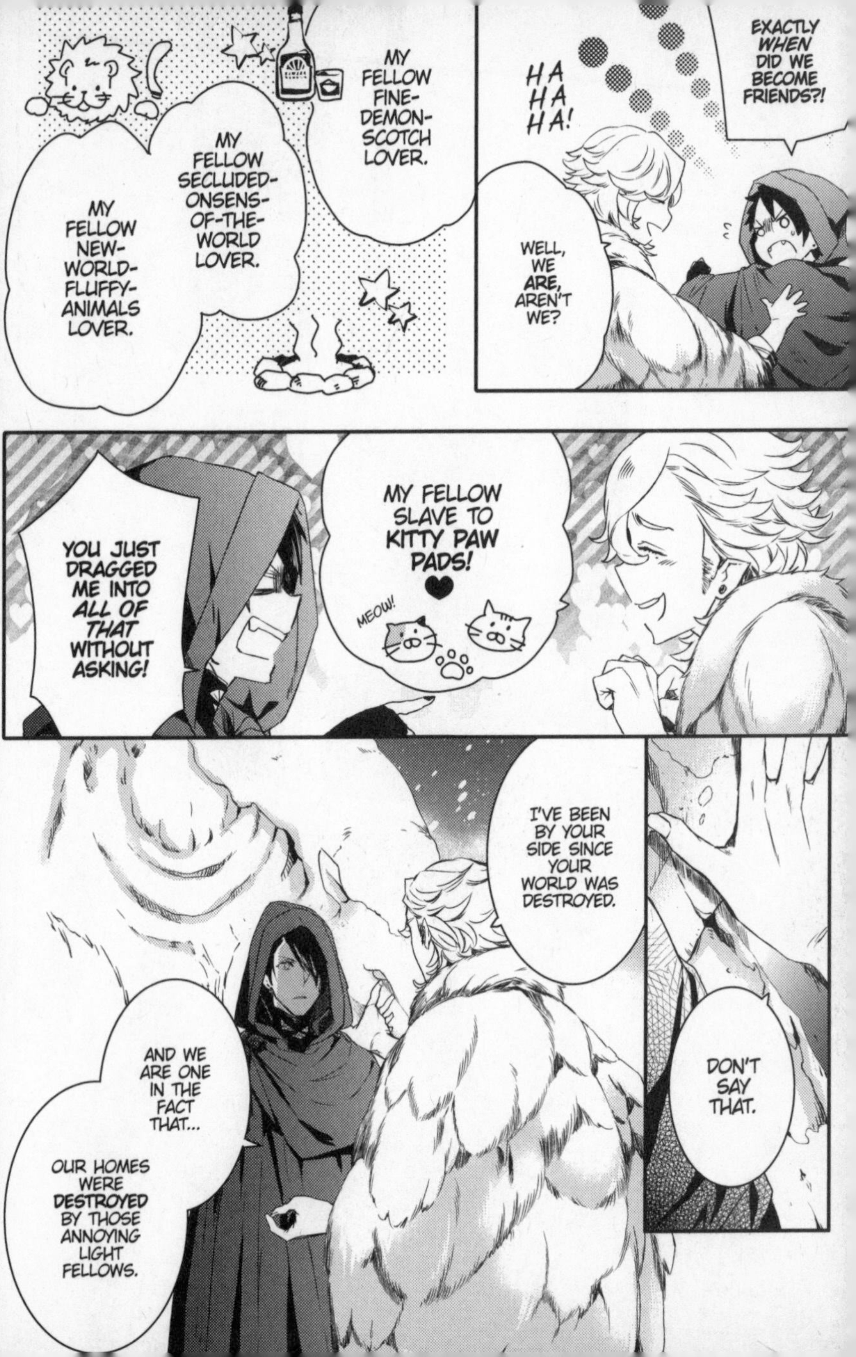
EXACTLY WHEN DID WE BECOME FRIENDS?!
HA HA HA!
WELL, WE ARE, AREN'T WE?
MY FELLOW FINE-DEMON-SCOTCH LOVER.
MY FELLOW SECLUDED-ONSENS-OF-THE-WORLD LOVER.
MY FELLOW NEW-WORLD-FLUFFY-ANIMALS LOVER.
MY FELLOW SLAVE TO KITTY PAW PADS! ♥
MEOW!
YOU JUST DRAGGED ME INTO ALL OF THAT WITHOUT ASKING!
DON'T SAY THAT.
I'VE BEEN BY YOUR SIDE SINCE YOUR WORLD WAS DESTROYED.
AND WE ARE ONE IN THE FACT THAT...
OUR HOMES WERE DESTROYED BY THOSE ANNOYING LIGHT FELLOWS.

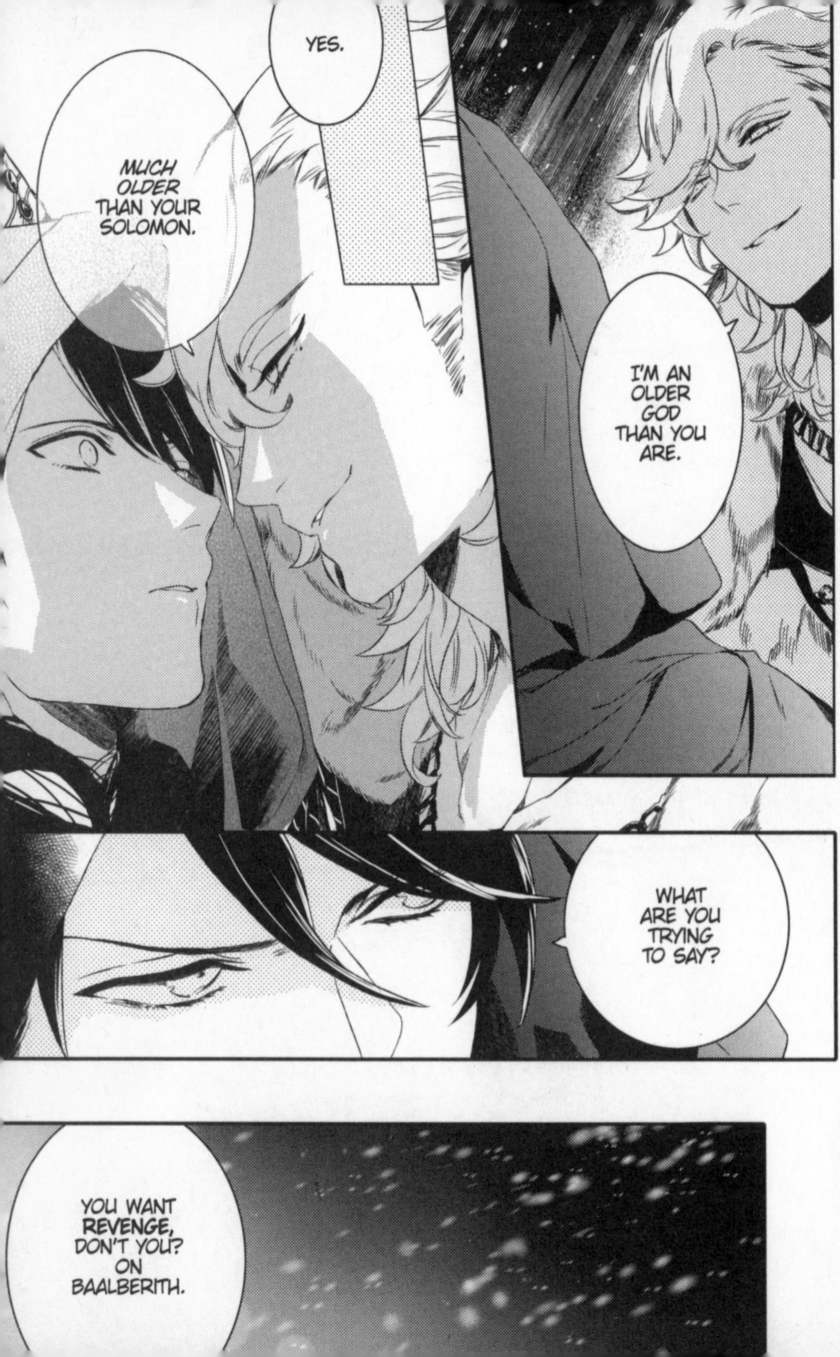
I'M AN OLDER GOD THAN YOU ARE.
YES.
MUCH OLDER THAN YOUR SOLOMON.
WHAT ARE YOU TRYING TO SAY?
YOU WANT REVENGE, DON'T YOU? ON BAALBERITH.

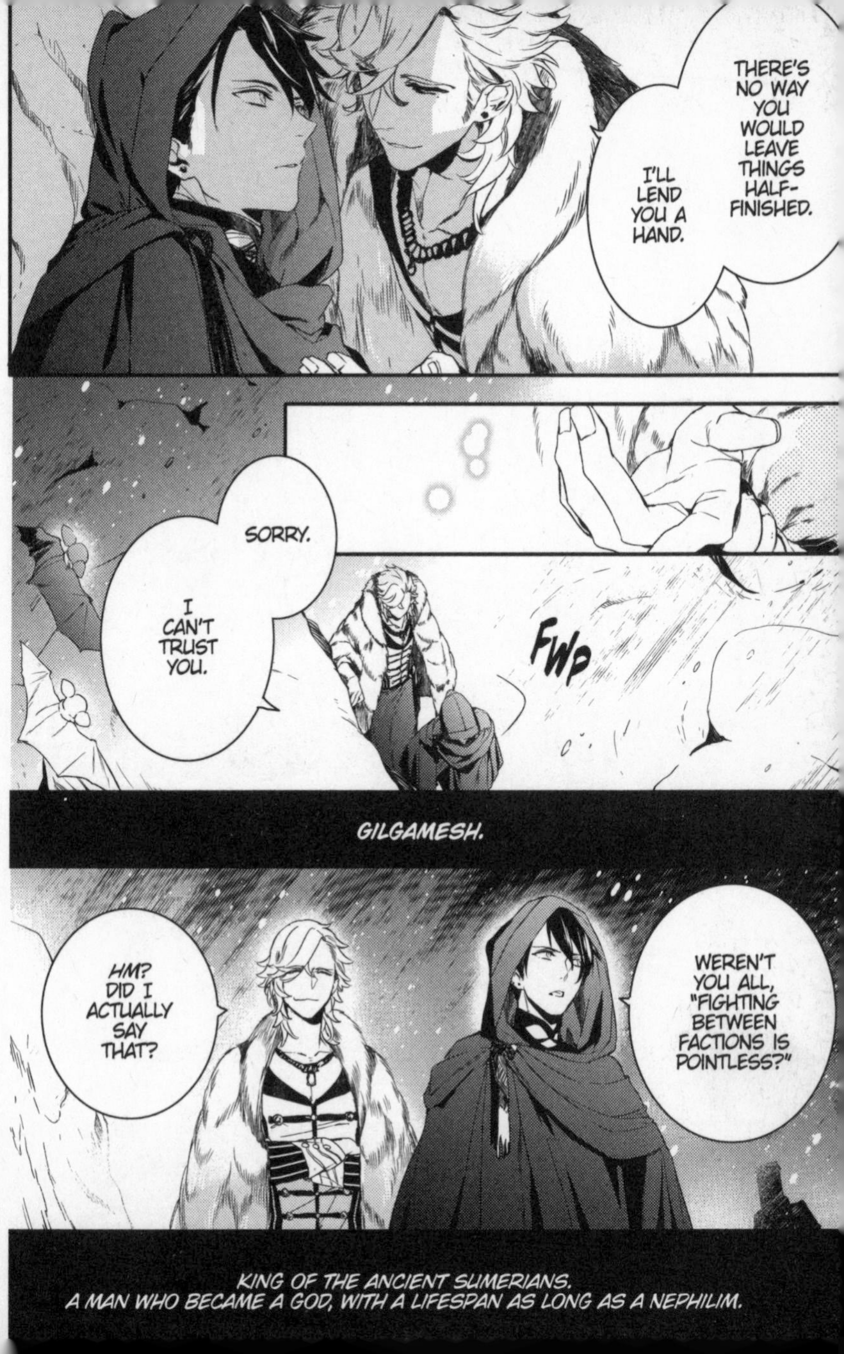
THERE'S NO WAY YOU WOULD LEAVE THINGS HALF-FINISHED.
I'LL LEND YOU A HAND.
FWP
SORRY.
I CAN'T TRUST YOU.
GILGAMESH.
WEREN'T YOU ALL, "FIGHTING BETWEEN FACTIONS IS POINTLESS?"
HM? DID I ACTUALLY SAY THAT?
KING OF THE ANCIENT SUMERIANS.
A MAN WHO BECAME A GOD, WITH A LIFESPAN AS LONG AS A NEPHILIM.

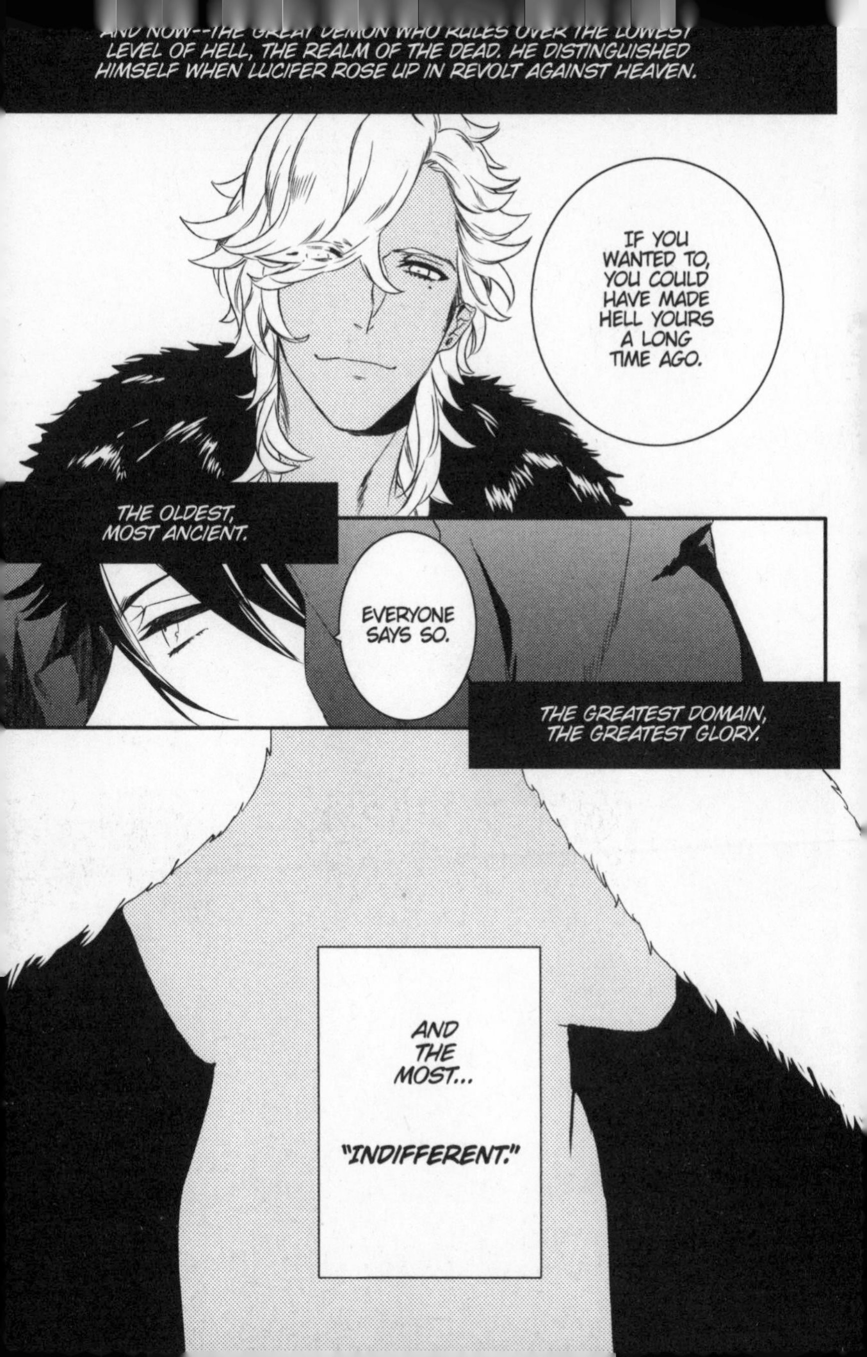
AND NOW--THE GREAT DEMON WHO RULES OVER THE LOWEST LEVEL OF HELL, THE REALM OF THE DEAD. HE DISTINGUISHED HIMSELF WHEN LUCIFER ROSE UP IN REVOLT AGAINST HEAVEN.
IF YOU WANTED TO, YOU COULD HAVE MADE HELL YOURS A LONG TIME AGO.
THE OLDEST, MOST ANCIENT.
EVERYONE SAYS SO.
THE GREATEST DOMAIN, THE GREATEST GLORY.
AND THE MOST...
"INDIFFERENT."

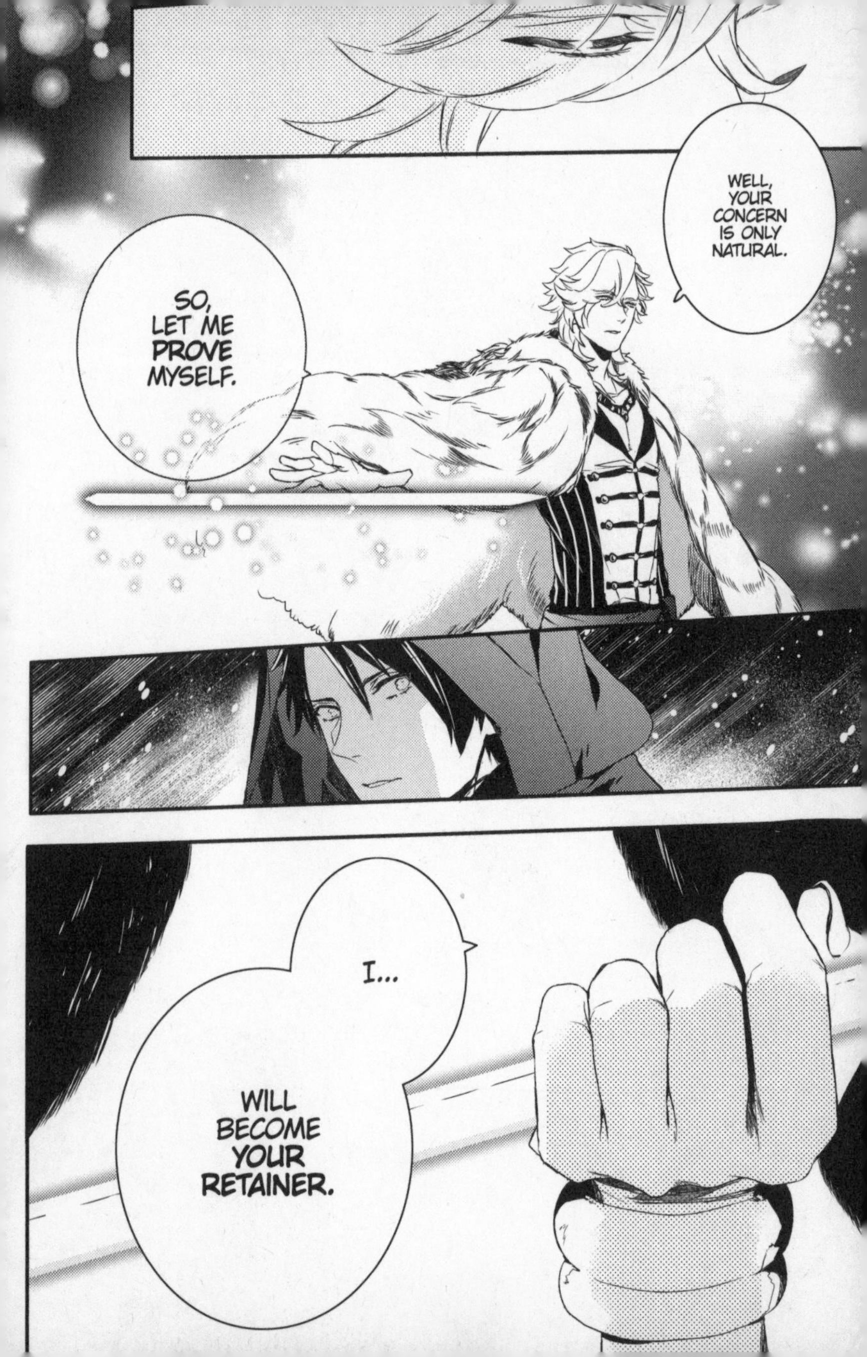
WELL, YOUR CONCERN IS ONLY NATURAL.
SO, LET ME PROVE MYSELF.
I...
WILL BECOME YOUR RETAINER.

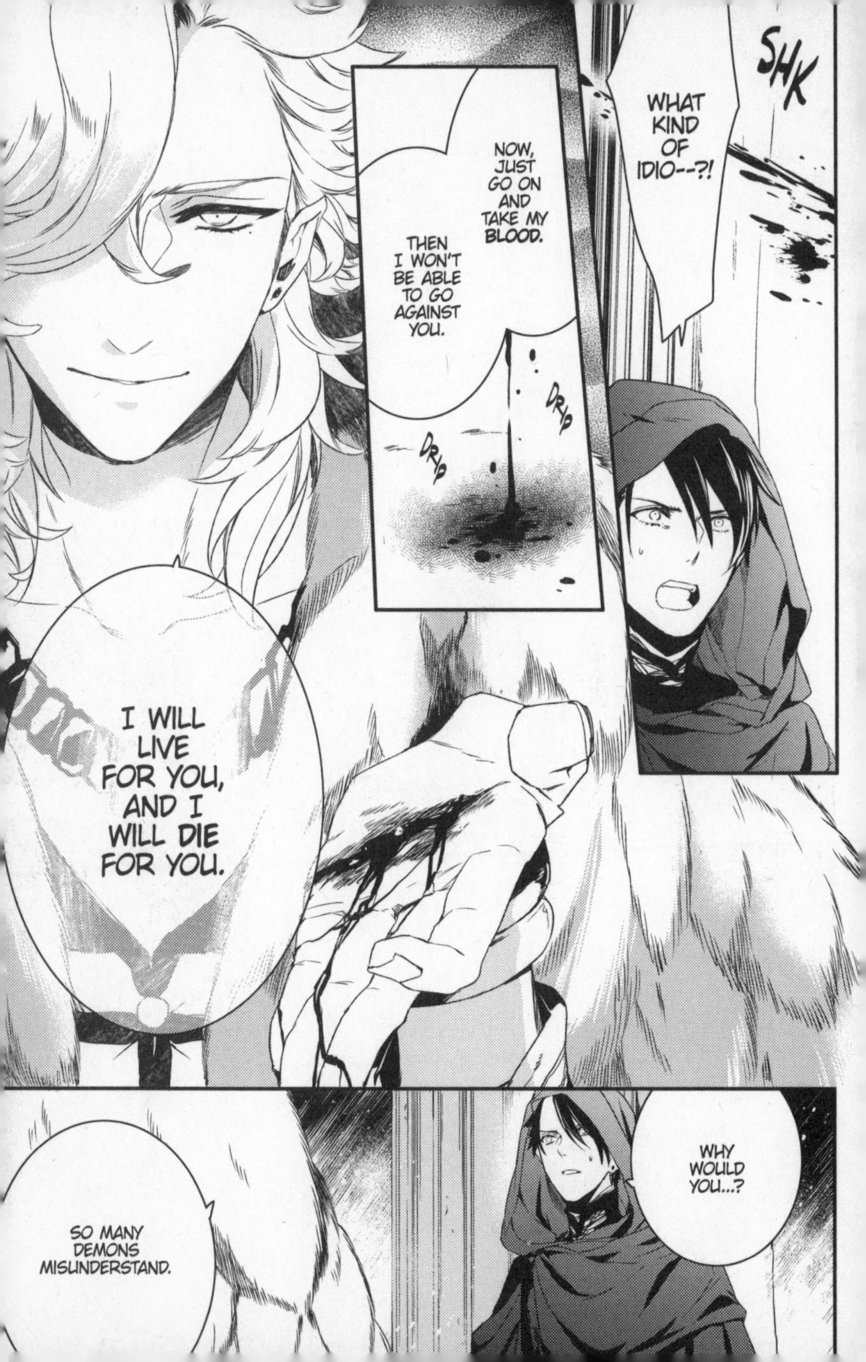
SHK
WHAT KIND OF IDIO--?!
NOW, JUST GO ON AND TAKE MY BLOOD.
THEN I WON'T BE ABLE TO GO AGAINST YOU.
DRIP
DRIP
I WILL LIVE FOR YOU, AND I WILL DIE FOR YOU.
WHY WOULD YOU...?
SO MANY DEMONS MISUNDERSTAND.

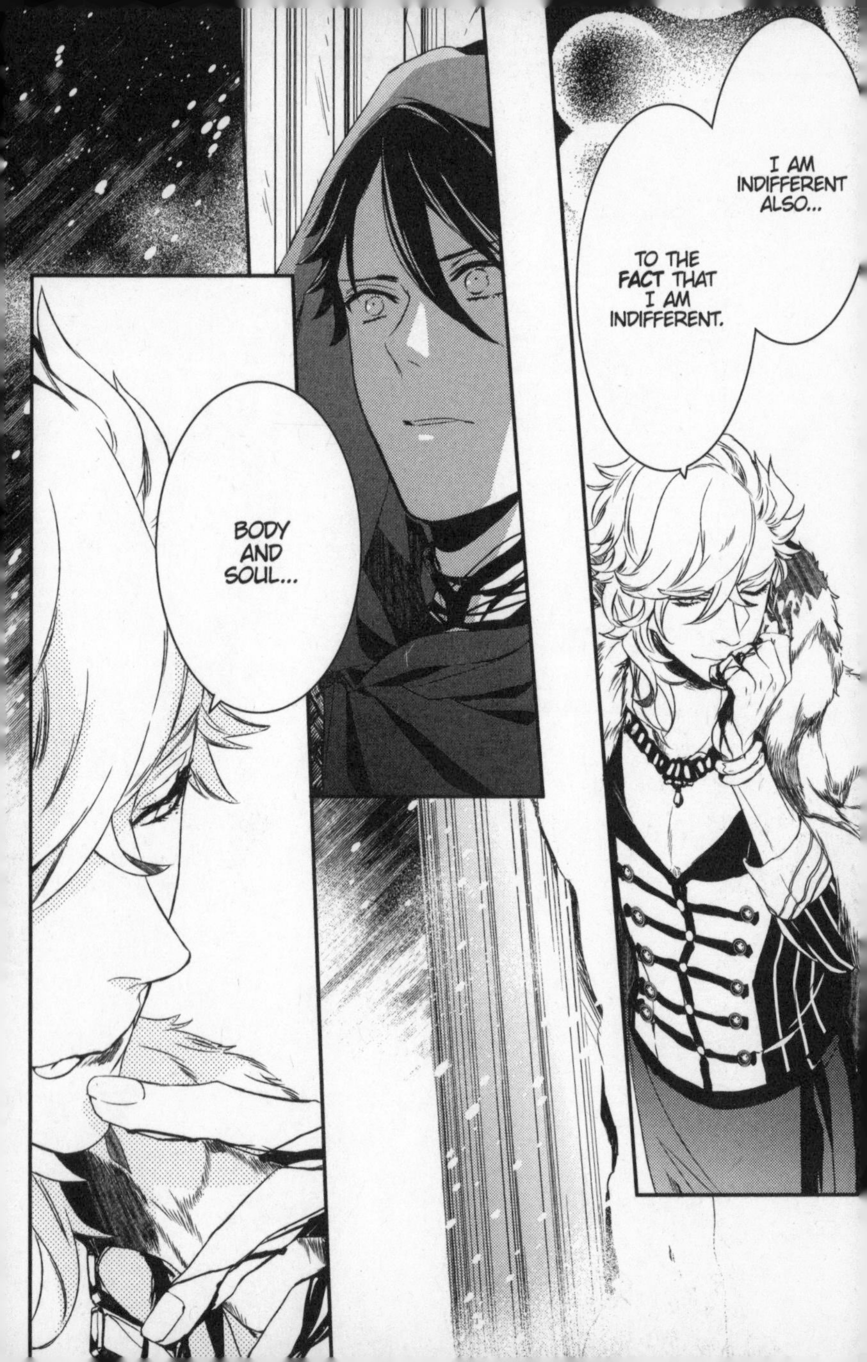
I AM INDIFFERENT ALSO...
TO THE FACT THAT I AM INDIFFERENT.
BODY AND SOUL...

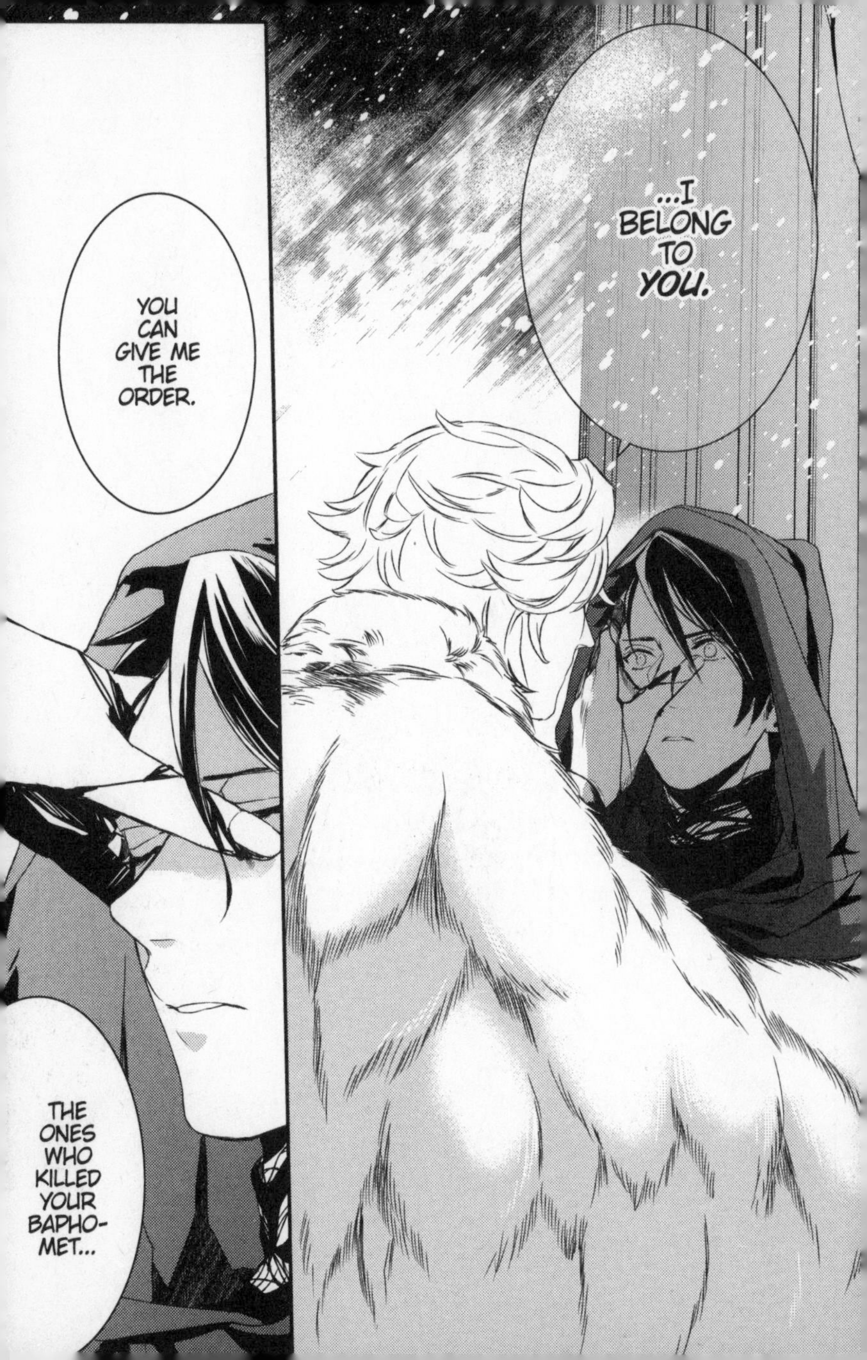
...I BELONG TO YOU.
YOU CAN GIVE ME THE ORDER.
THE ONES WHO KILLED YOUR BAPHO-MET...

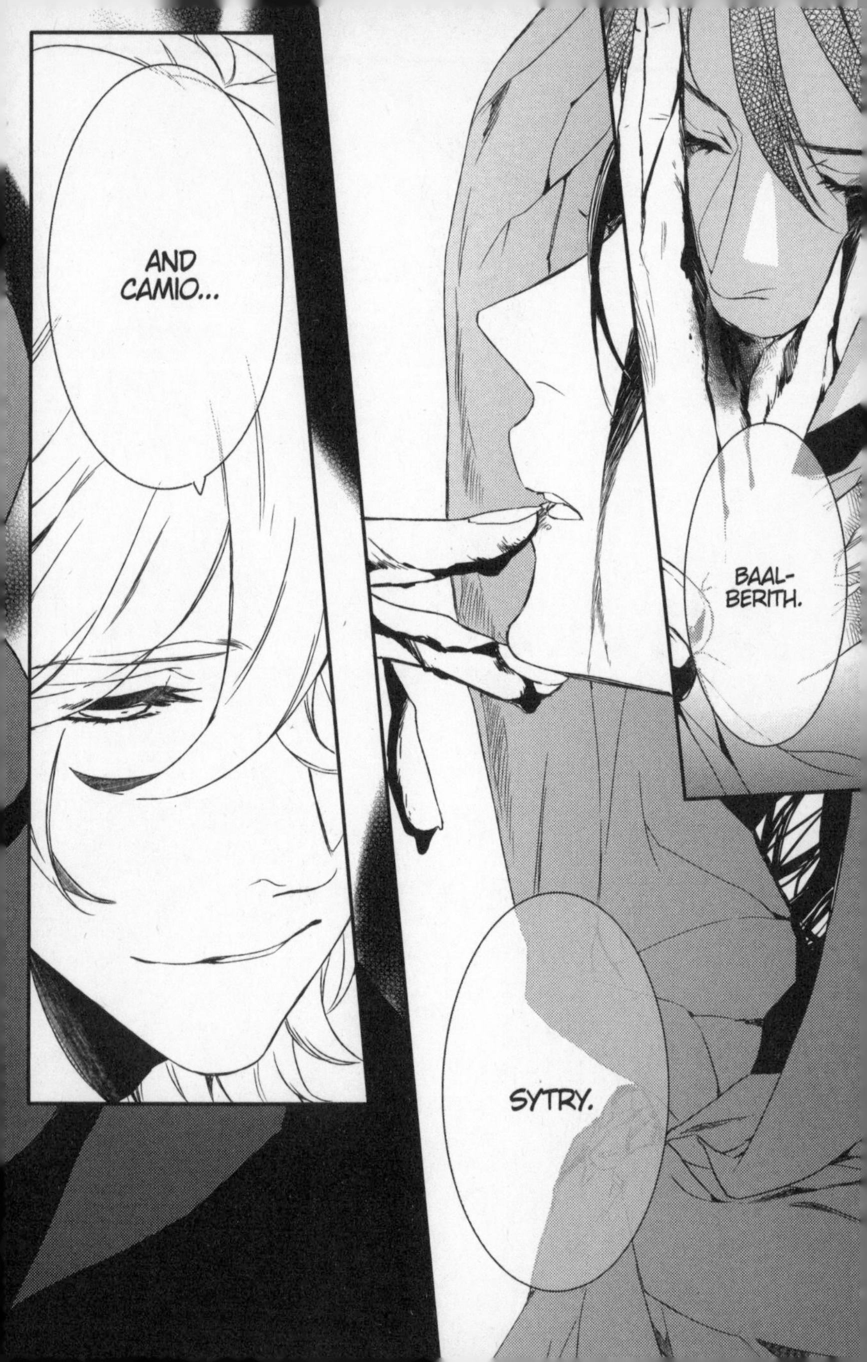
BAAL-BERITH.
SYTRY.
AND CAMIO...

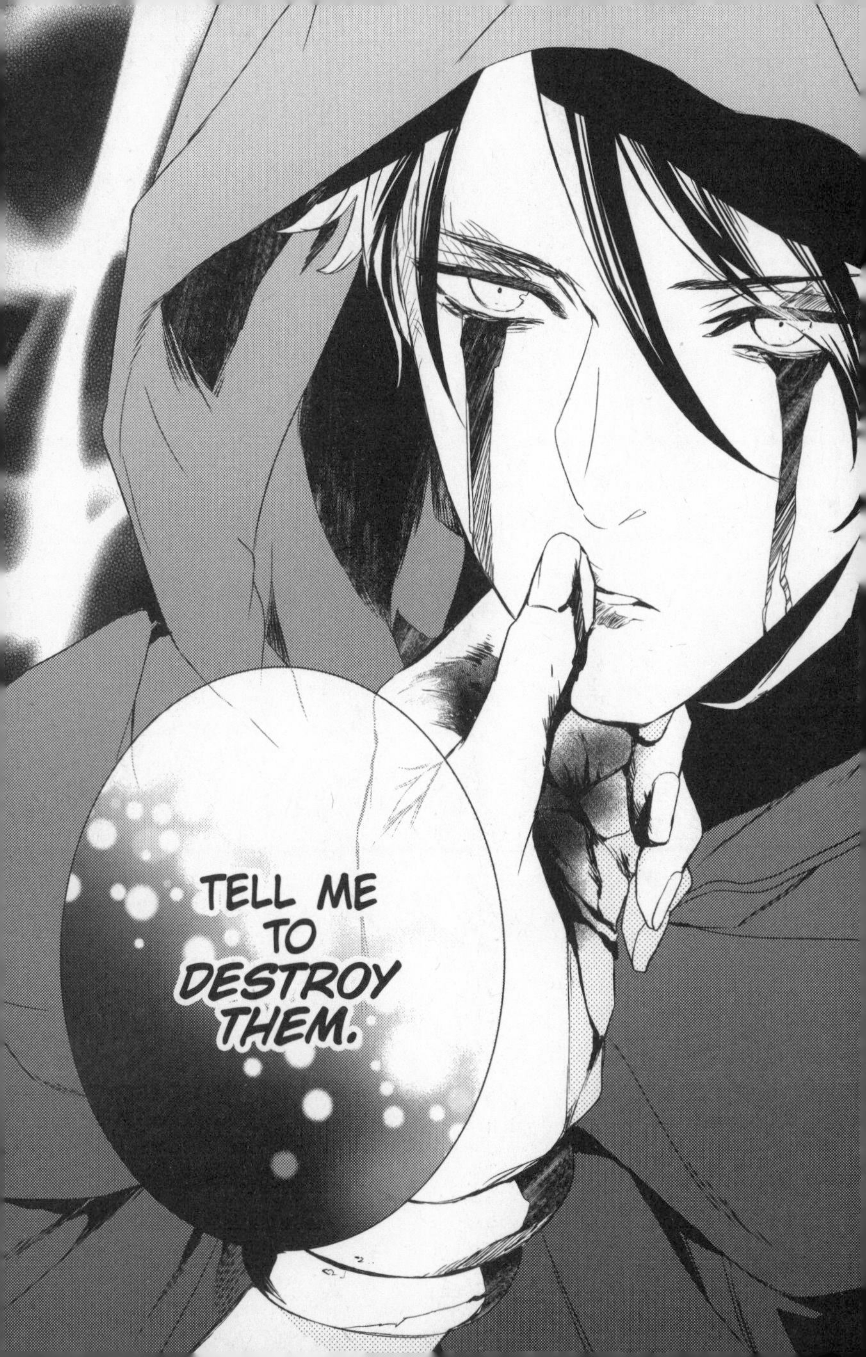
TELL ME TO DESTROY THEM.

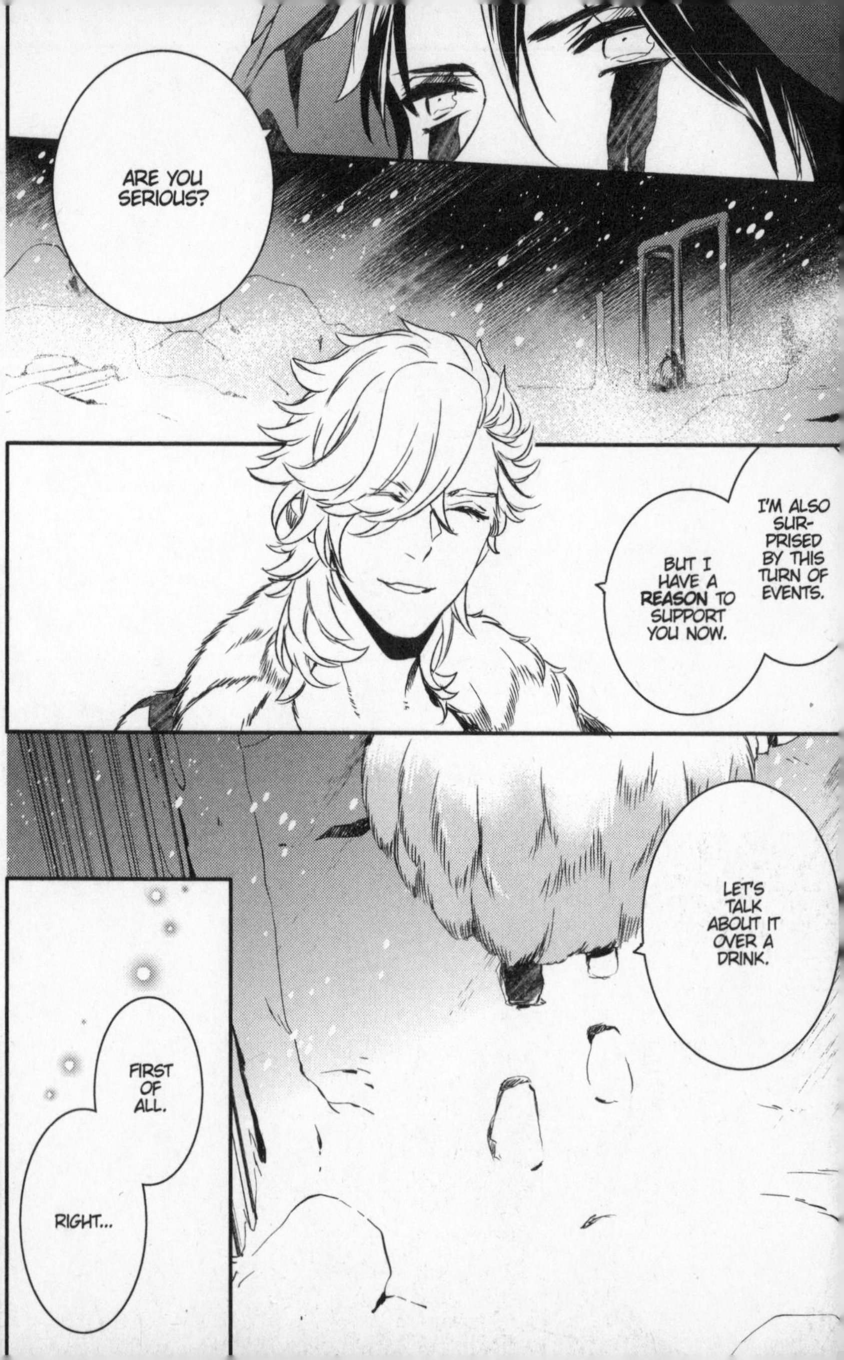
ARE YOU SERIOUS?
I'M ALSO SURPRISED BY THIS TURN OF EVENTS.
BUT I HAVE A **REASON** TO SUPPORT YOU NOW.
LET'S TALK ABOUT IT OVER A DRINK.
FIRST OF ALL.
RIGHT...

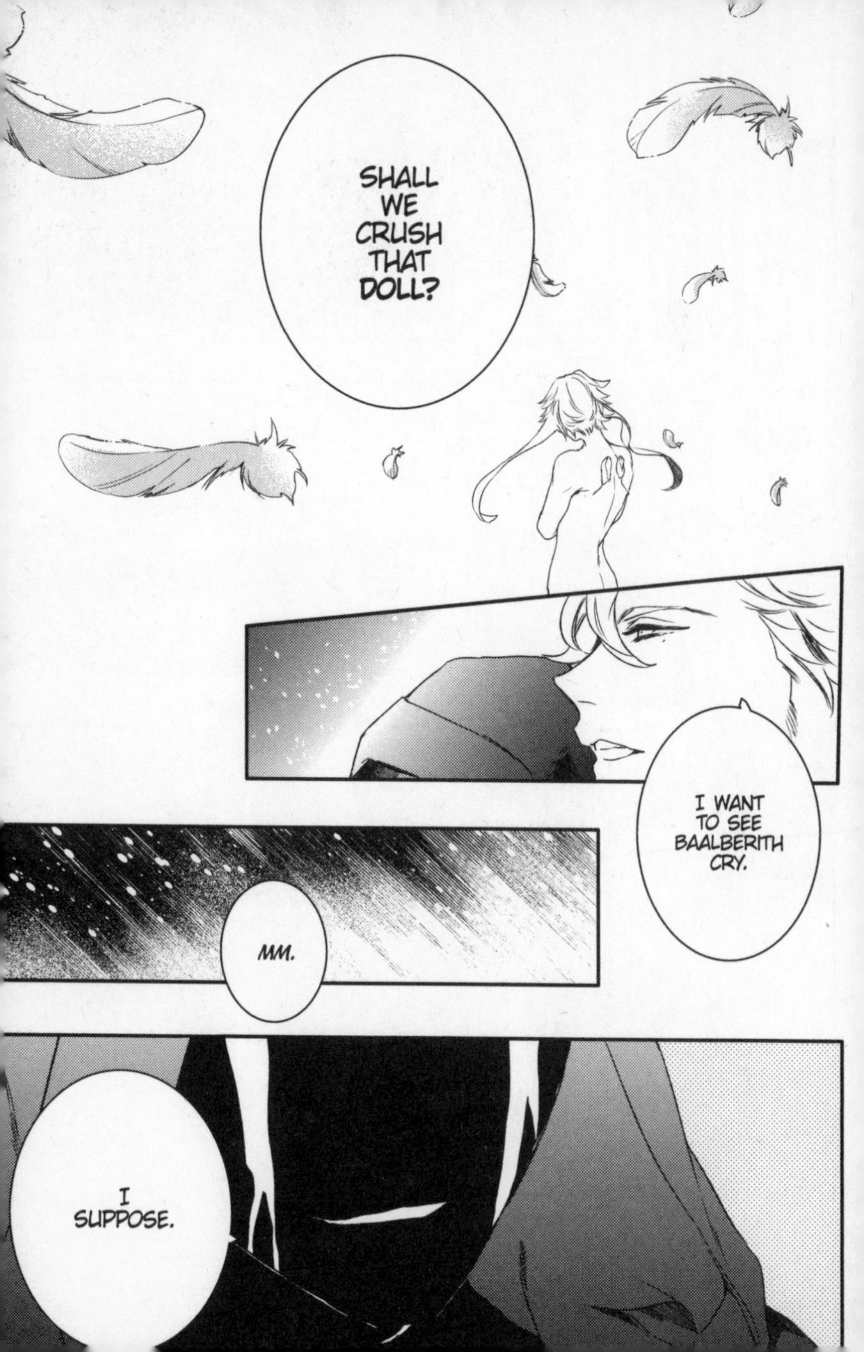
SHALL WE CRUSH THAT DOLL?
I WANT TO SEE BAALBERITH CRY.
MM.
I SUPPOSE.

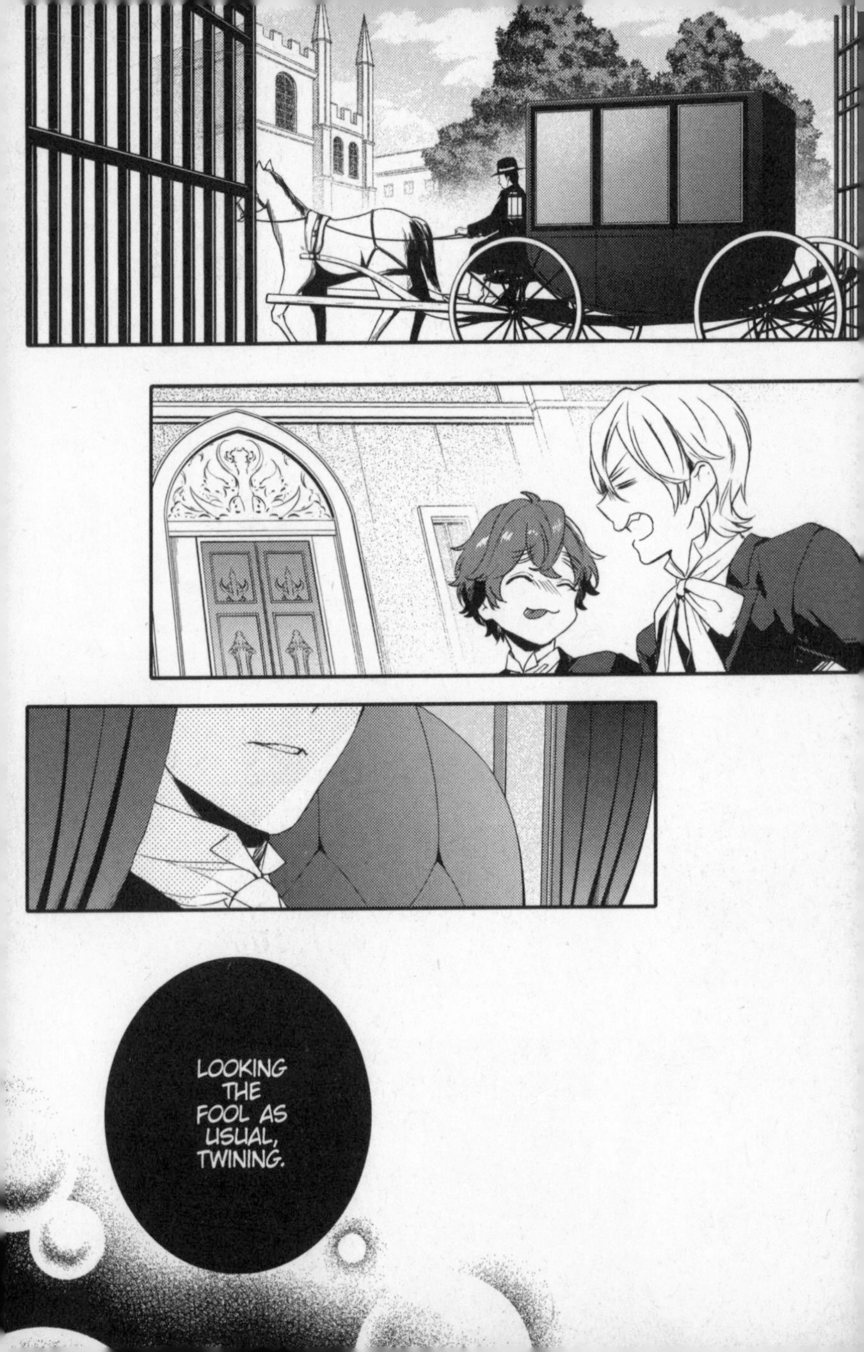
LOOKING THE FOOL AS USUAL, TWINING.

魔界王子

devils and realist

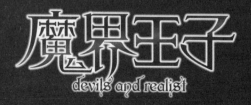

魔界王子

devils and realist

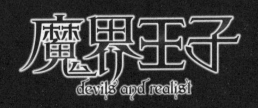

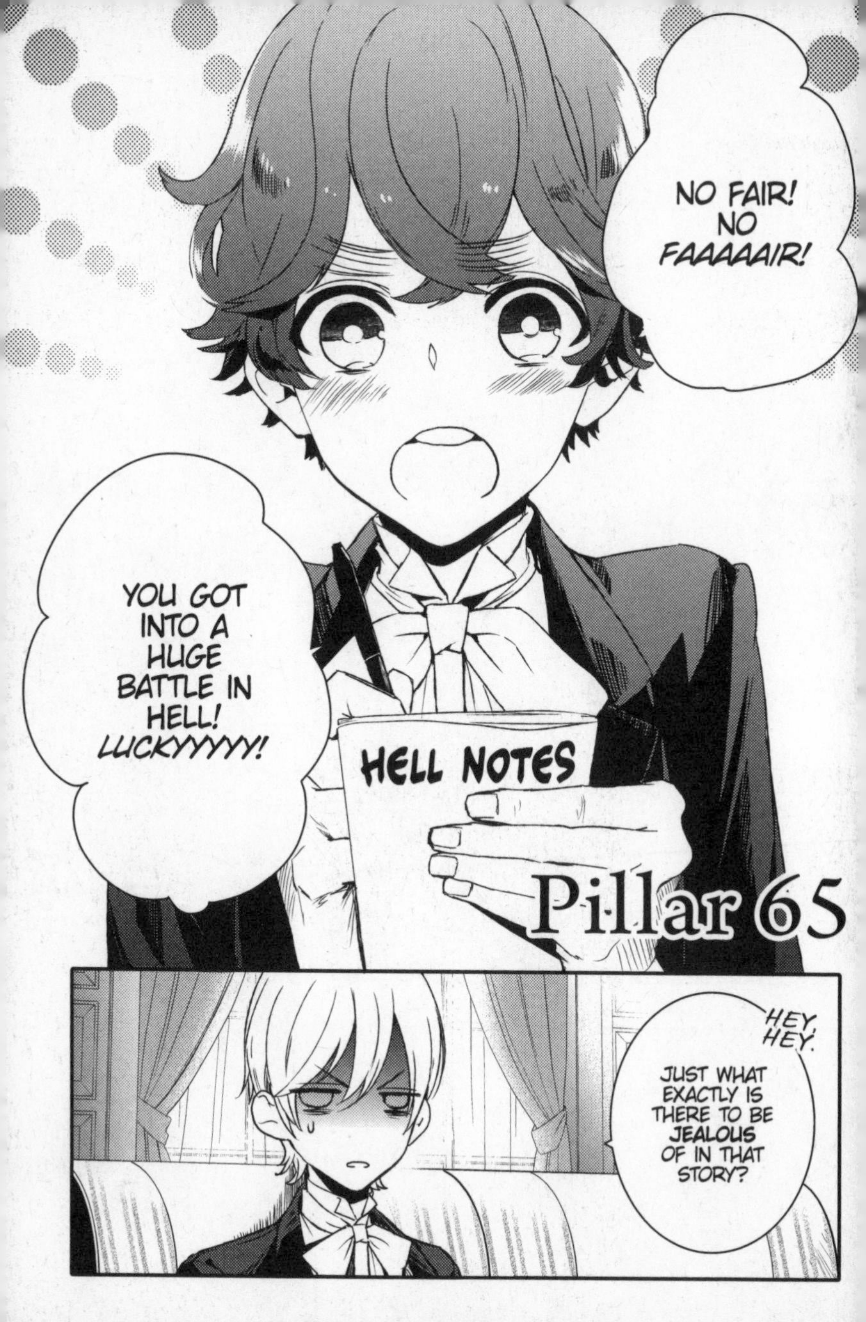
NO FAIR! NO FAAAAAIR!
YOU GOT INTO A HUGE BATTLE IN HELL! LUCKYYYYY!
HELL NOTES
Pillar 65
HEY, HEY.
JUST WHAT EXACTLY IS THERE TO BE JEALOUS OF IN THAT STORY?

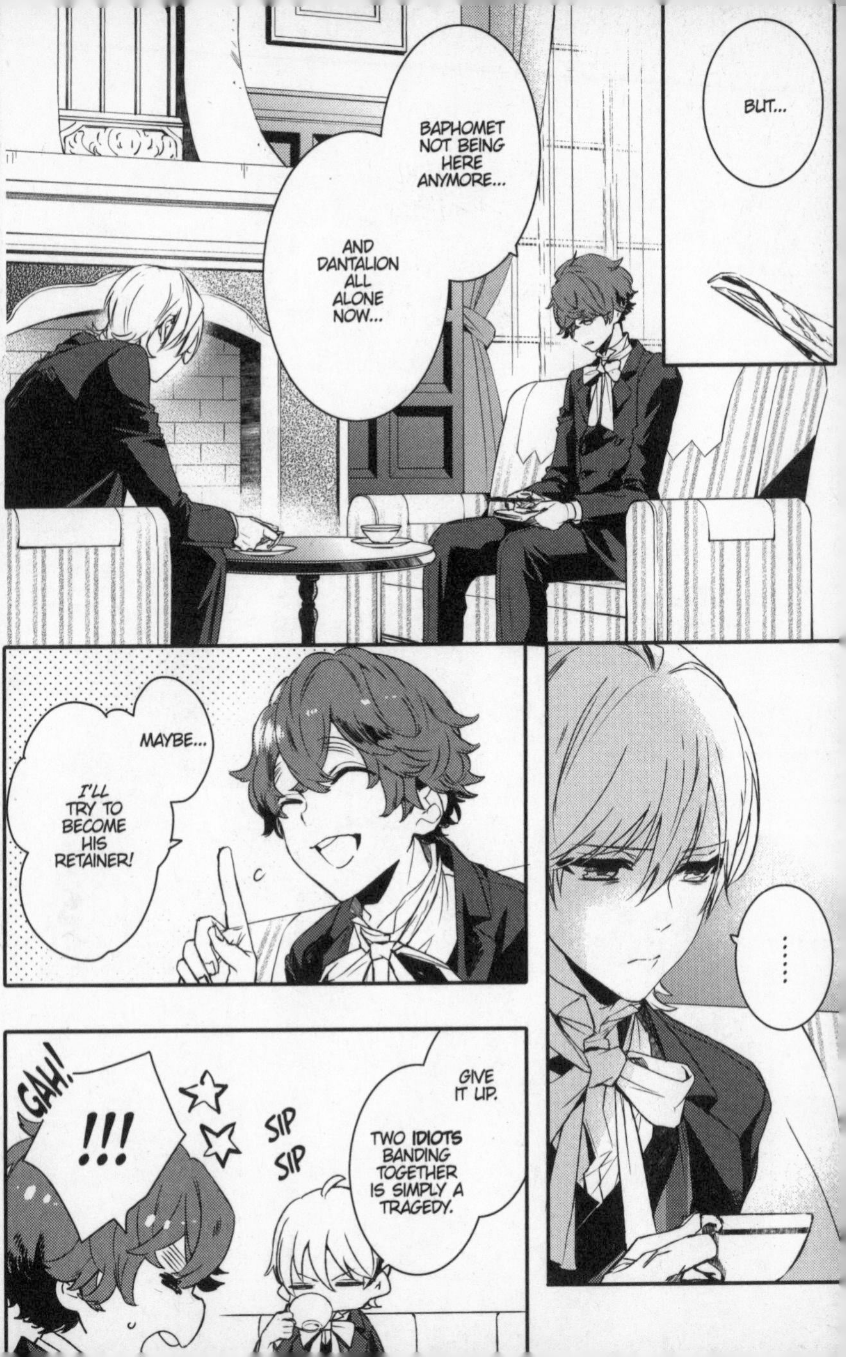
BUT...
BAPHOMET NOT BEING HERE ANYMORE...
AND DANTALION ALL ALONE NOW...
......
MAYBE...
I'LL TRY TO BECOME HIS RETAINER!
GIVE IT UP.
TWO IDIOTS BANDING TOGETHER IS SIMPLY A TRAGEDY.
SIP SIP
GAH!
!!!

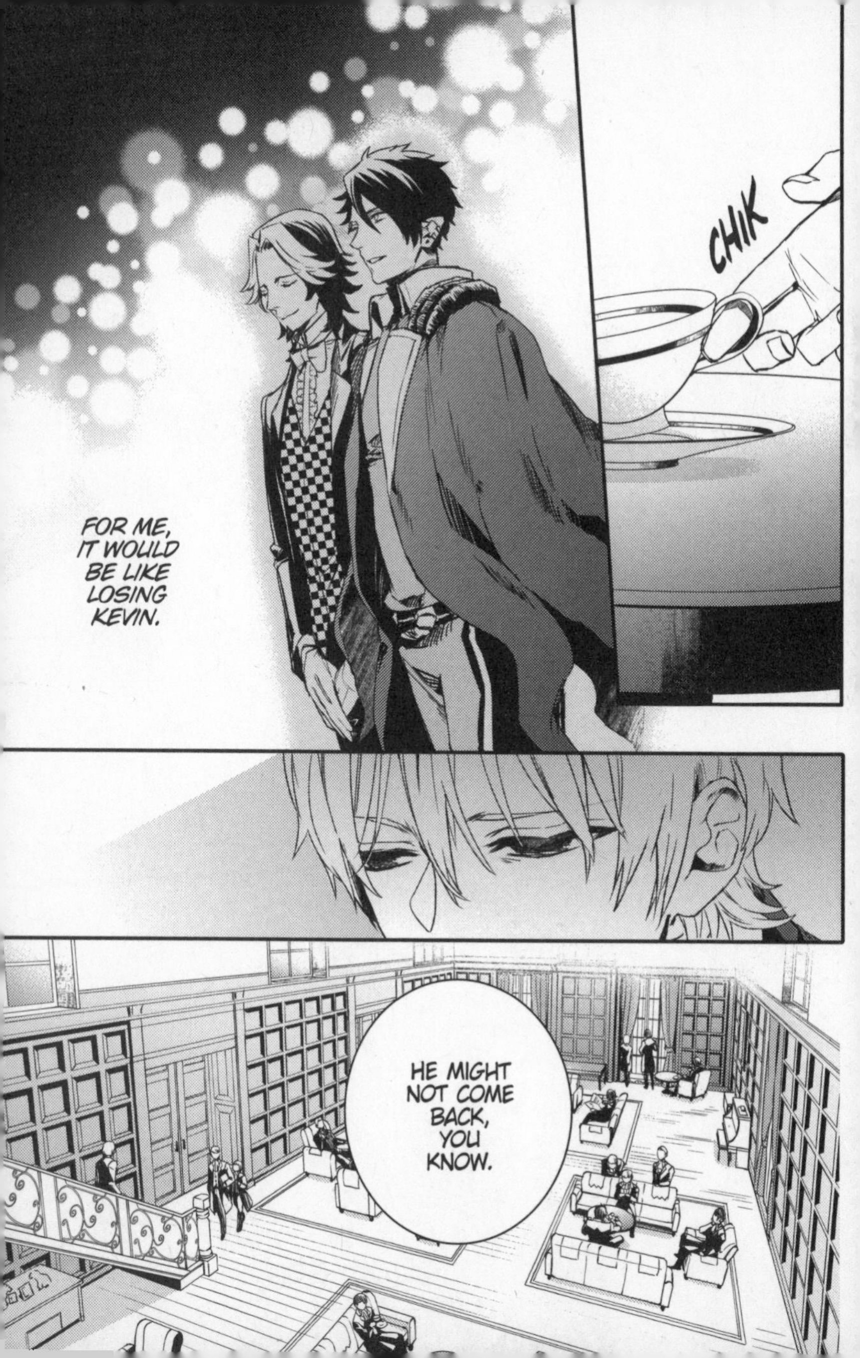
CHIK
FOR ME, IT WOULD BE LIKE LOSING KEVIN.
HE MIGHT NOT COME BACK, YOU KNOW.

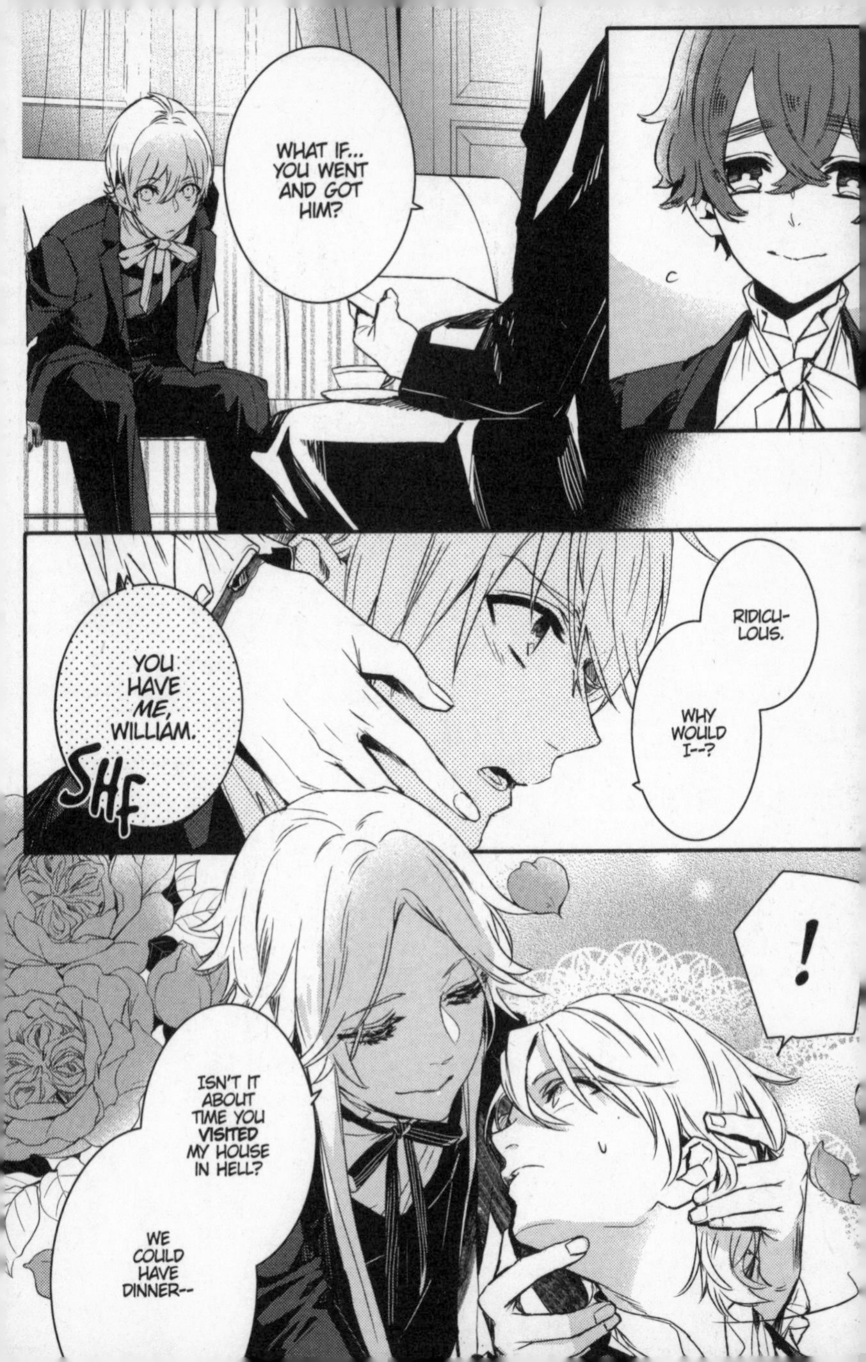
WHAT IF... YOU WENT AND GOT HIM?
RIDICU-LOUS.
WHY WOULD I--?
YOU HAVE *ME*, WILLIAM.
SHF
!
ISN'T IT ABOUT TIME YOU **VISITED** MY HOUSE IN HELL?
WE COULD HAVE DINNER--

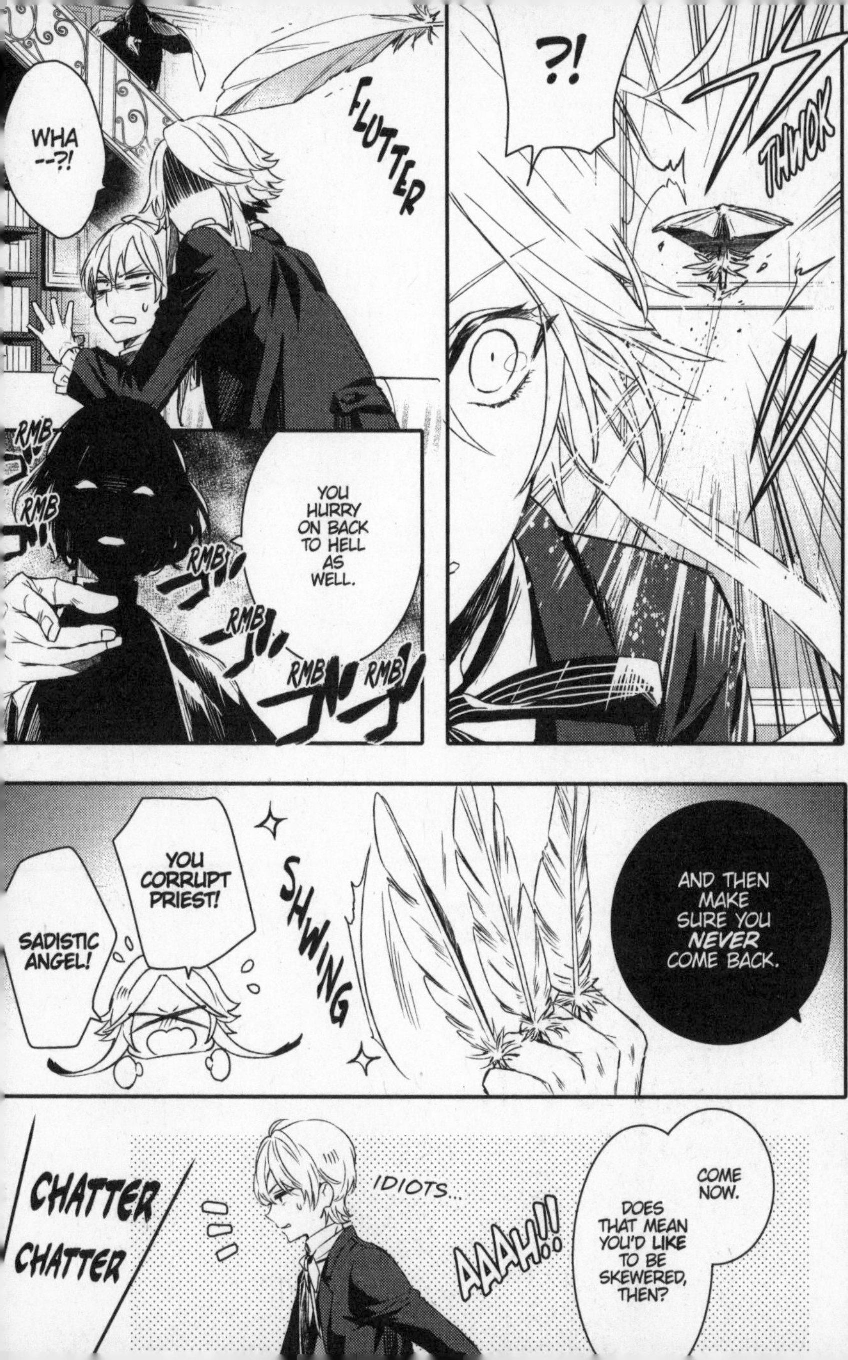
?!
THWOK
FLUTTER
WHA --?!
YOU HURRY ON BACK TO HELL AS WELL.
RMB RMB RMB RMB RMB RMB
AND THEN MAKE SURE YOU *NEVER* COME BACK.
SHWING
YOU CORRUPT PRIEST!
SADISTIC ANGEL!
COME NOW. DOES THAT MEAN YOU'D LIKE TO BE SKEWERED, THEN?
AAAH!!
IDIOTS...
CHATTER CHATTER

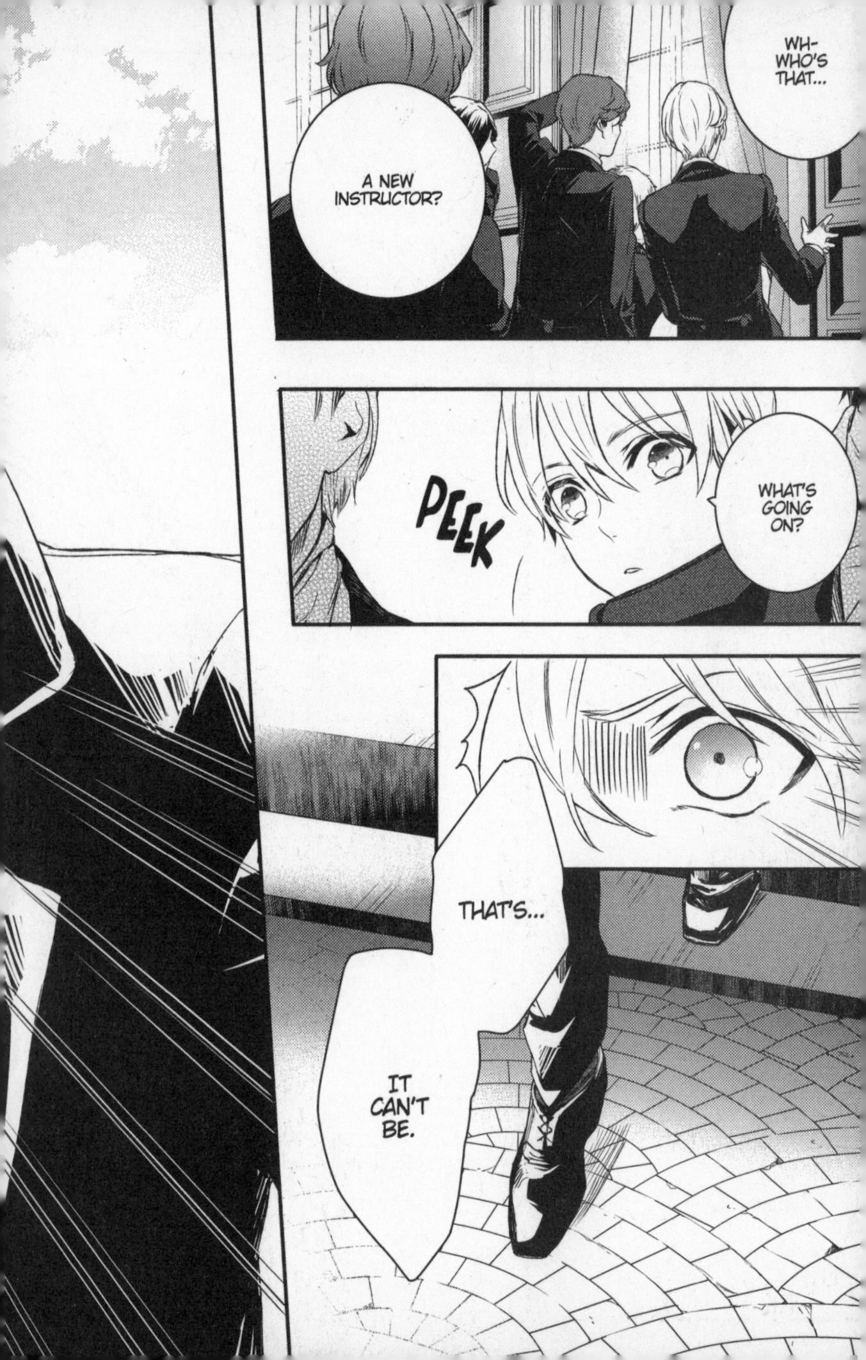
WH-WHO'S THAT...
A NEW INSTRUCTOR?
WHAT'S GOING ON?
PEEK
THAT'S...
IT CAN'T BE.

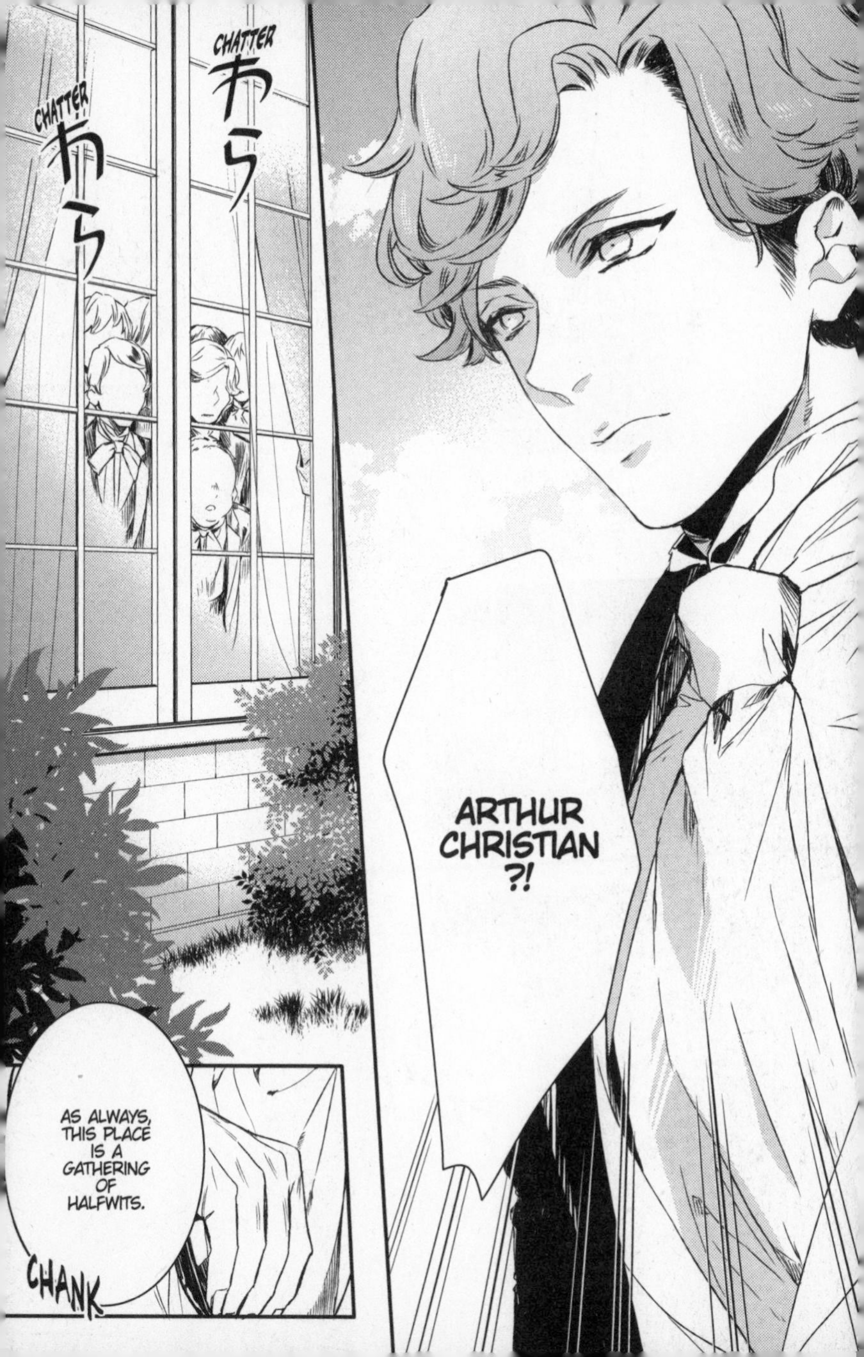
ARTHUR CHRISTIAN ?!
CHATTER
CHATTER
AS ALWAYS, THIS PLACE IS A GATHERING OF HALFWITS.
CHANK

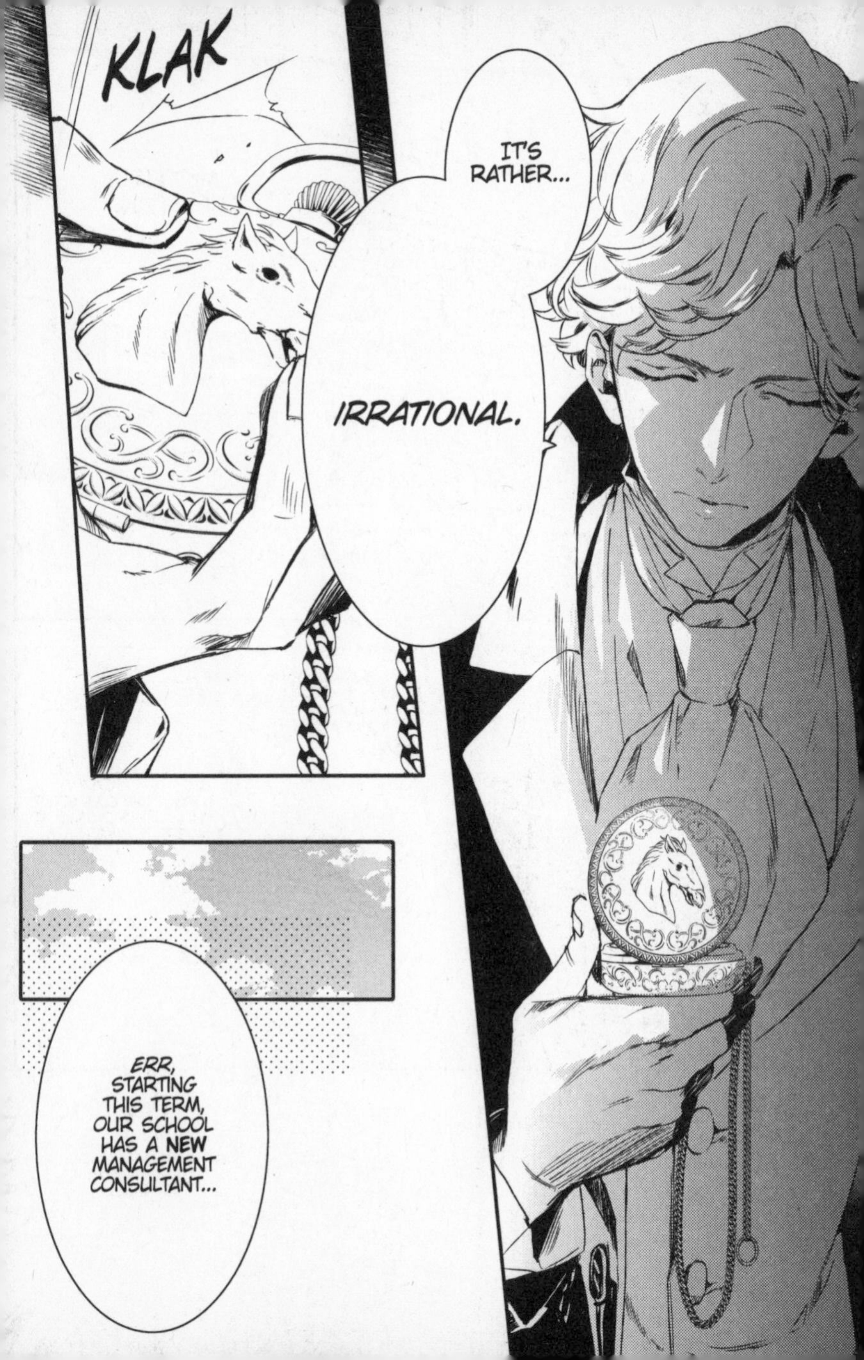
IT'S RATHER...
IRRATIONAL.
KLAK
ERR, STARTING THIS TERM, OUR SCHOOL HAS A NEW MANAGEMENT CONSULTANT...

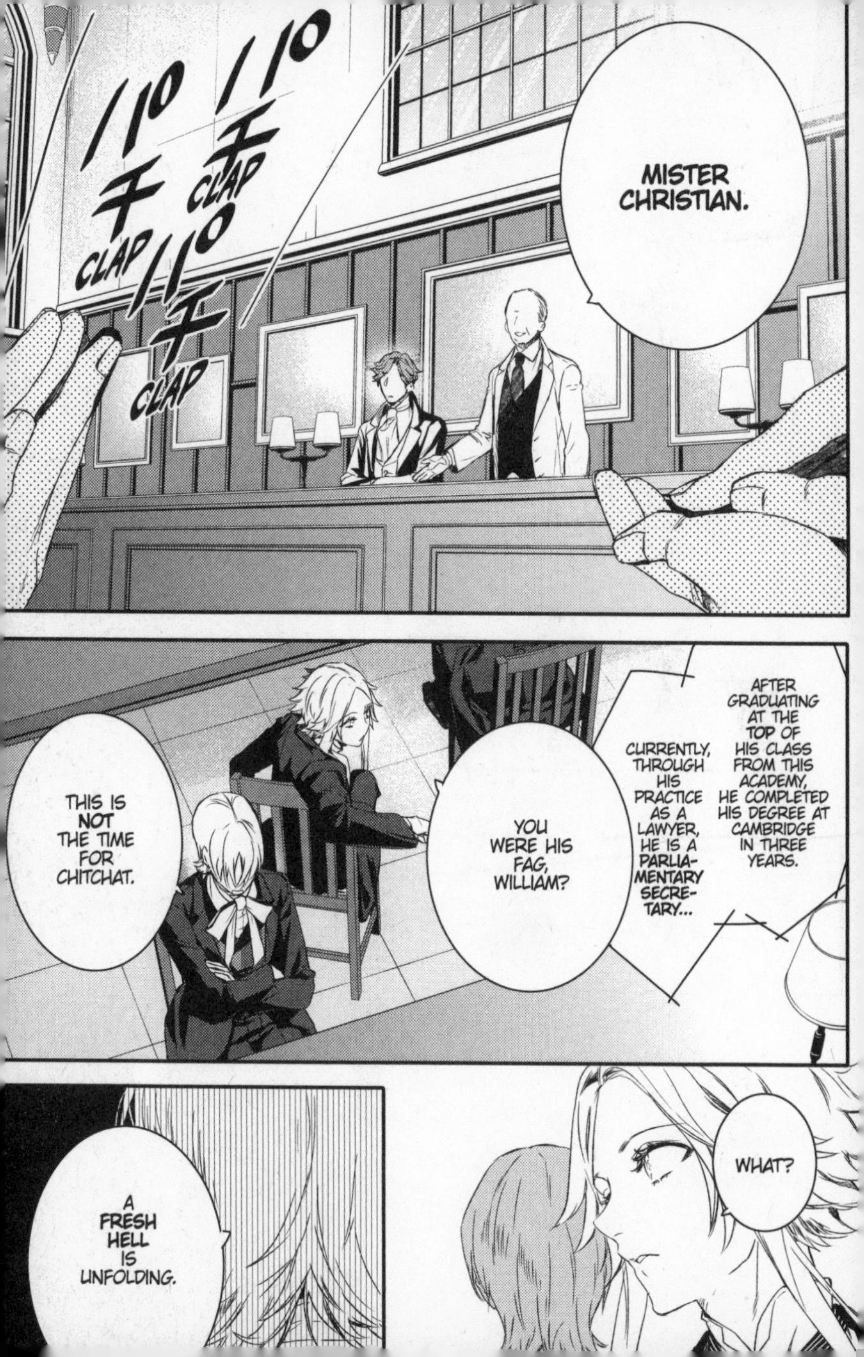
MISTER CHRISTIAN.
パチ CLAP
パチ CLAP
パチ CLAP
AFTER GRADUATING AT THE TOP OF HIS CLASS FROM THIS ACADEMY, HE COMPLETED HIS DEGREE AT CAMBRIDGE IN THREE YEARS.
CURRENTLY, THROUGH HIS PRACTICE AS A LAWYER, HE IS A PARLIAMENTARY SECRETARY...
YOU WERE HIS FAG, WILLIAM?
THIS IS NOT THE TIME FOR CHITCHAT.
WHAT?
A FRESH HELL IS UNFOLDING.

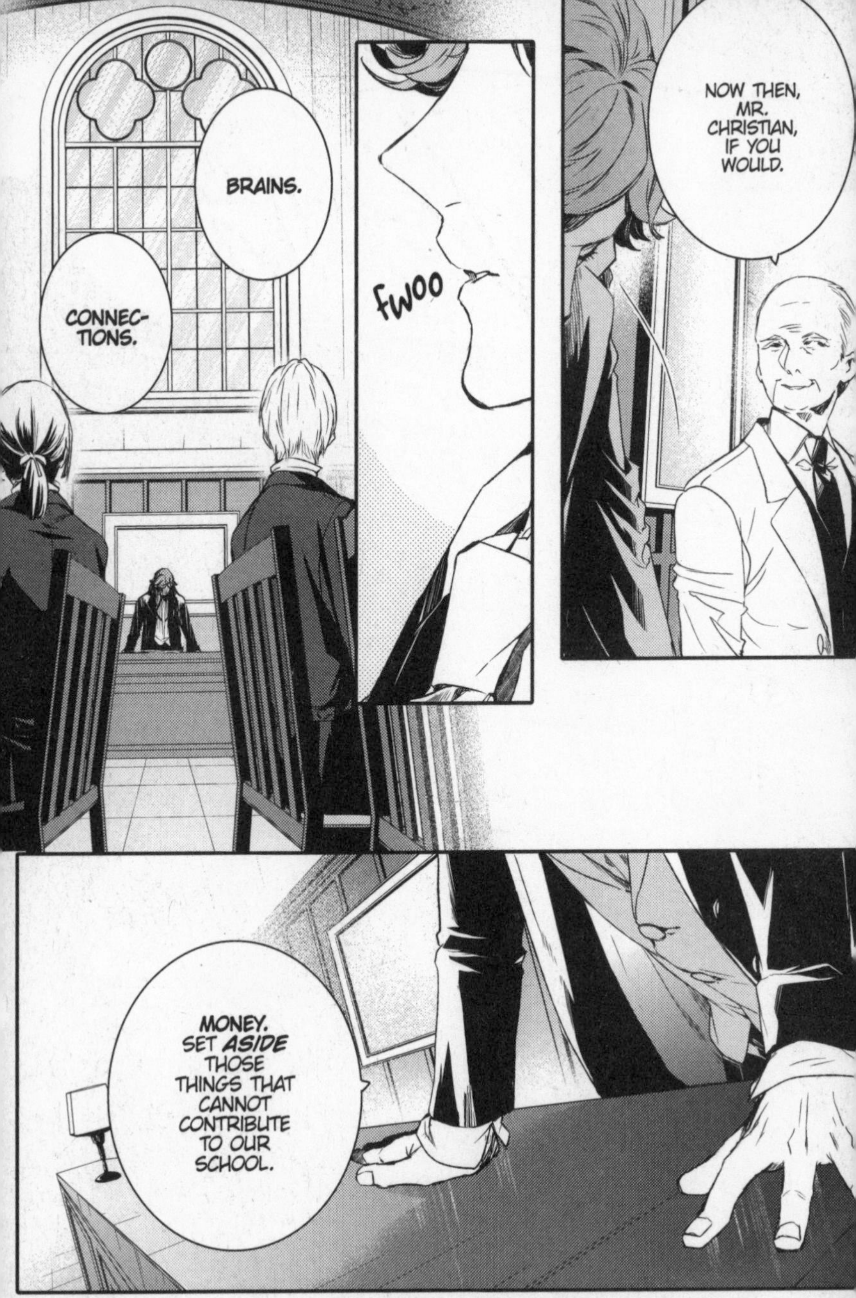
NOW THEN, MR. CHRISTIAN, IF YOU WOULD.
FWOO
BRAINS.
CONNEC-TIONS.
MONEY. SET *ASIDE* THOSE THINGS THAT CANNOT CONTRIBUTE TO OUR SCHOOL.

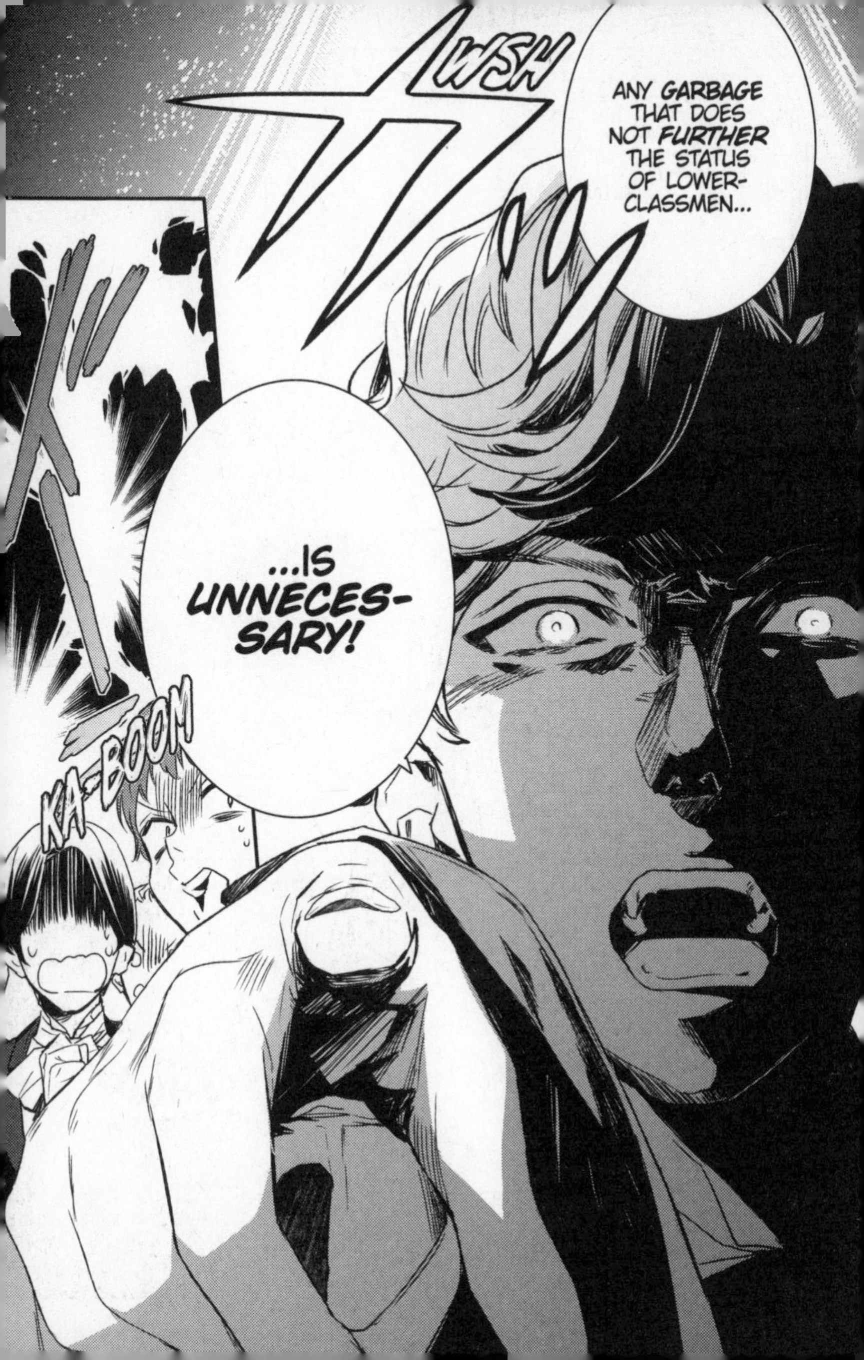
WSH
ANY GARBAGE THAT DOES NOT FURTHER THE STATUS OF LOWER-CLASSMEN...
...IS UNNECES-SARY!
KA-BOOM

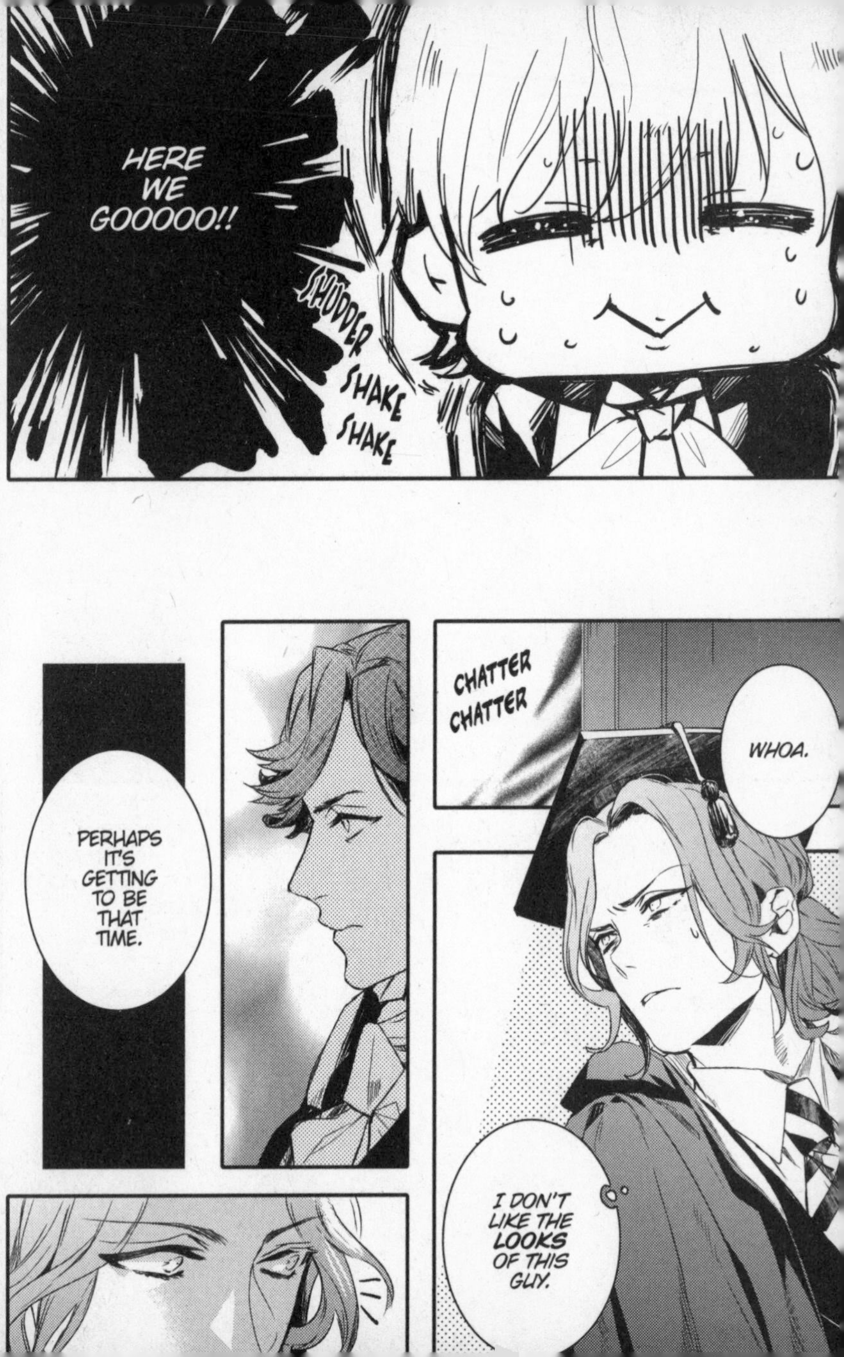
HERE WE GOOOOO!!
SHUDDER
SHAKE SHAKE
CHATTER CHATTER
WHOA.
I DON'T LIKE THE LOOKS OF THIS GUY.
PERHAPS IT'S GETTING TO BE THAT TIME.

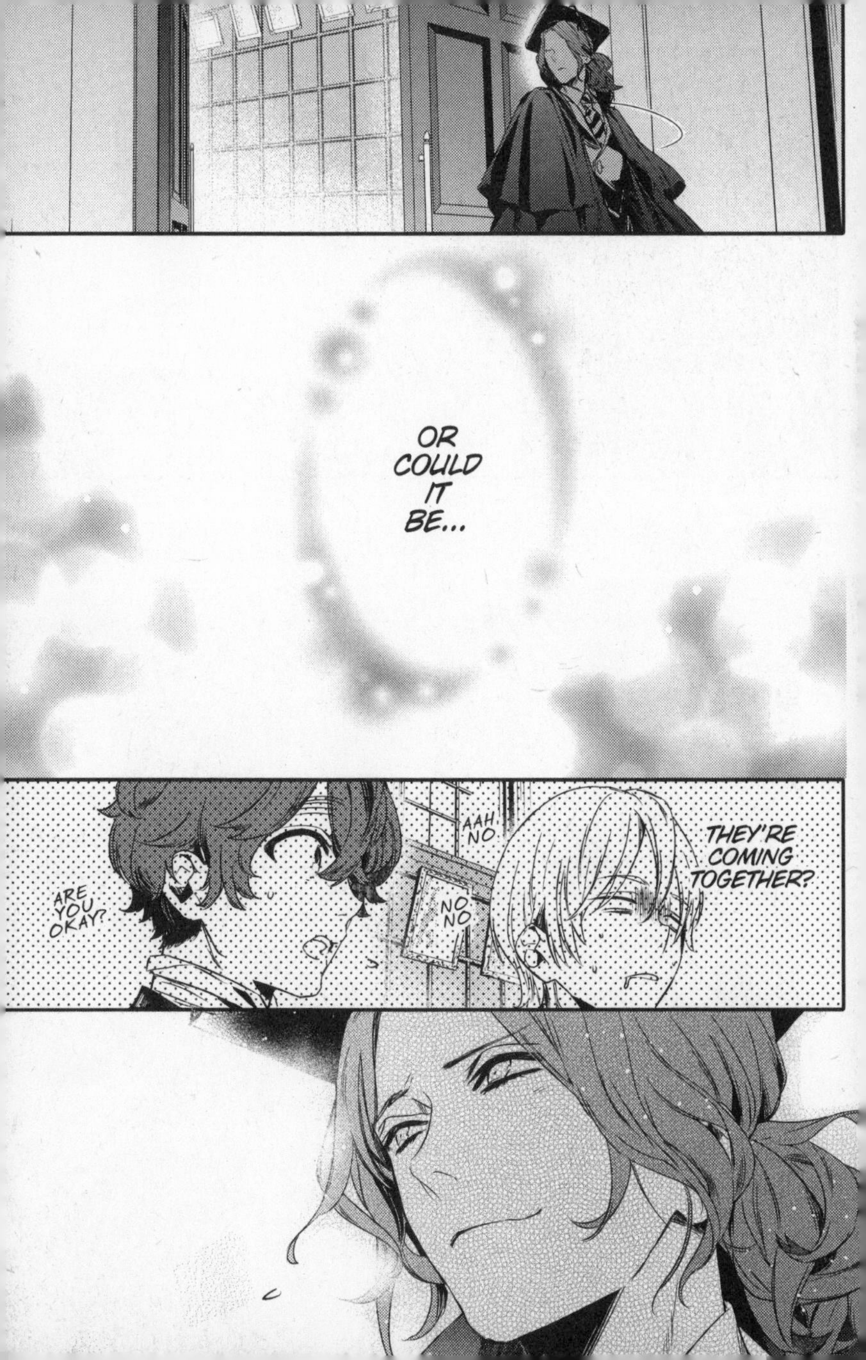
OR COULD IT BE...
THEY'RE COMING TOGETHER?
AAH NO
NO NO
ARE YOU OKAY?

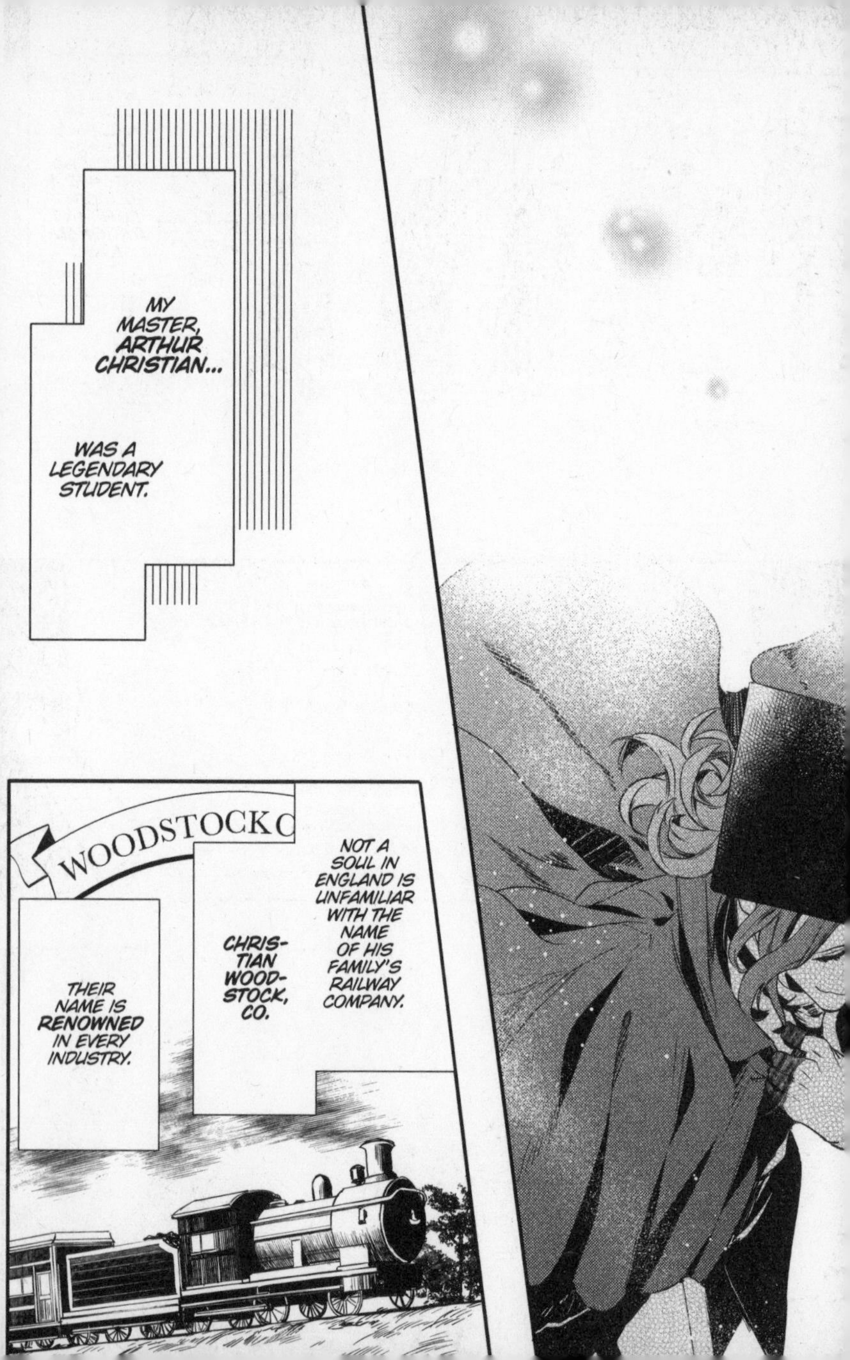
MY MASTER, ARTHUR CHRISTIAN...
WAS A LEGENDARY STUDENT.
NOT A SOUL IN ENGLAND IS UNFAMILIAR WITH THE NAME OF HIS FAMILY'S RAILWAY COMPANY.
CHRIS-TIAN WOOD-STOCK, CO.
WOODSTOCK C
WOODSTOCK
THEIR NAME IS RENOWNED IN EVERY INDUSTRY.

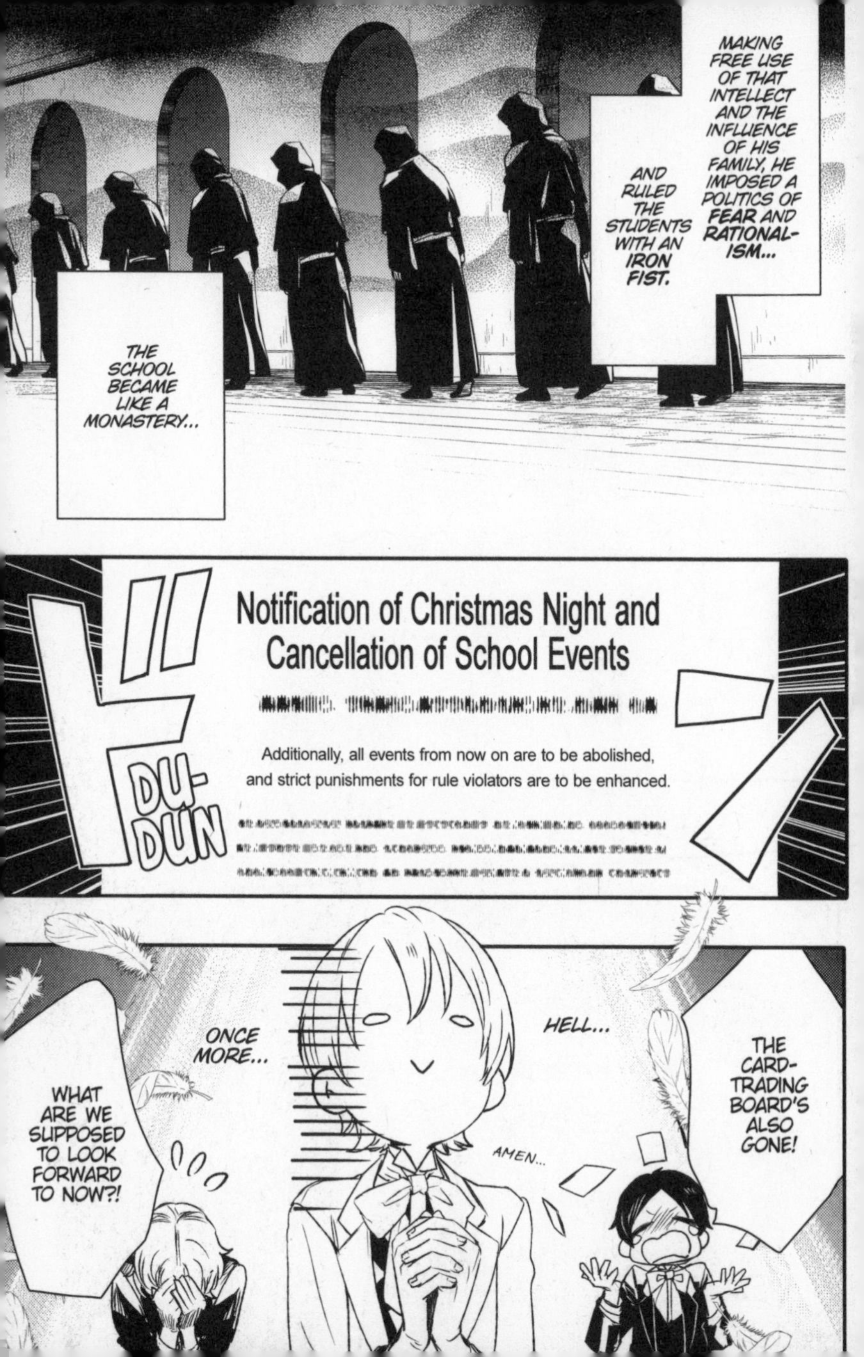
MAKING FREE USE OF THAT INTELLECT AND THE INFLUENCE OF HIS FAMILY, HE IMPOSED A POLITICS OF FEAR AND RATIONALISM...
AND RULED THE STUDENTS WITH AN IRON FIST.
THE SCHOOL BECAME LIKE A MONASTERY...
Notification of Christmas Night and Cancellation of School Events
Additionally, all events from now on are to be abolished, and strict punishments for rule violators are to be enhanced.
DU-DUN
THE CARD-TRADING BOARD'S ALSO GONE!
HELL...
ONCE MORE...
AMEN...
WHAT ARE WE SUPPOSED TO LOOK FORWARD TO NOW?!

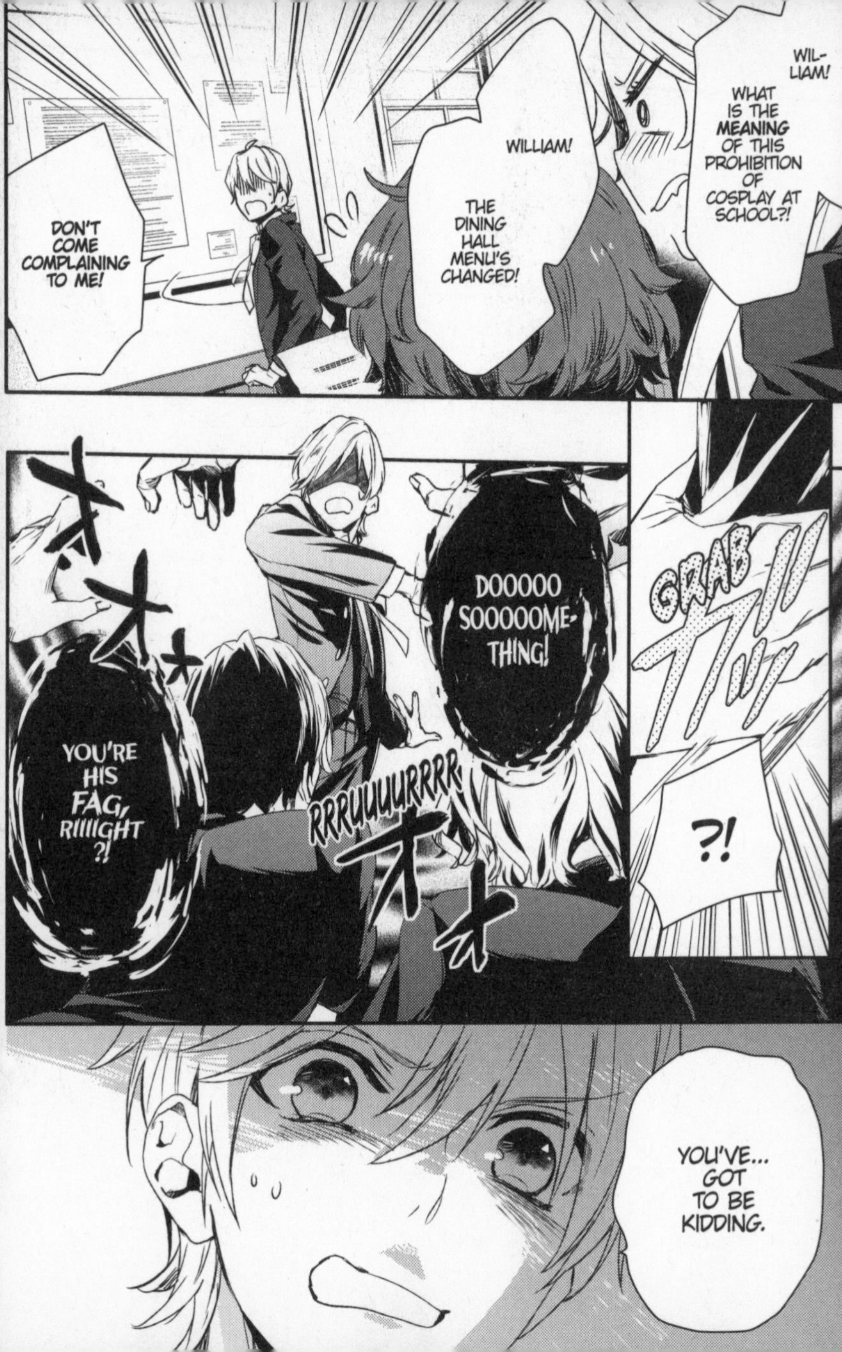
WIL-LIAM!
WHAT IS THE MEANING OF THIS PROHIBITION OF COSPLAY AT SCHOOL?!
WILLIAM!
THE DINING HALL MENU'S CHANGED!
DON'T COME COMPLAINING TO ME!
GRAB
?!
DOOOOO SOOOOOME-THING!
RRRYUUUURRRR
YOU'RE HIS FAG, RIIIIGHT?!
YOU'VE... GOT TO BE KIDDING.

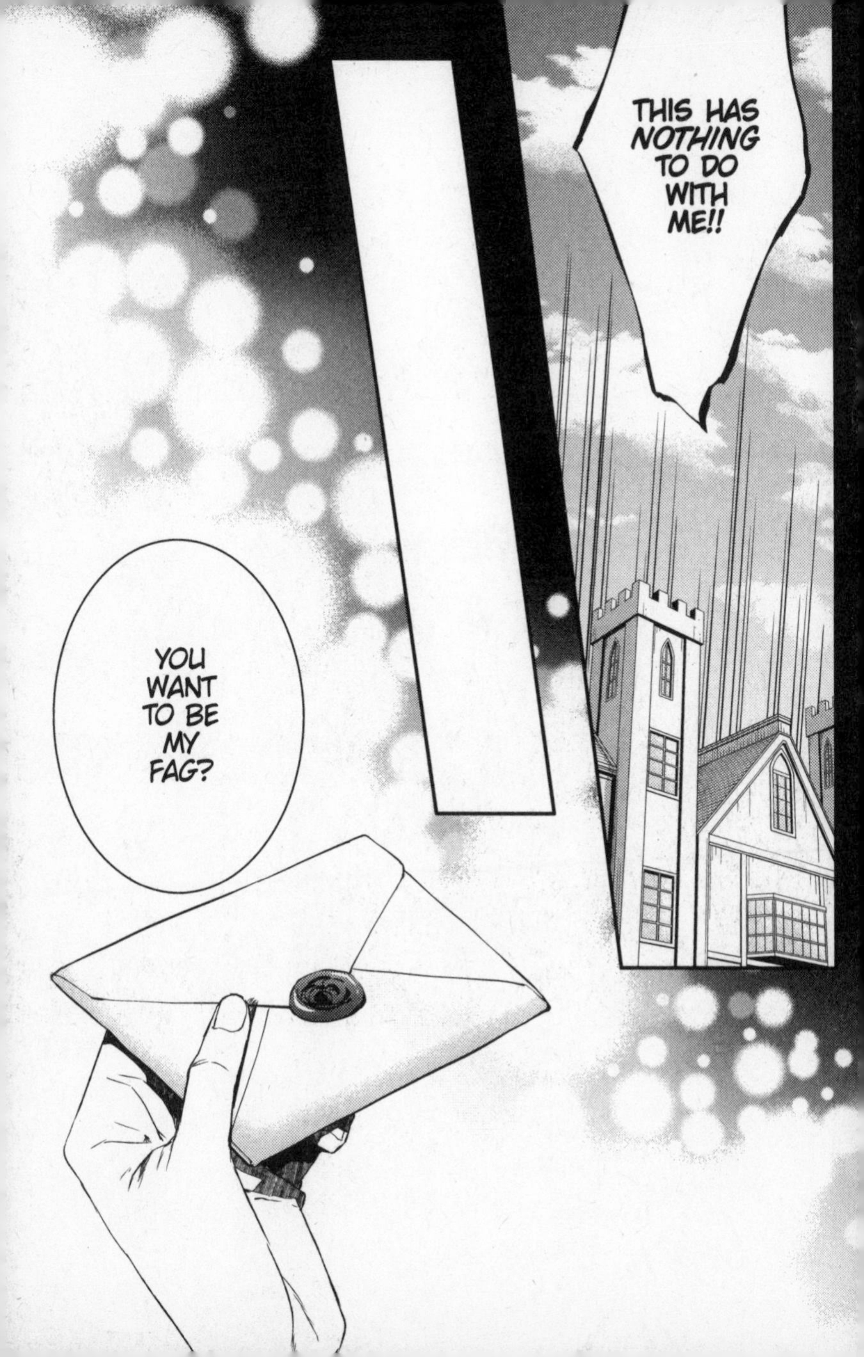
THIS HAS NOTHING TO DO WITH ME!!
YOU WANT TO BE MY FAG?

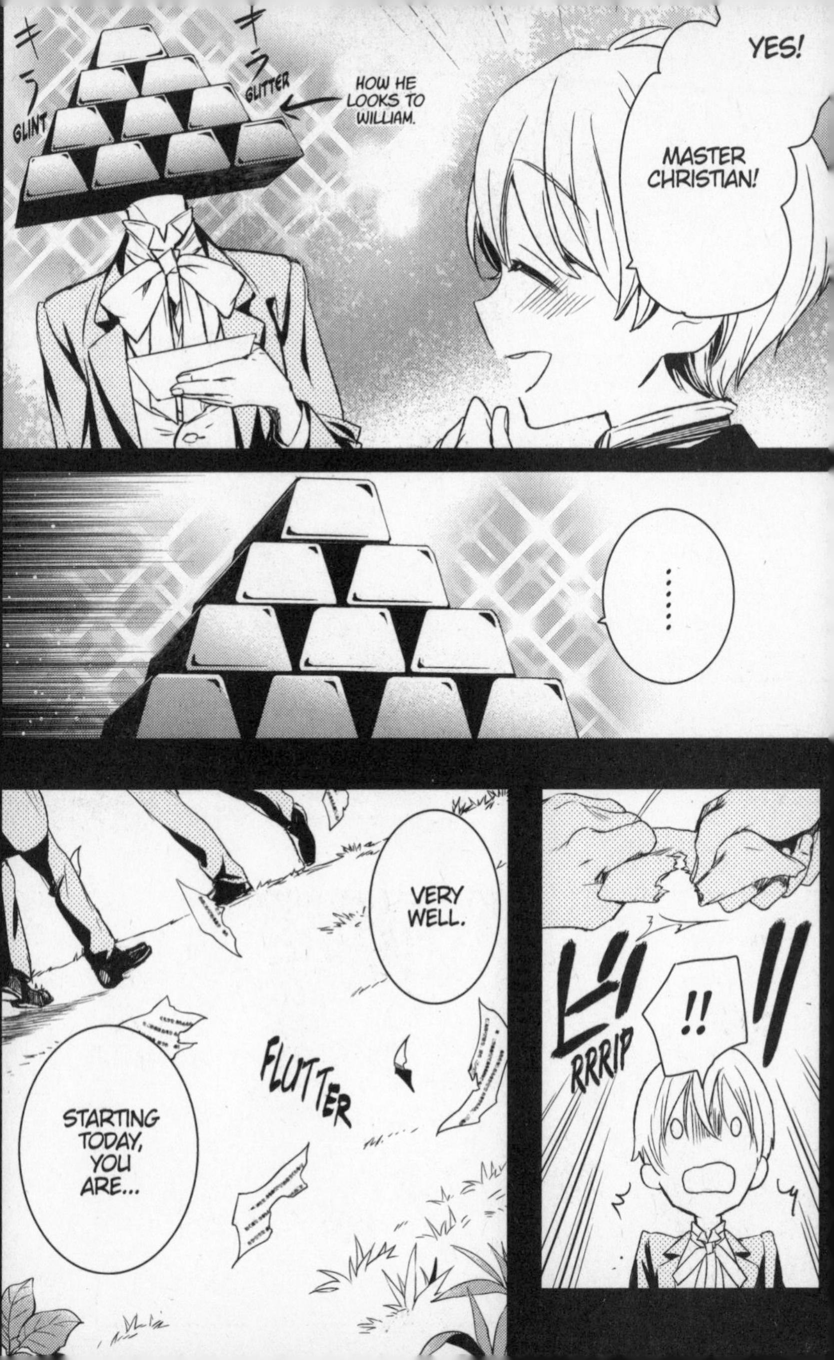
YES!
MASTER CHRISTIAN!
HOW HE LOOKS TO WILLIAM.
キラ
GLITTER
キラ
GLINT
......
ビリ
RRRIP
!!
VERY WELL.
FLUTTER
STARTING TODAY, YOU ARE...

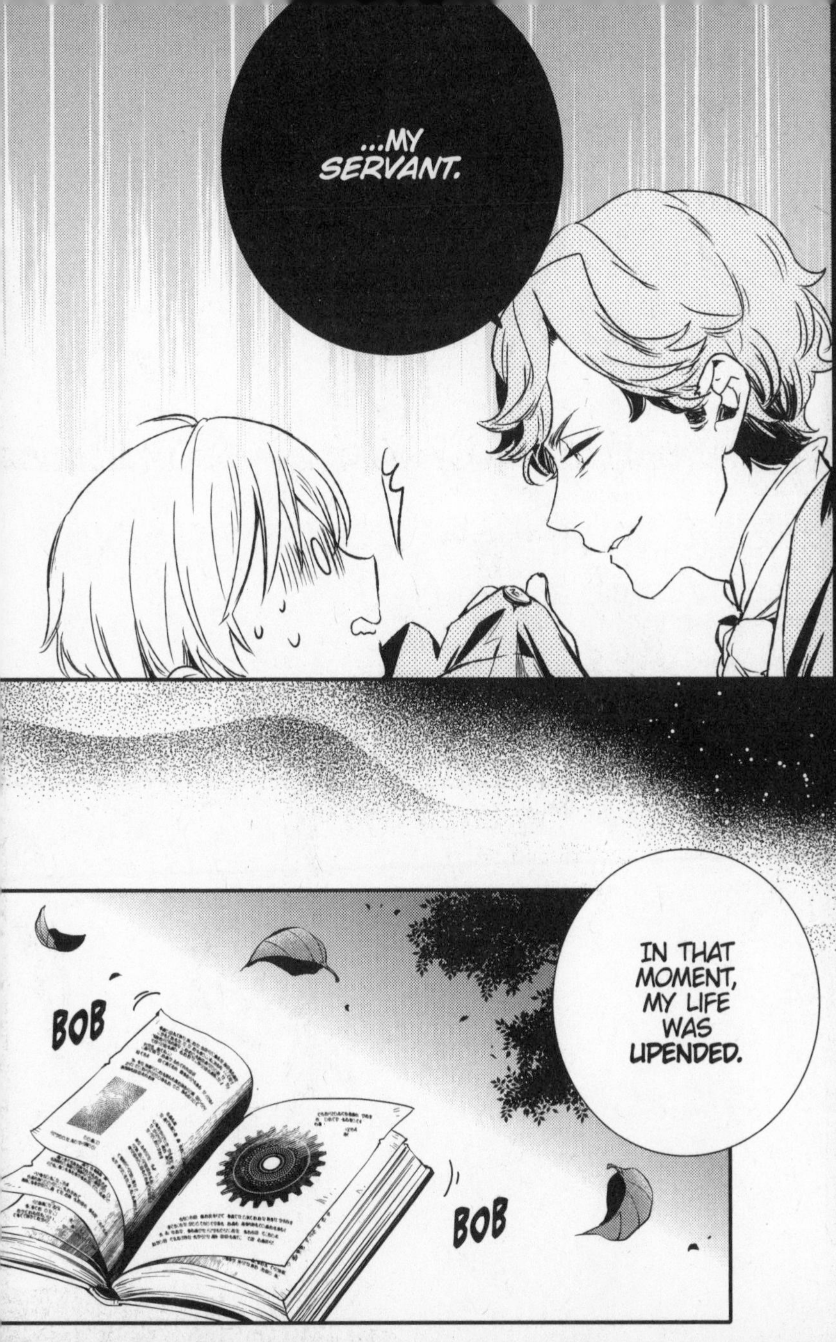
...MY SERVANT.
IN THAT MOMENT, MY LIFE WAS UPENDED.
BOB
BOB

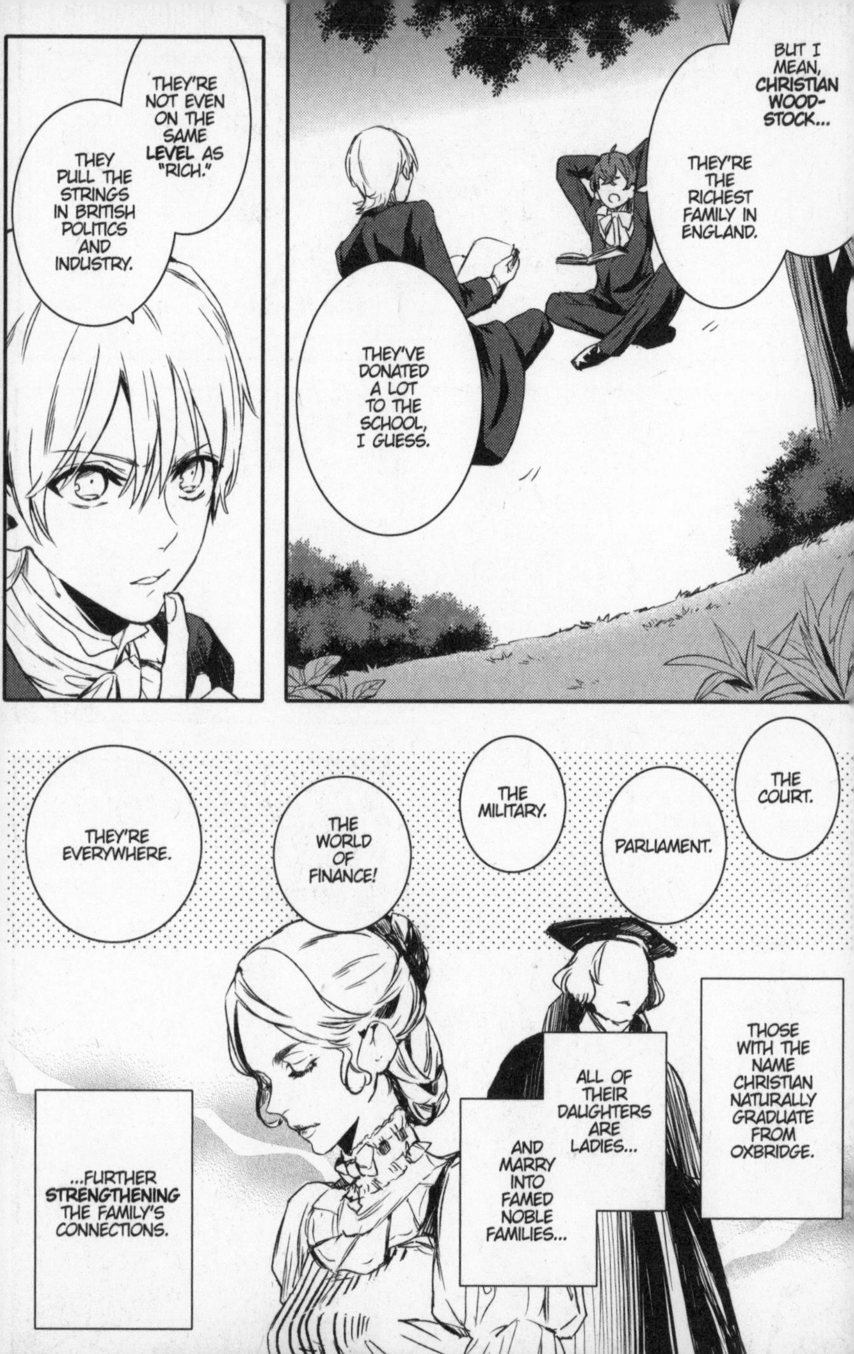
BUT I MEAN, CHRISTIAN WOOD-STOCK...
THEY'RE THE RICHEST FAMILY IN ENGLAND.
THEY'VE DONATED A LOT TO THE SCHOOL, I GUESS.
THEY'RE NOT EVEN ON THE SAME **LEVEL** AS "RICH."
THEY PULL THE STRINGS IN BRITISH POLITICS AND INDUSTRY.
THE COURT.
PARLIAMENT.
THE MILITARY.
THE WORLD OF FINANCE!
THEY'RE EVERYWHERE.
THOSE WITH THE NAME CHRISTIAN NATURALLY GRADUATE FROM OXBRIDGE.
ALL OF THEIR DAUGHTERS ARE LADIES...
AND MARRY INTO FAMED NOBLE FAMILIES...
...FURTHER **STRENGTHENING** THE FAMILY'S CONNECTIONS.

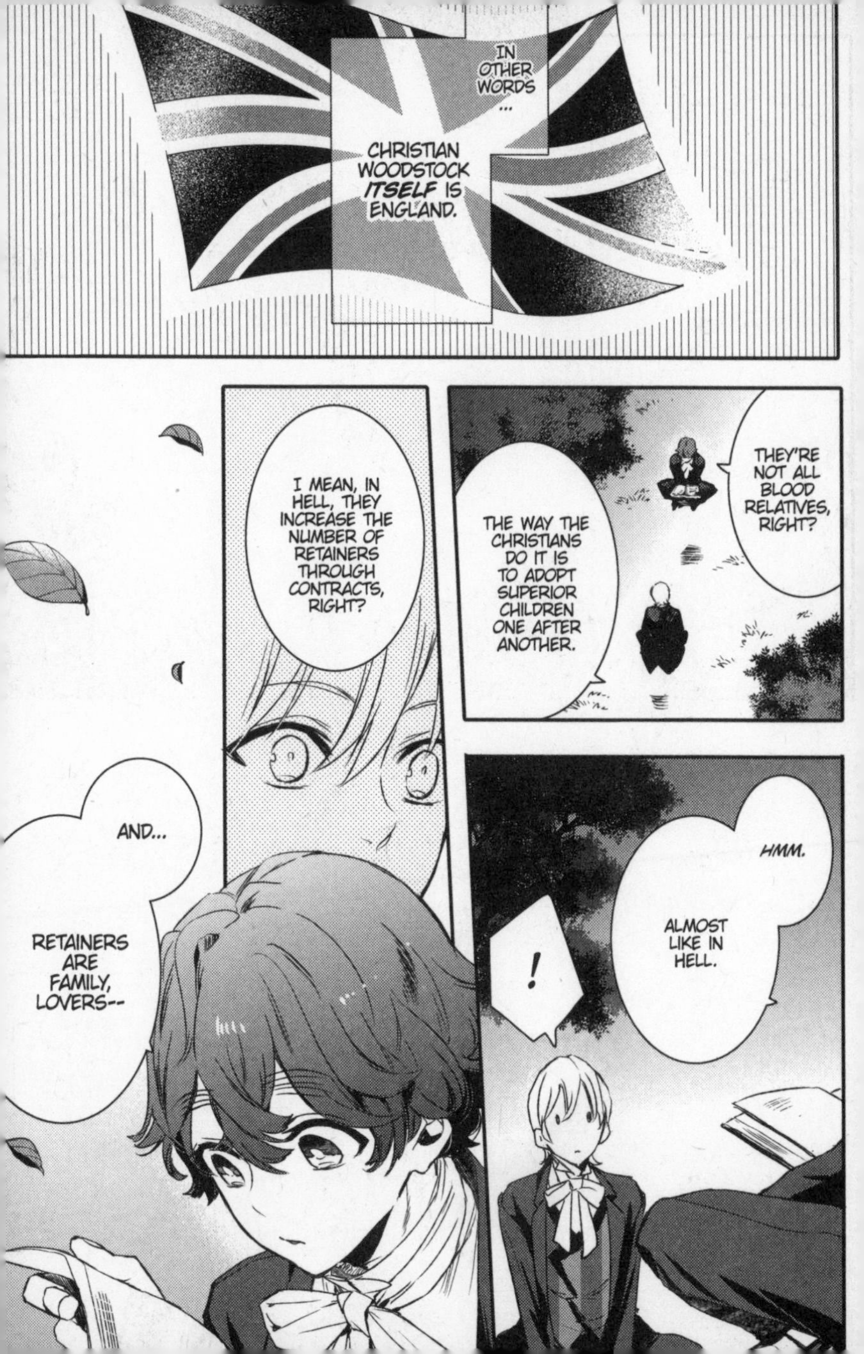
IN OTHER WORDS...
CHRISTIAN WOODSTOCK *ITSELF* IS ENGLAND.
THEY'RE NOT ALL BLOOD RELATIVES, RIGHT?
THE WAY THE CHRISTIANS DO IT IS TO ADOPT SUPERIOR CHILDREN ONE AFTER ANOTHER.
I MEAN, IN HELL, THEY INCREASE THE NUMBER OF RETAINERS THROUGH CONTRACTS, RIGHT?
HMM.
ALMOST LIKE IN HELL.
!
AND...
RETAINERS ARE FAMILY, LOVERS--

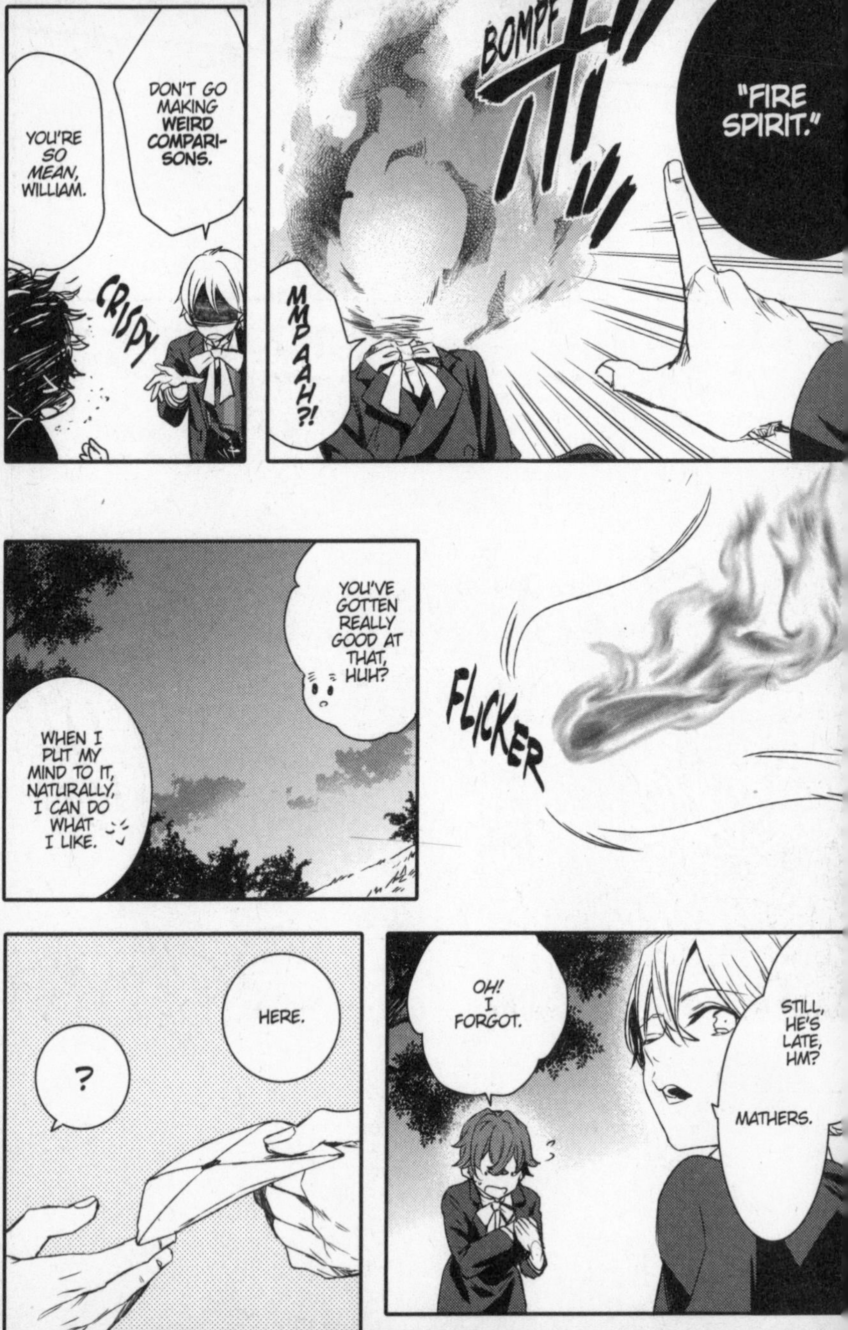
"FIRE SPIRIT."
BOMPF
MMPAAH?!
DON'T GO MAKING WEIRD COMPARISONS.
YOU'RE SO MEAN, WILLIAM.
CRISPY
FLICKER
YOU'VE GOTTEN REALLY GOOD AT THAT, HUH?
WHEN I PUT MY MIND TO IT, NATURALLY, I CAN DO WHAT I LIKE.
STILL, HE'S LATE, HM?
MATHERS.
OH! I FORGOT.
HERE.
?

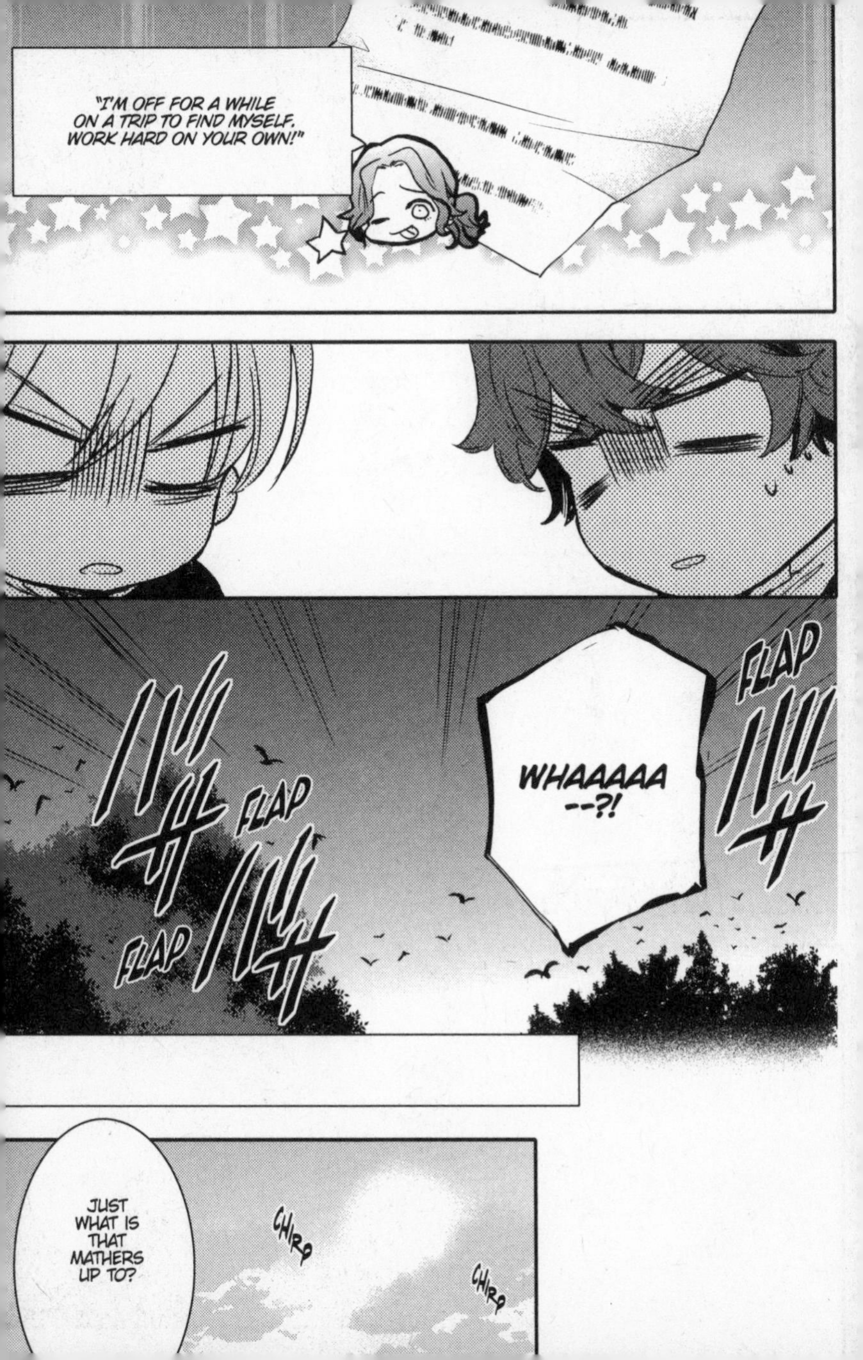
"I'M OFF FOR A WHILE ON A TRIP TO FIND MYSELF. WORK HARD ON YOUR OWN!"
FLAP
WHAAAAA --?!
FLAP
FLAP
CHIRP
CHIRP
JUST WHAT IS THAT MATHERS UP TO?

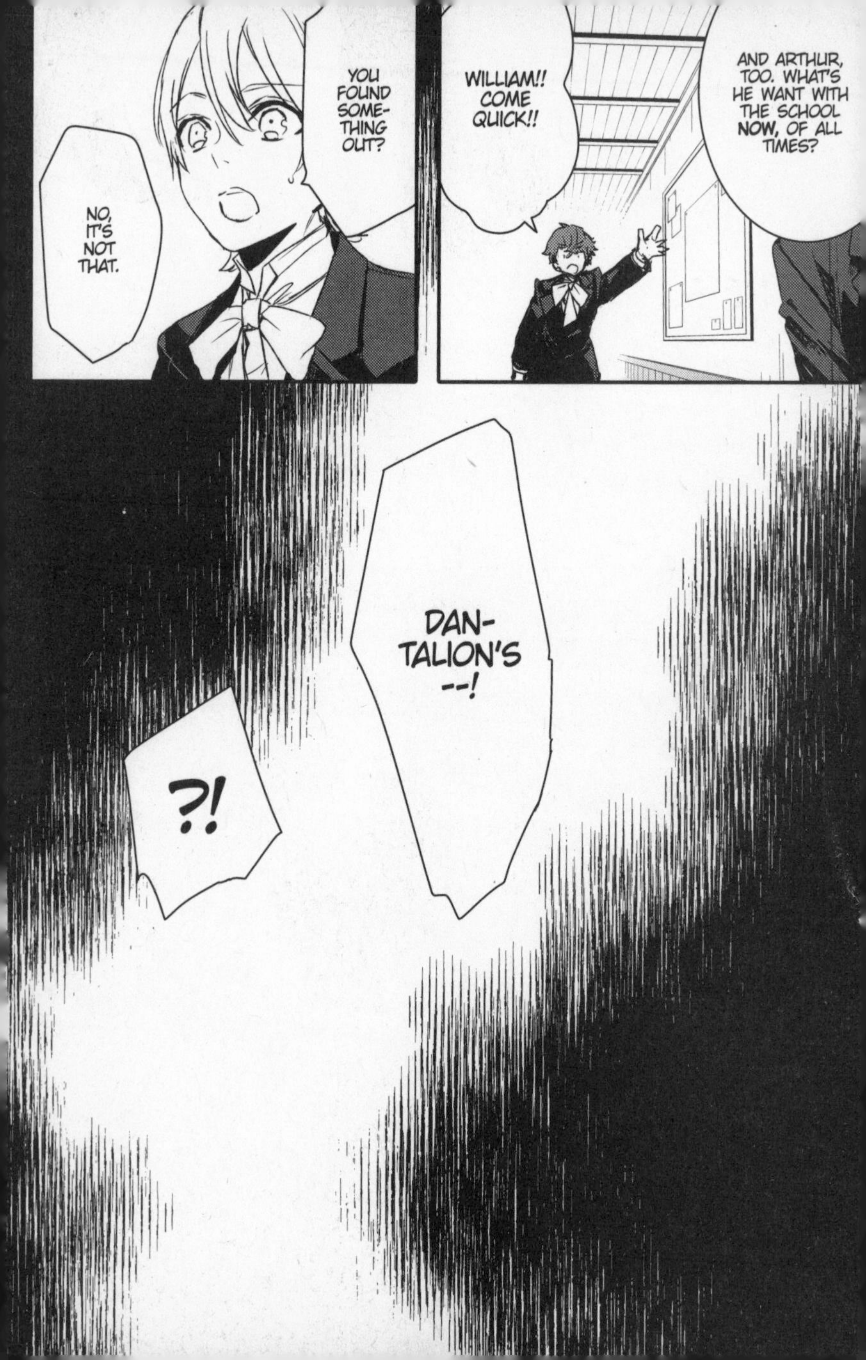

AND ARTHUR, TOO. WHAT'S HE WANT WITH THE SCHOOL NOW, OF ALL TIMES?
WILLIAM!! COME QUICK!!
YOU FOUND SOME-THING OUT?
NO, IT'S NOT THAT.
DAN-TALION'S --!
?!

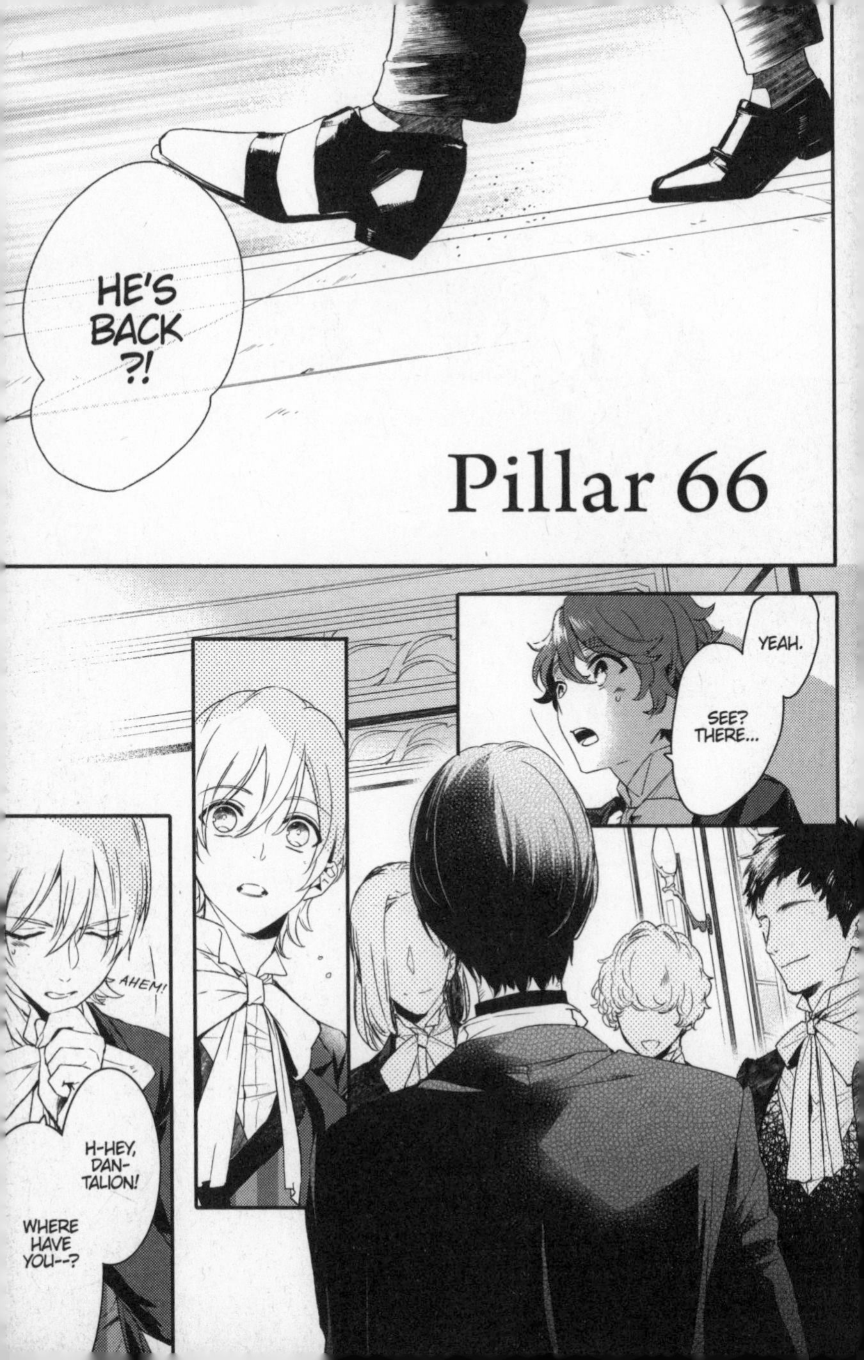
HE'S BACK?!
Pillar 66
YEAH.
SEE? THERE...
AHEM!
H-HEY, DAN-TALION!
WHERE HAVE YOU--?

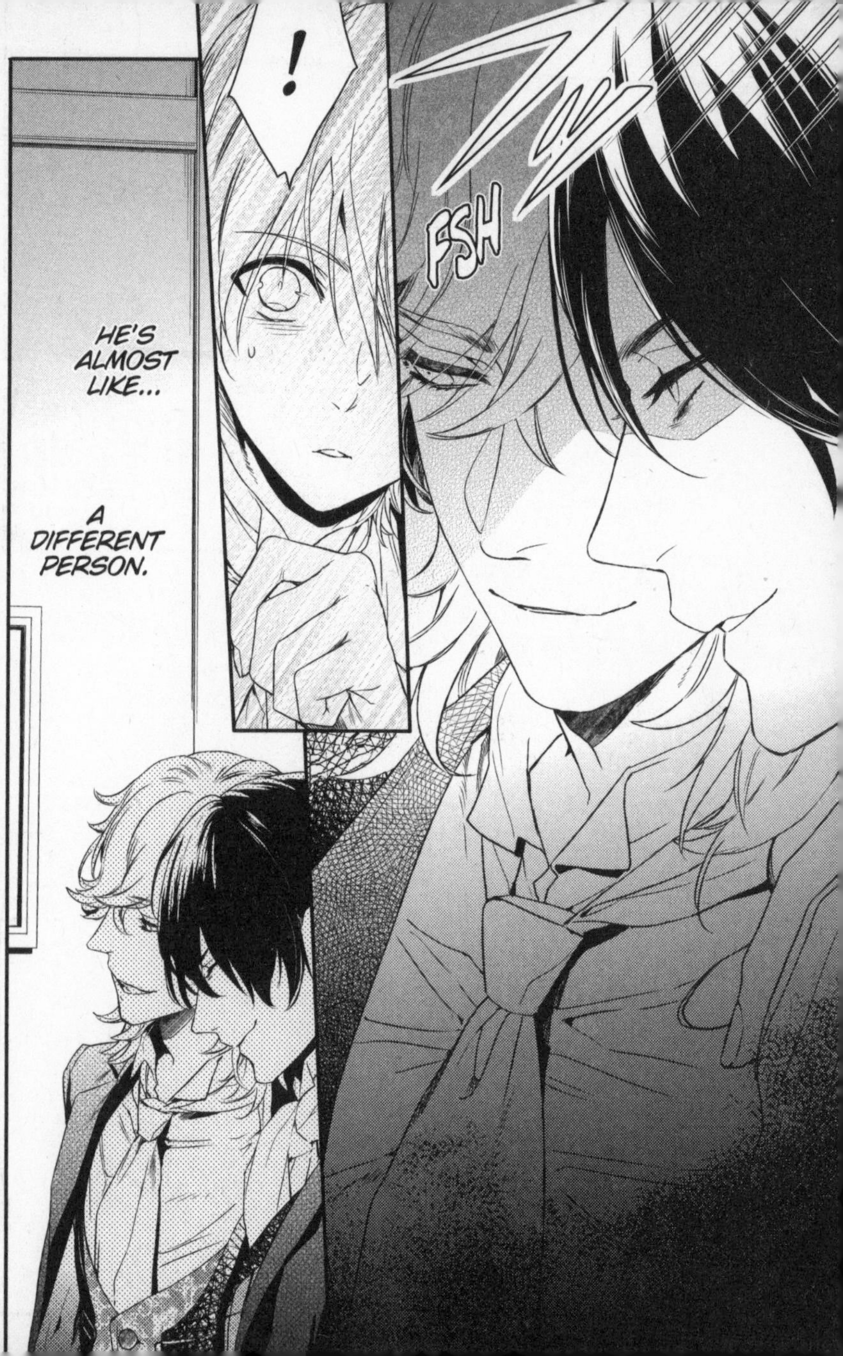
FSH
!
HE'S ALMOST LIKE...
A DIFFERENT PERSON.

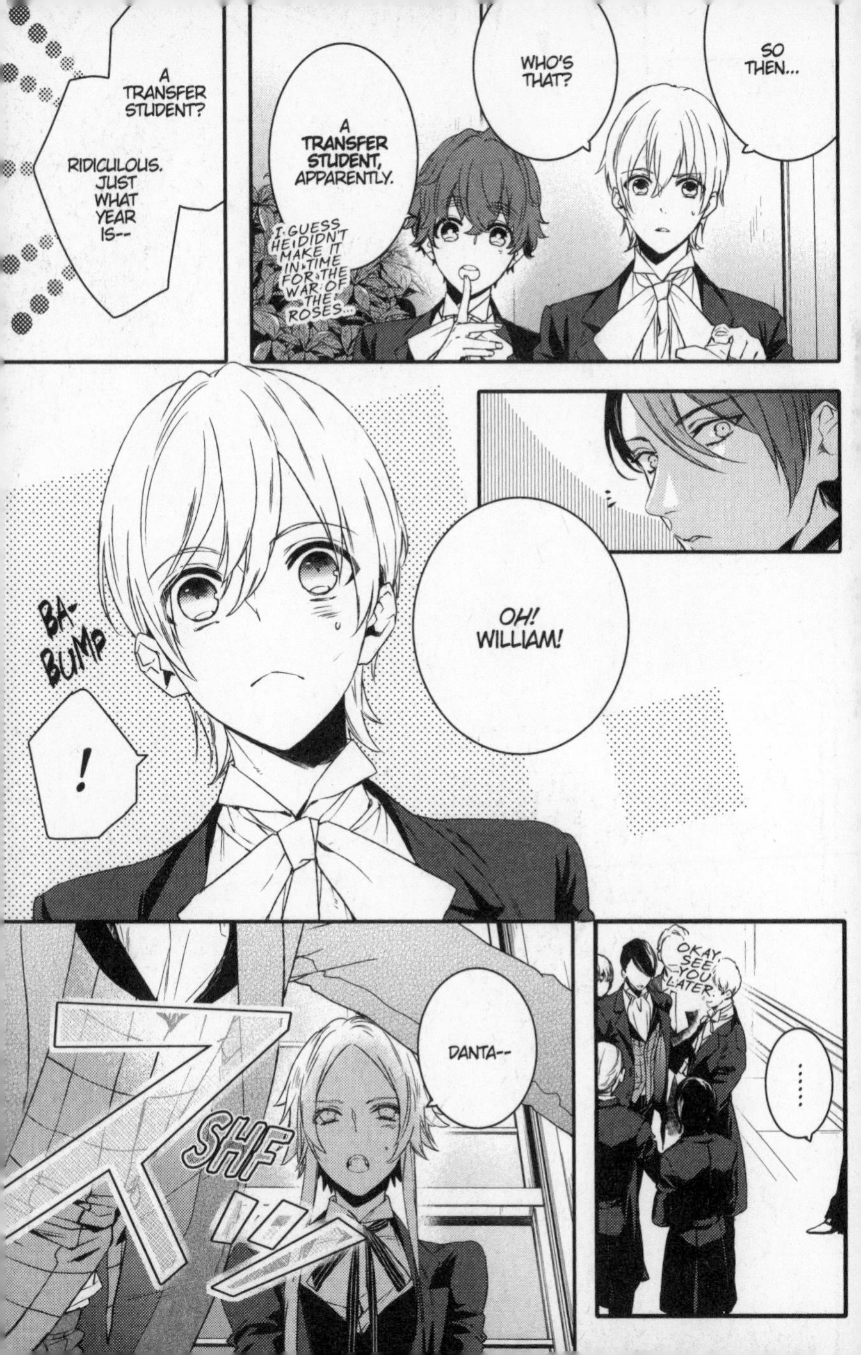
SO THEN...
WHO'S THAT?
A TRANSFER STUDENT, APPARENTLY.
I GUESS HE DIDN'T MAKE IT IN TIME FOR THE WAR OF THE ROSES...
A TRANSFER STUDENT?
RIDICULOUS. JUST WHAT YEAR IS--
OH! WILLIAM!
BA-BUMP
!
OKAY, SEE YOU LATER.
......
DANTA--
SHF

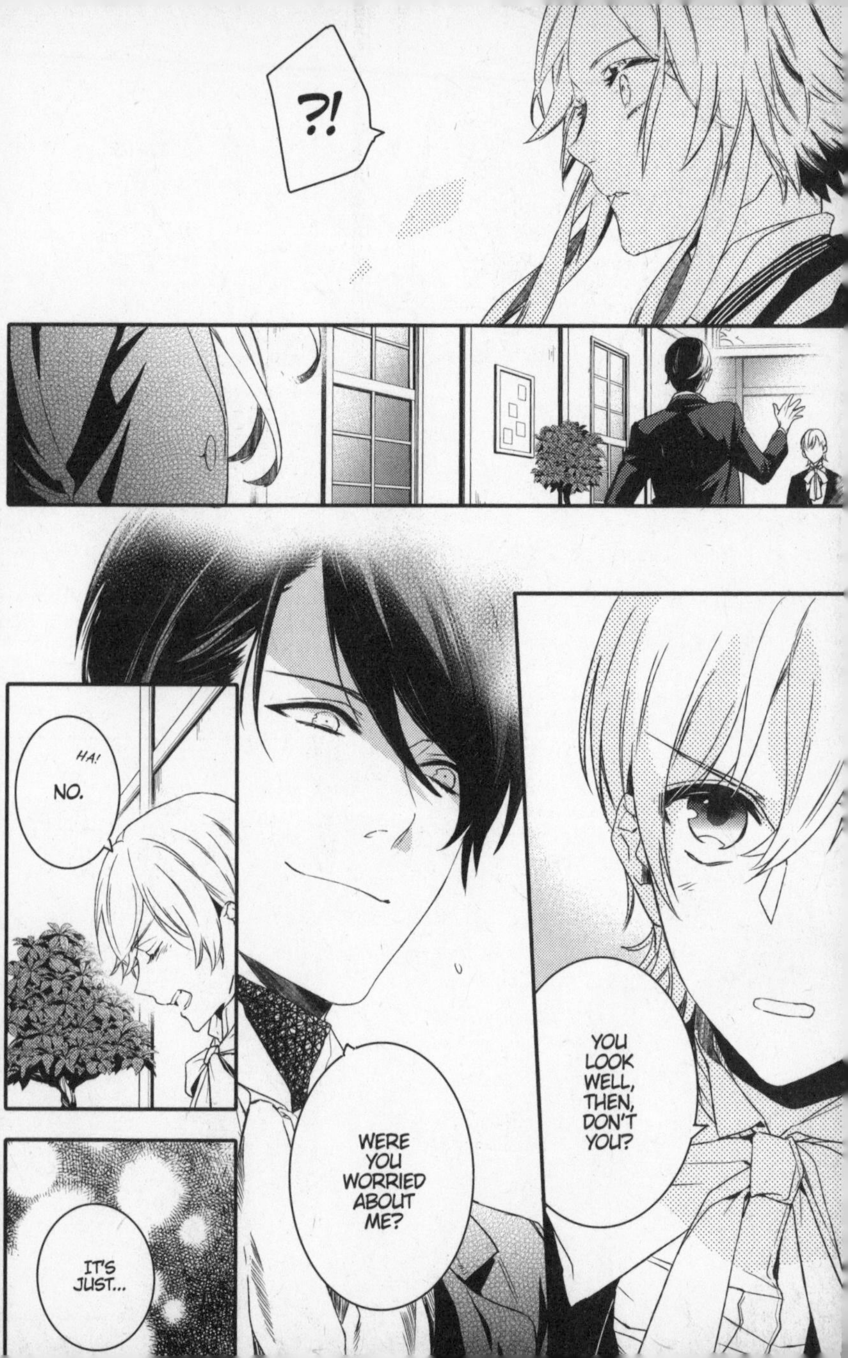
?!
YOU LOOK WELL, THEN, DON'T YOU?
WERE YOU WORRIED ABOUT ME?
HA!
NO.
IT'S JUST...

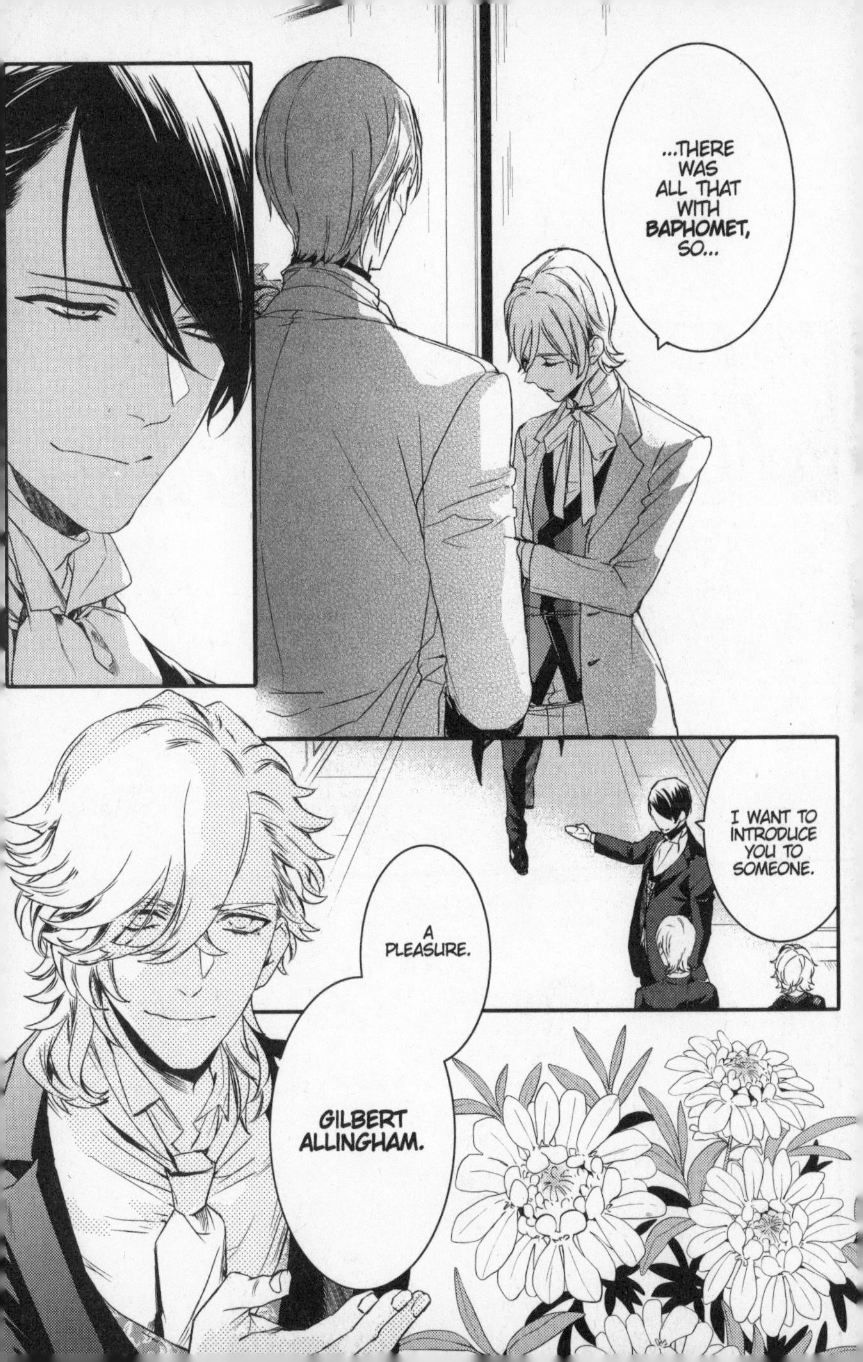
...THERE WAS ALL THAT WITH BAPHOMET, SO...
I WANT TO INTRODUCE YOU TO SOMEONE.
A PLEASURE.
GILBERT ALLINGHAM.

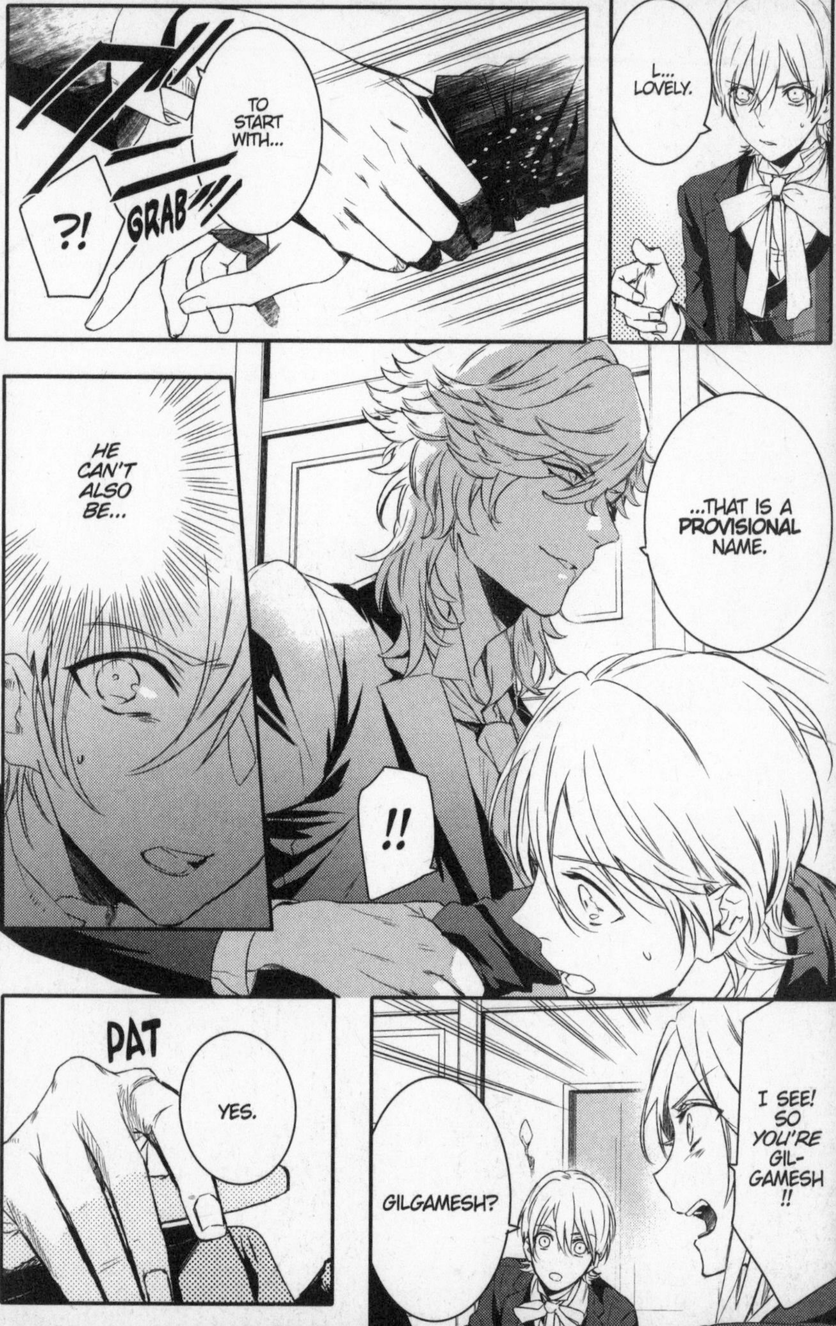
L... LOVELY.
TO START WITH...
GRAB
?!
...THAT IS A PROVISIONAL NAME.
!!
HE CAN'T ALSO BE...
I SEE! SO YOU'RE GIL-GAMESH !!
GILGAMESH?
PAT
YES.

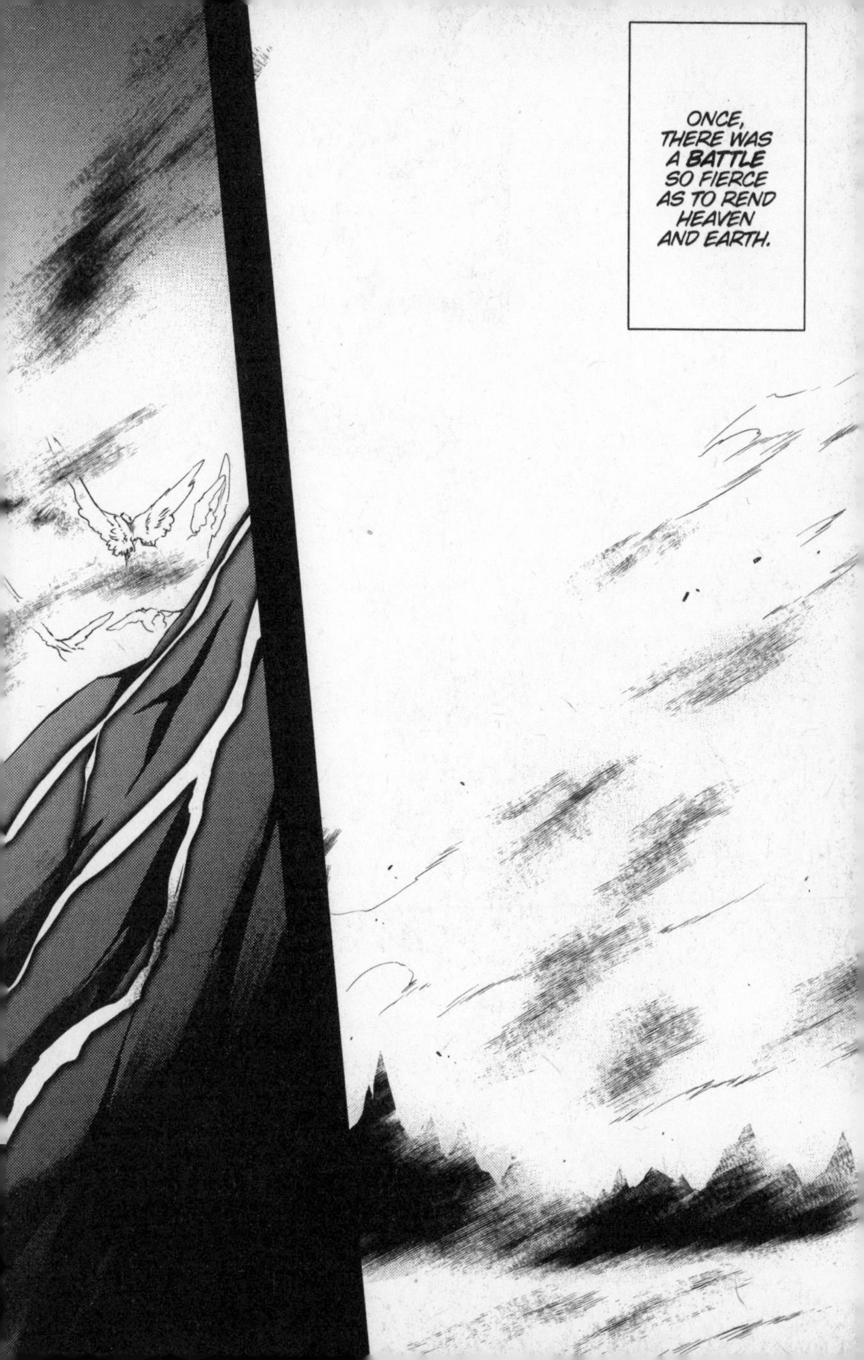
ONCE, THERE WAS A BATTLE SO FIERCE AS TO REND HEAVEN AND EARTH.

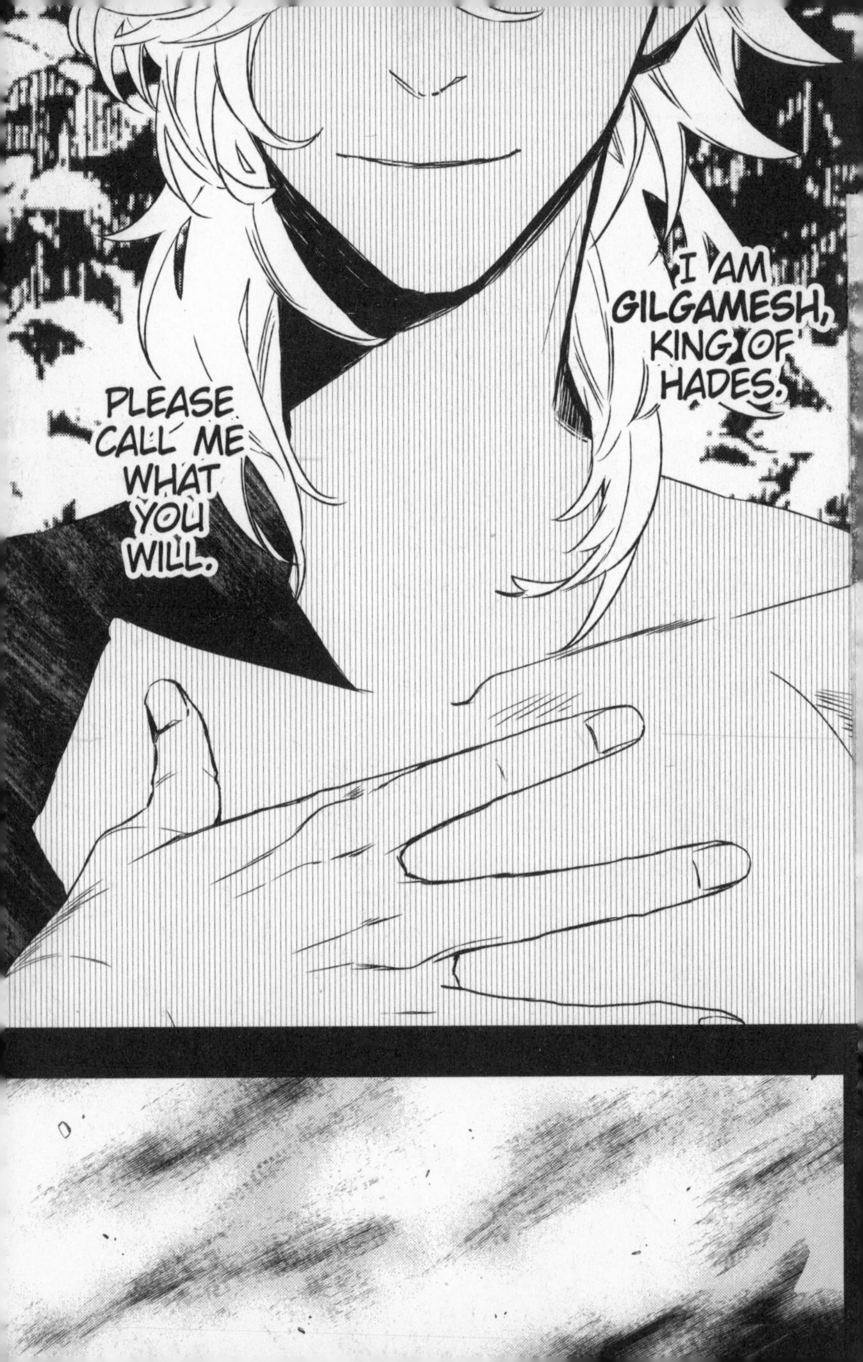
I AM GILGAMESH, KING OF HADES.
PLEASE CALL ME WHAT YOU WILL.

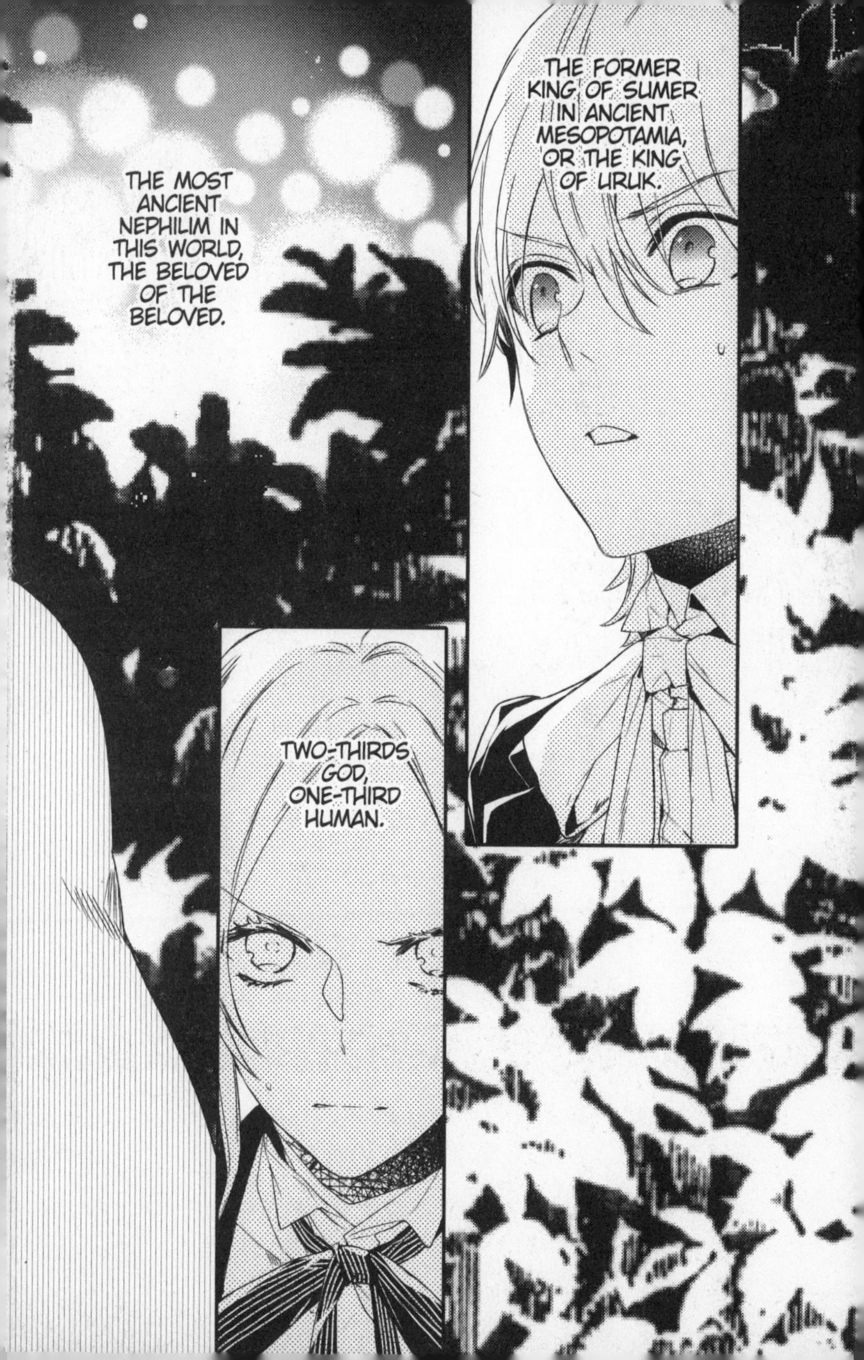
THE FORMER KING OF SUMER IN ANCIENT MESOPOTAMIA, OR THE KING OF URUK.
THE MOST ANCIENT NEPHILIM IN THIS WORLD, THE BELOVED OF THE BELOVED.
TWO-THIRDS GOD, ONE-THIRD HUMAN.

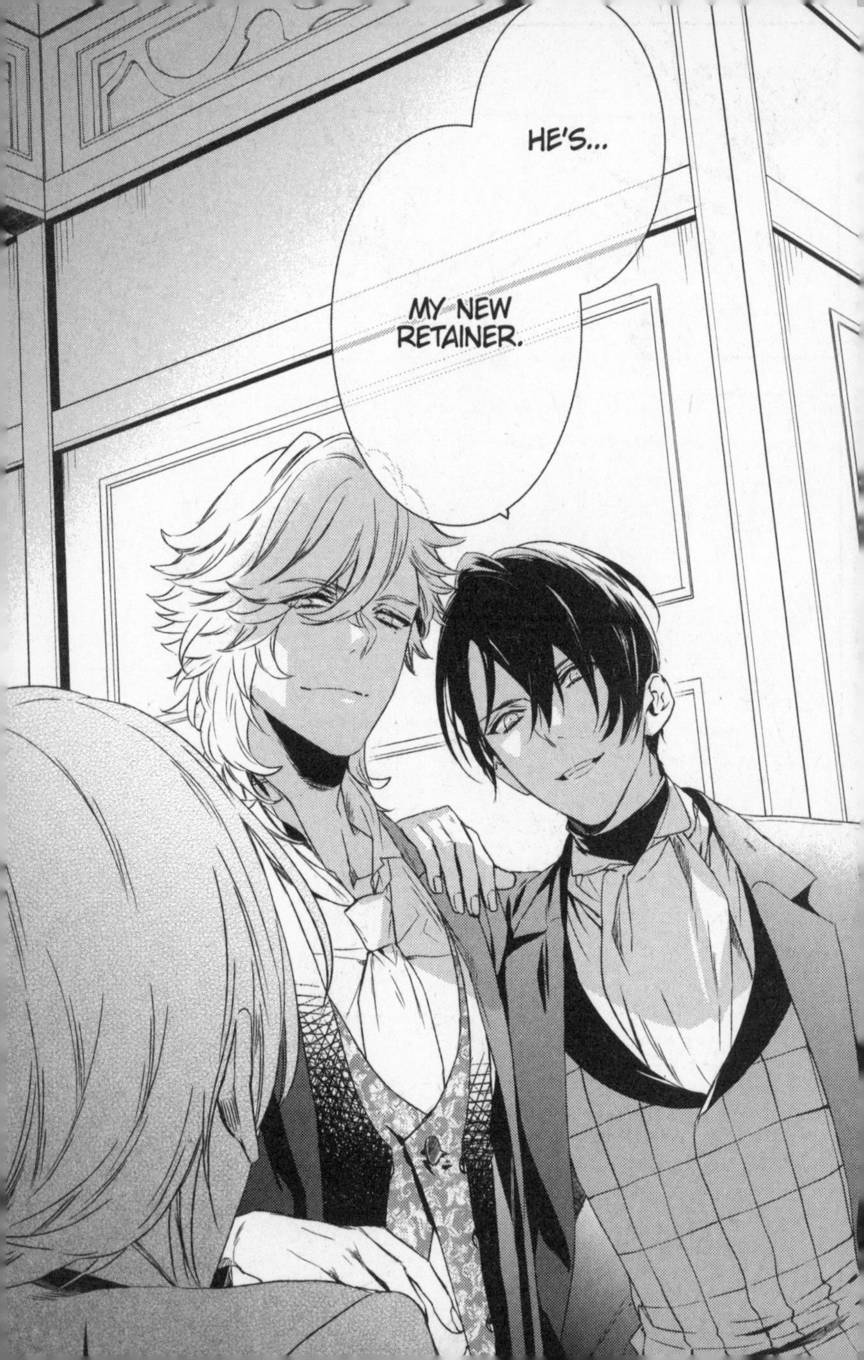
HE'S...
MY NEW RETAINER.

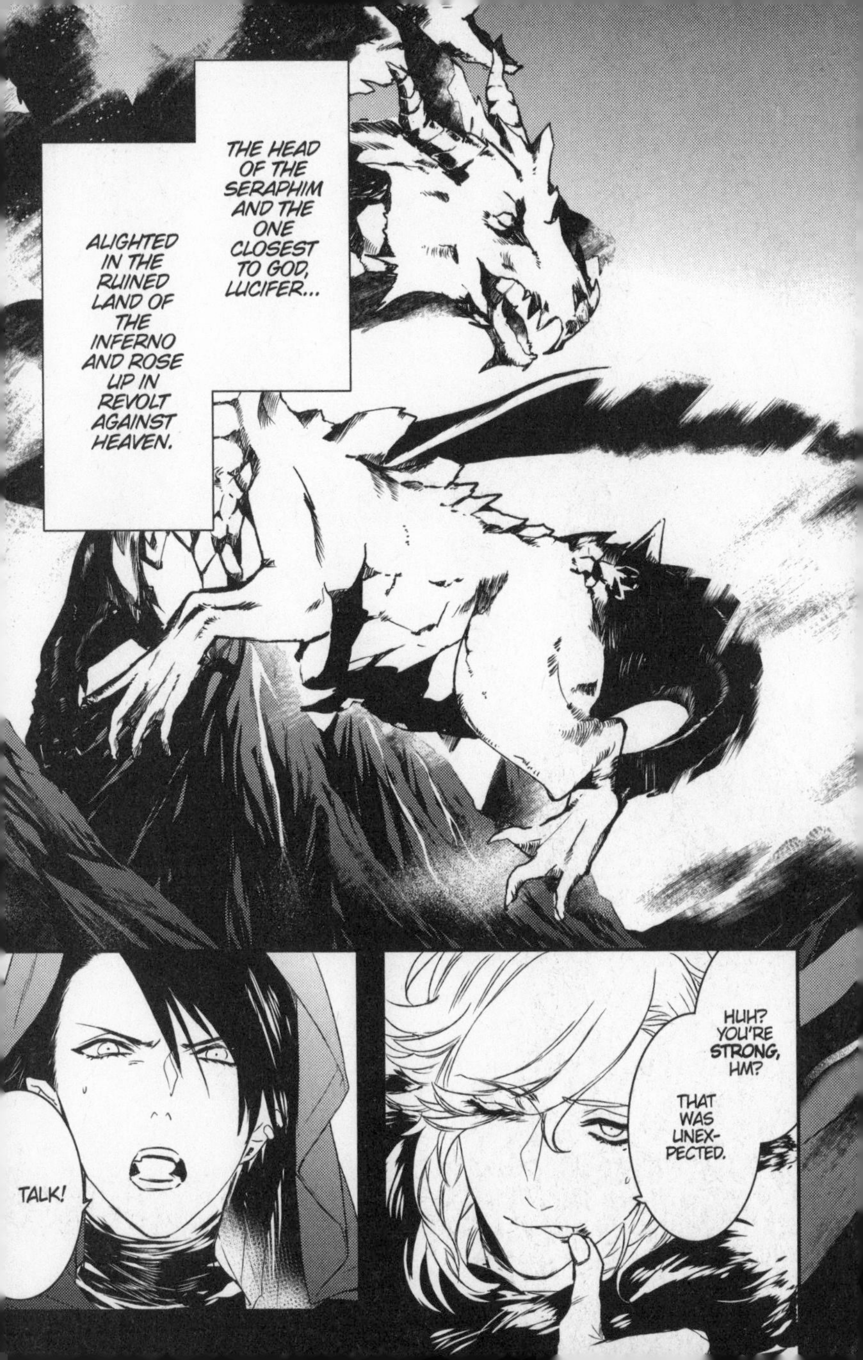
THE HEAD OF THE SERAPHIM AND THE ONE CLOSEST TO GOD, LUCIFER...
ALIGHTED IN THE RUINED LAND OF THE INFERNO AND ROSE UP IN REVOLT AGAINST HEAVEN.
HUH? YOU'RE STRONG, HM?
THAT WAS UNEX-PECTED.
TALK!

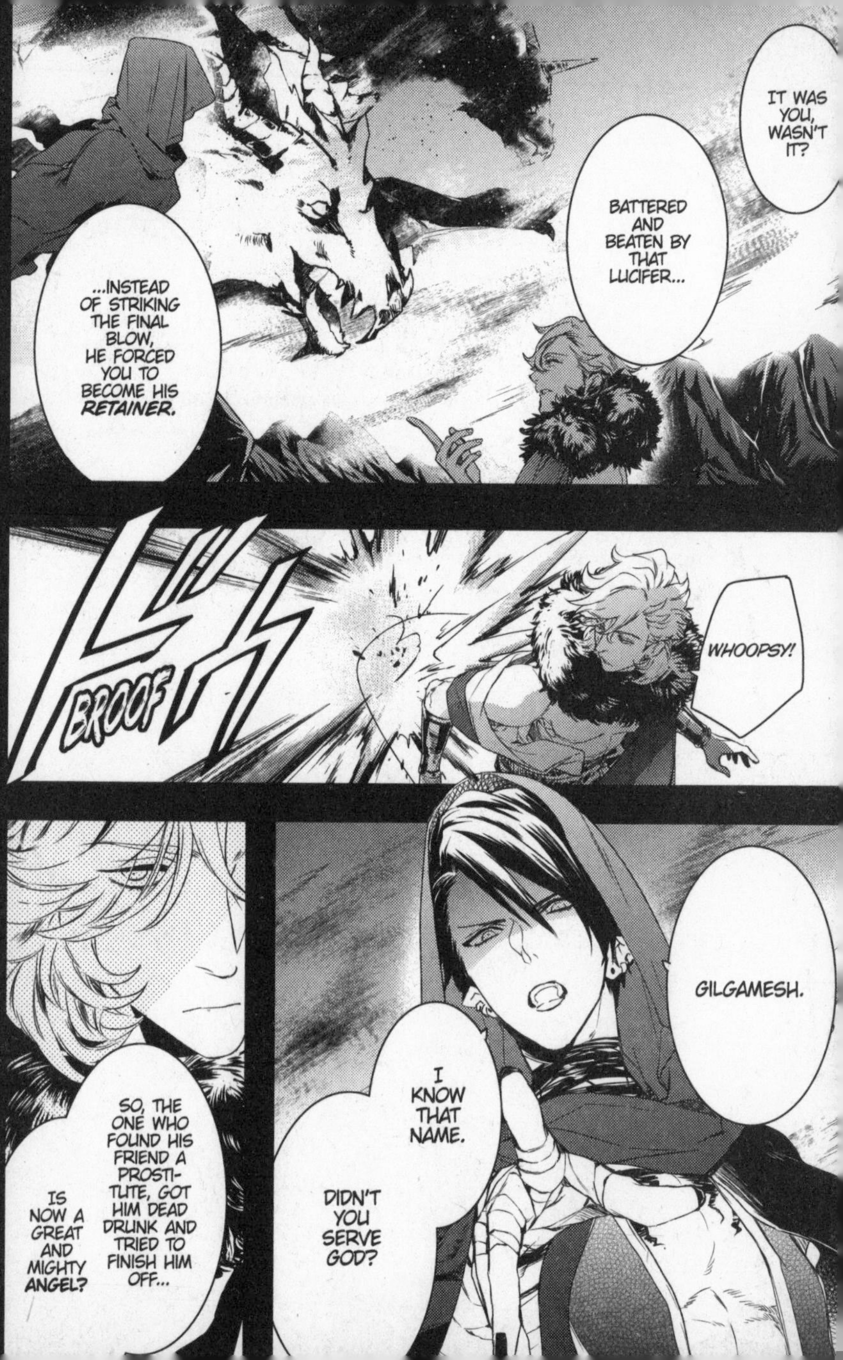
IT WAS YOU, WASN'T IT?
BATTERED AND BEATEN BY THAT LUCIFER...
...INSTEAD OF STRIKING THE FINAL BLOW, HE FORCED YOU TO BECOME HIS *RETAINER.*
WHOOPSY!
BROOF
GILGAMESH.
I KNOW THAT NAME.
DIDN'T YOU SERVE GOD?
SO, THE ONE WHO FOUND HIS FRIEND A PROSTI-TUTE, GOT HIM DEAD DRUNK AND TRIED TO FINISH HIM OFF...
IS NOW A GREAT AND MIGHTY ANGEL?

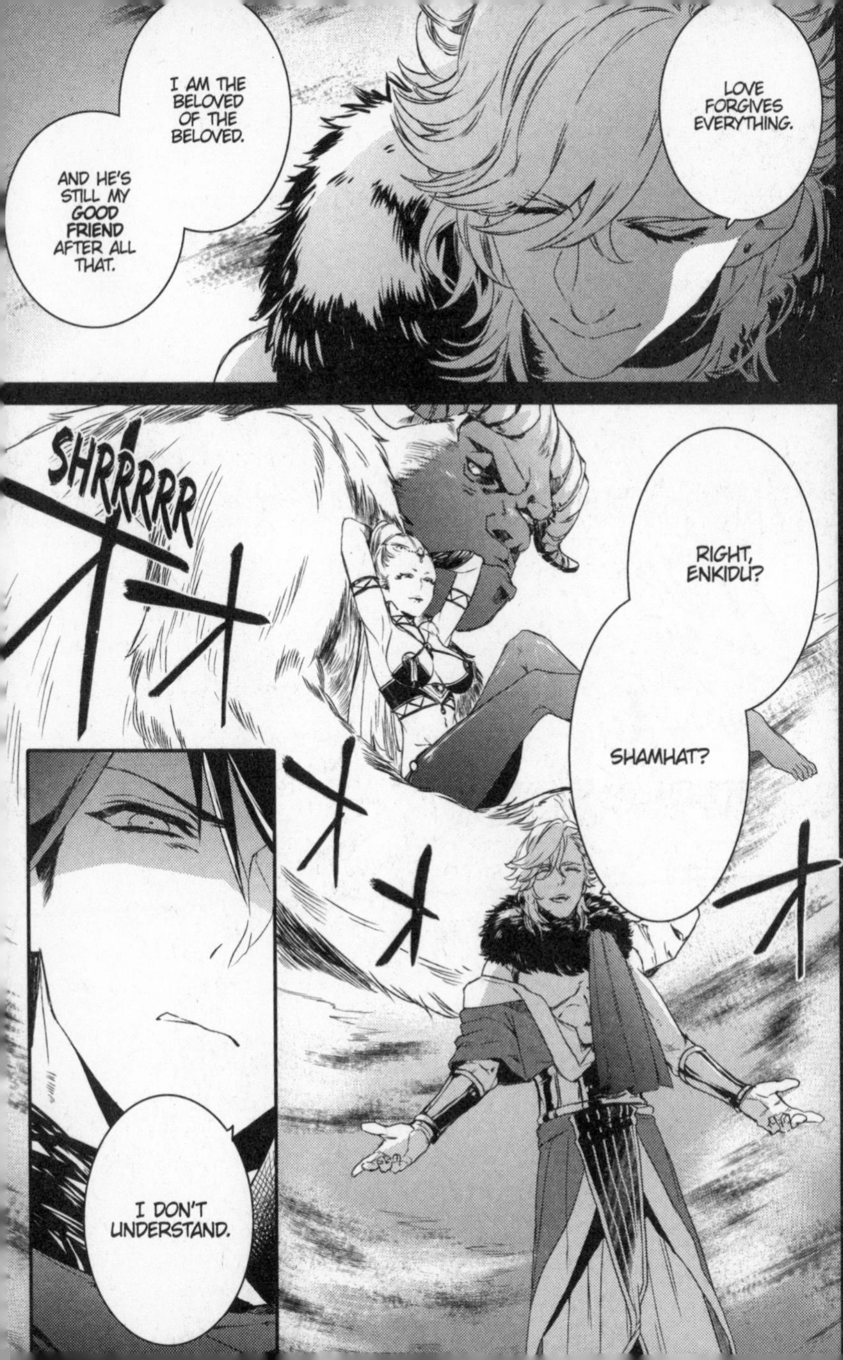
LOVE FORGIVES EVERYTHING.
I AM THE BELOVED OF THE BELOVED.
AND HE'S STILL MY GOOD FRIEND AFTER ALL THAT.
SHRRRRR
RIGHT, ENKIDU?
SHAMHAT?
I DON'T UNDERSTAND.

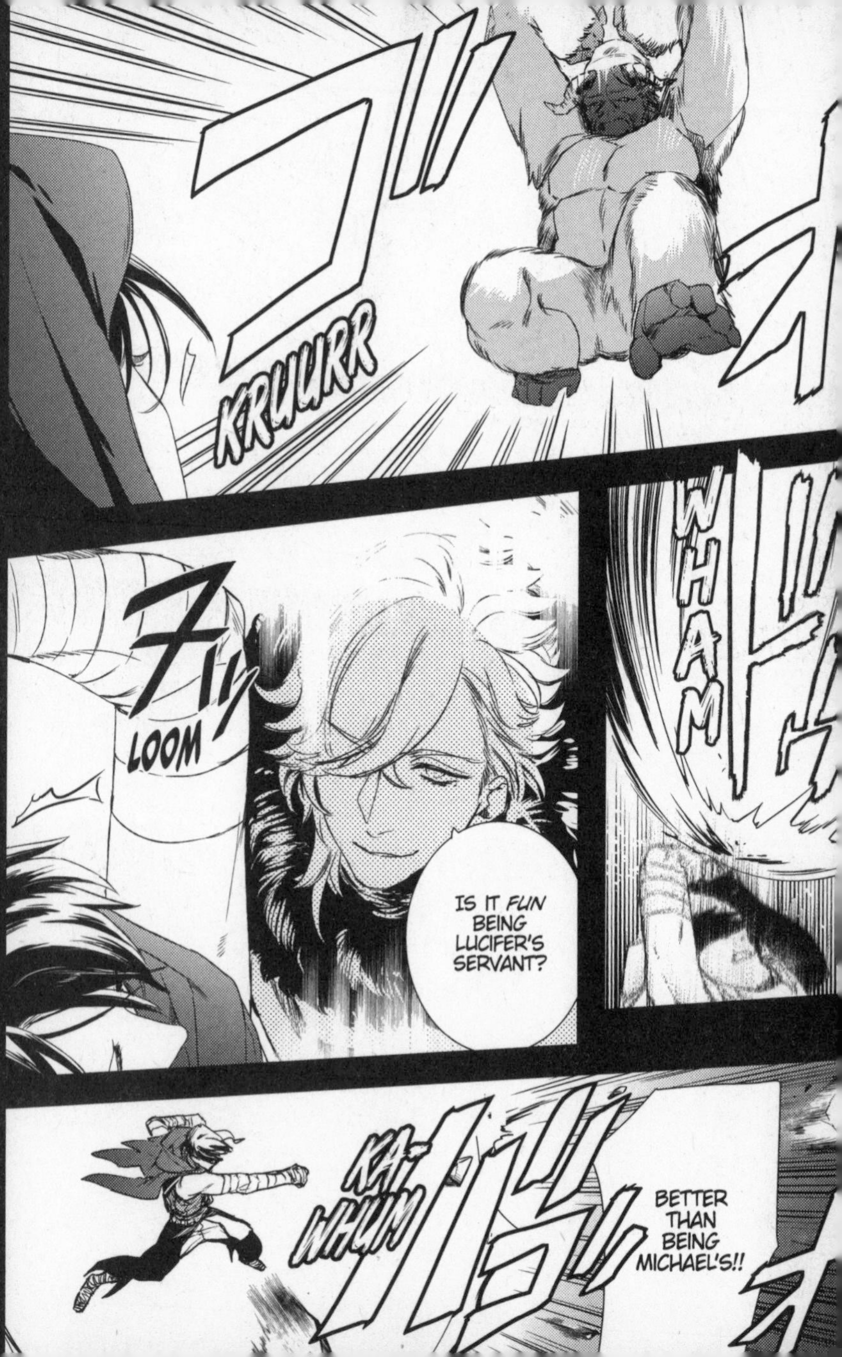
KRUURR
WHAM
FLOOM
IS IT *FUN* BEING LUCIFER'S SERVANT?
BETTER THAN BEING MICHAEL'S!!
KA-WHUM

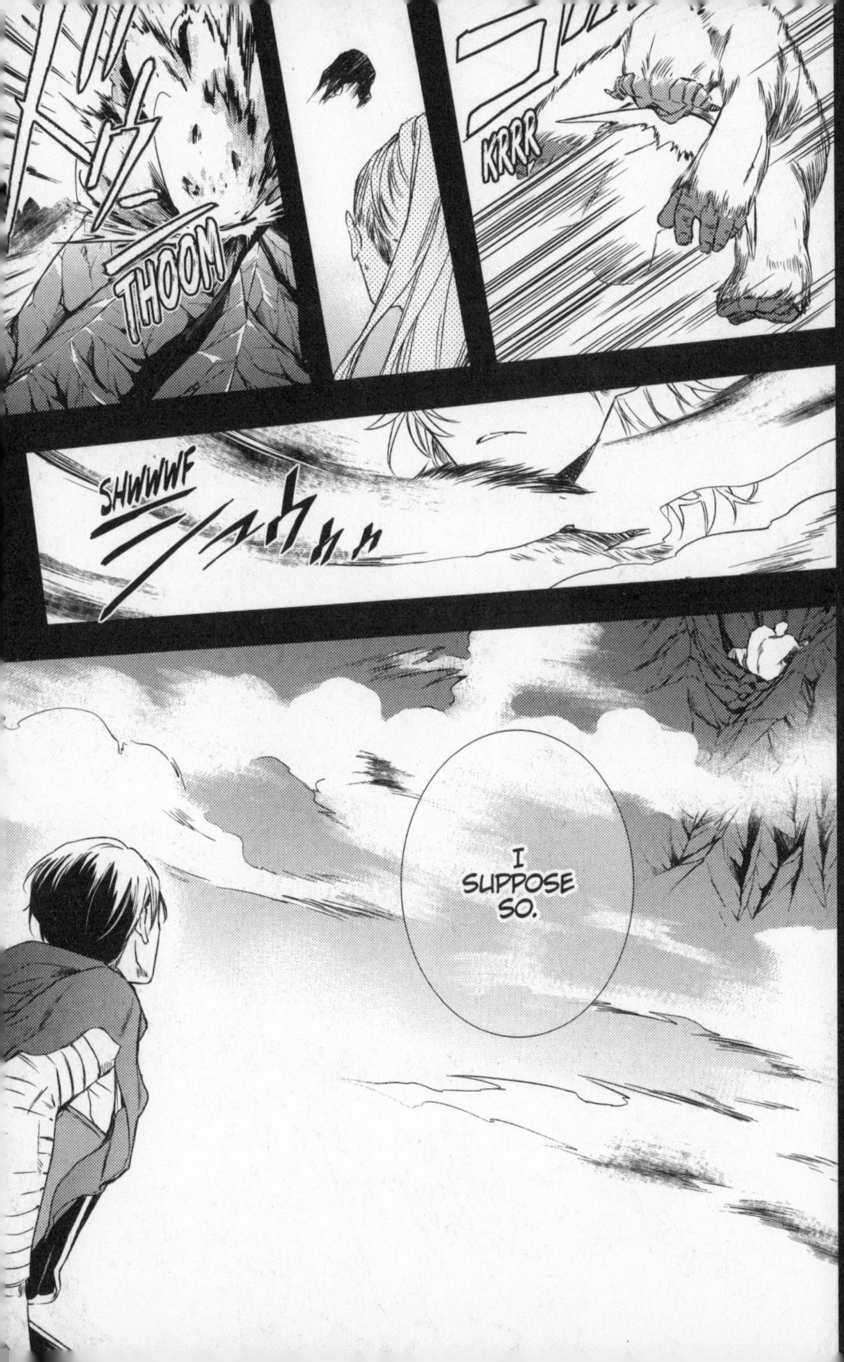
KRRR
THOOM
SHWWWF
I SUPPOSE SO.

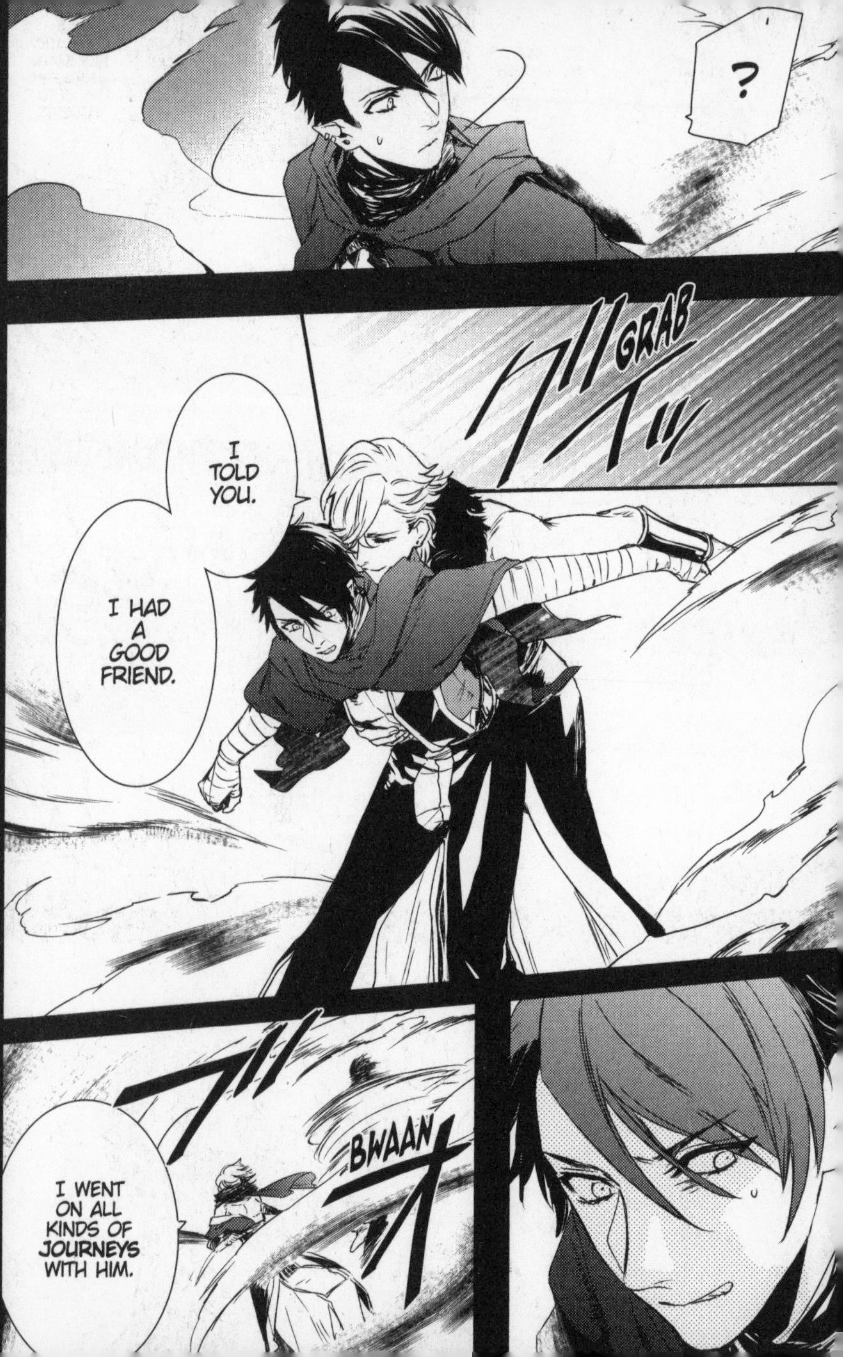
?
GRAB
I TOLD YOU.
I HAD A GOOD FRIEND.
I WENT ON ALL KINDS OF JOURNEYS WITH HIM.
BWAAN

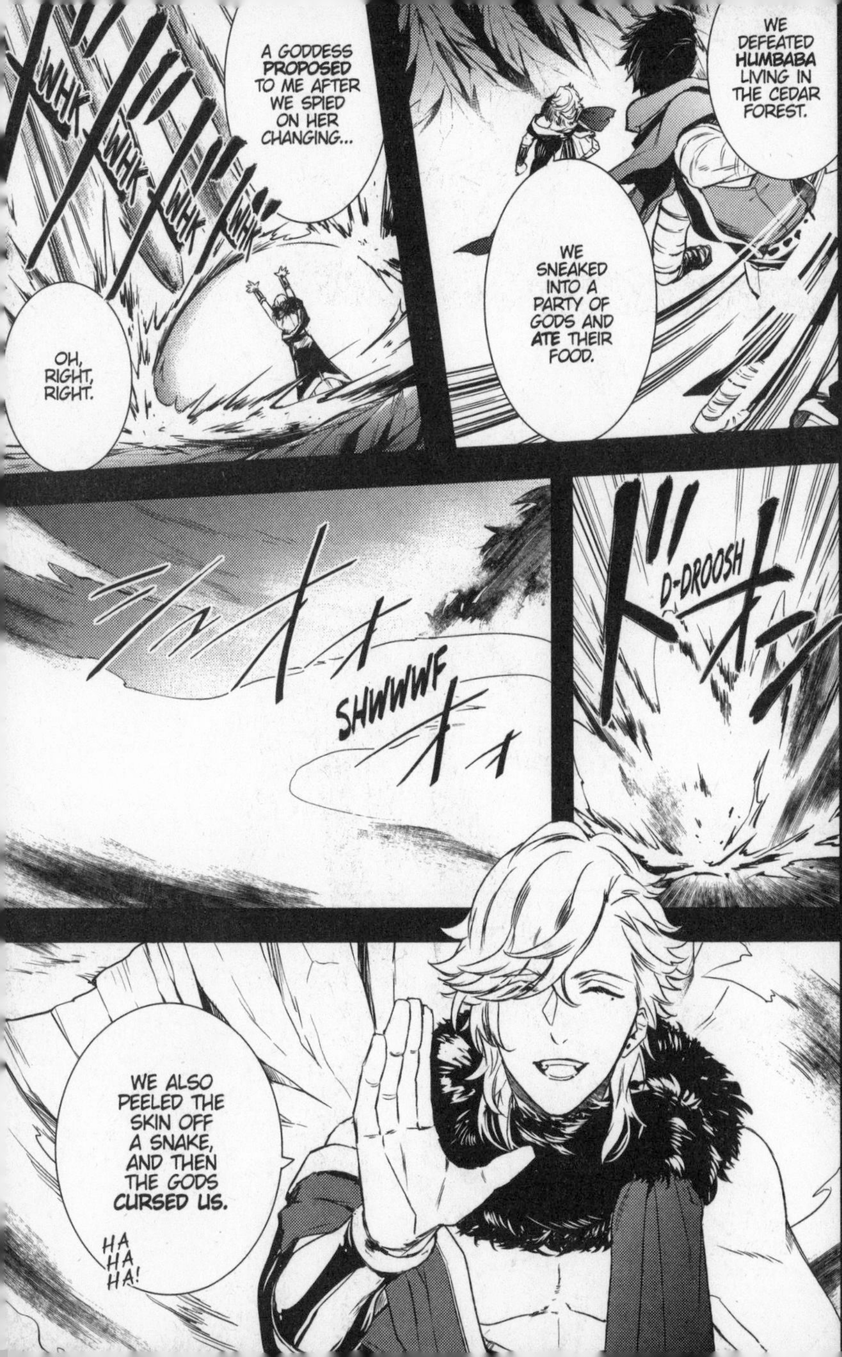
WE DEFEATED HUMBABA LIVING IN THE CEDAR FOREST.
WE SNEAKED INTO A PARTY OF GODS AND ATE THEIR FOOD.
WHK WHK WHK WHK
A GODDESS PROPOSED TO ME AFTER WE SPIED ON HER CHANGING...
OH, RIGHT, RIGHT.
D-DROOSH
SHWWWF
WE ALSO PEELED THE SKIN OFF A SNAKE, AND THEN THE GODS CURSED US.
HA HA HA!

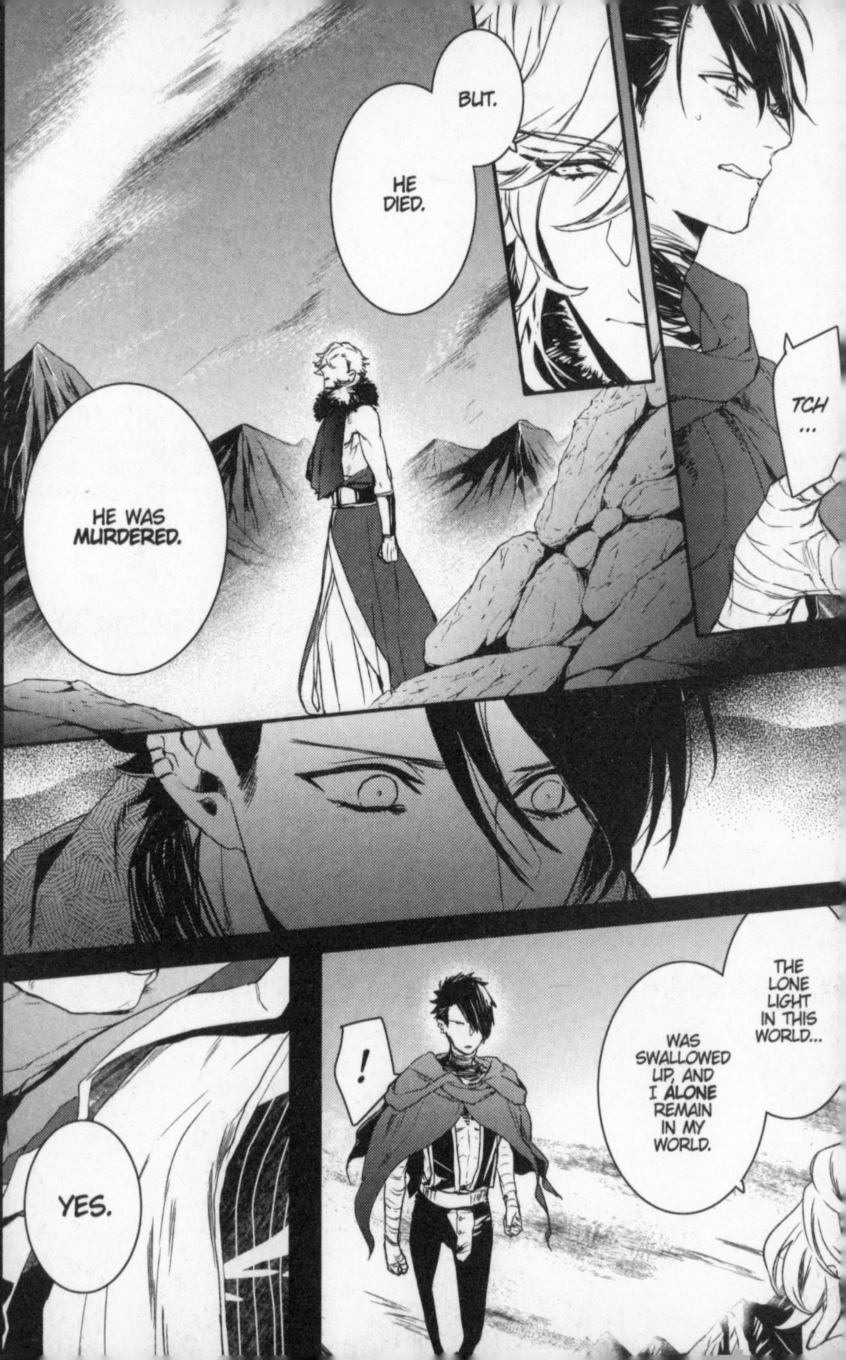

BUT.
HE DIED.
TCH ...
HE WAS MURDERED.
THE LONE LIGHT IN THIS WORLD...
WAS SWALLOWED UP, AND I ALONE REMAIN IN MY WORLD.
!
YES.

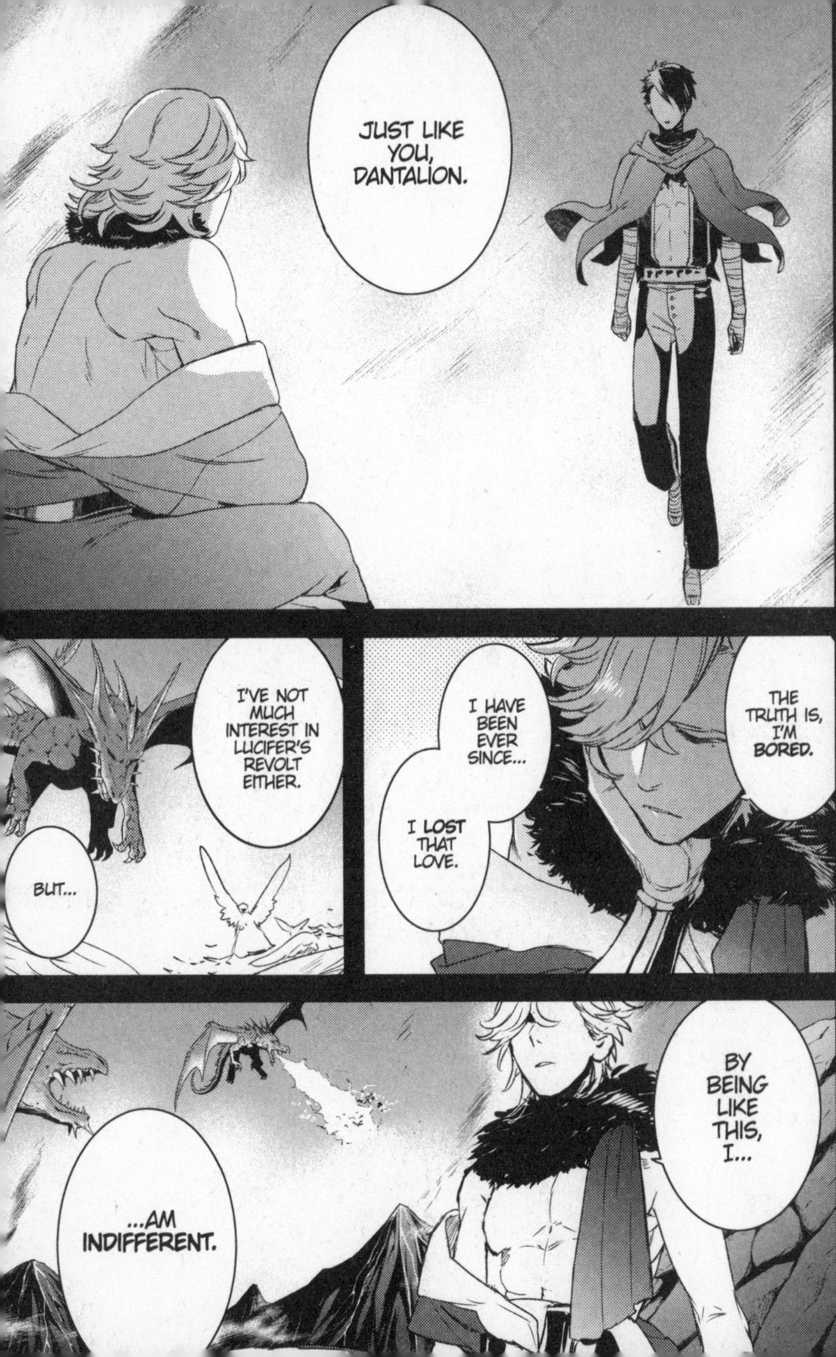
JUST LIKE YOU, DANTALION.
THE TRUTH IS, I'M BORED.
I HAVE BEEN EVER SINCE...
I LOST THAT LOVE.
I'VE NOT MUCH INTEREST IN LUCIFER'S REVOLT EITHER.
BUT...
BY BEING LIKE THIS, I...
...AM INDIFFERENT.

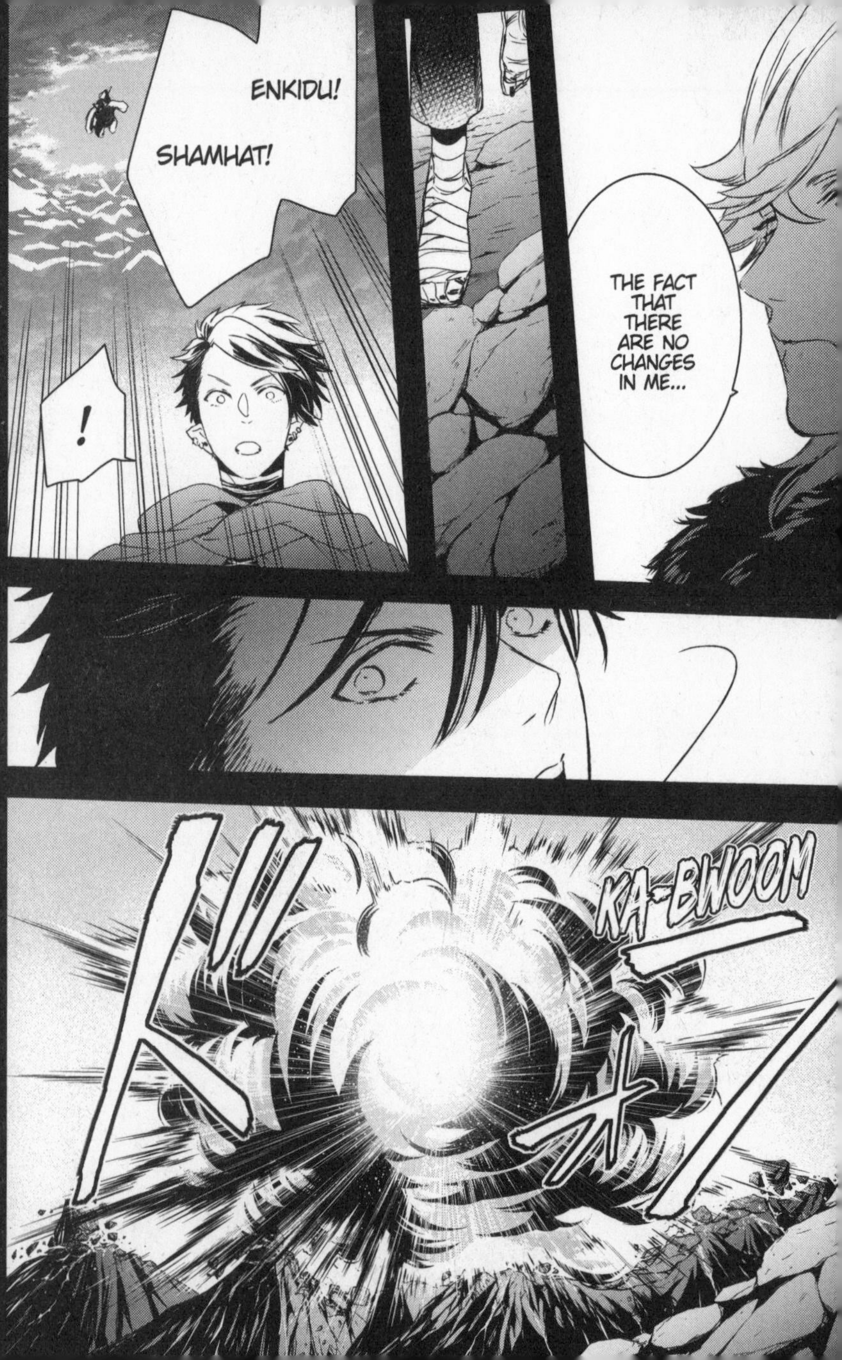
THE FACT THAT THERE ARE NO CHANGES IN ME...
ENKIDU!
SHAMHAT!
!
KA-BWOOM

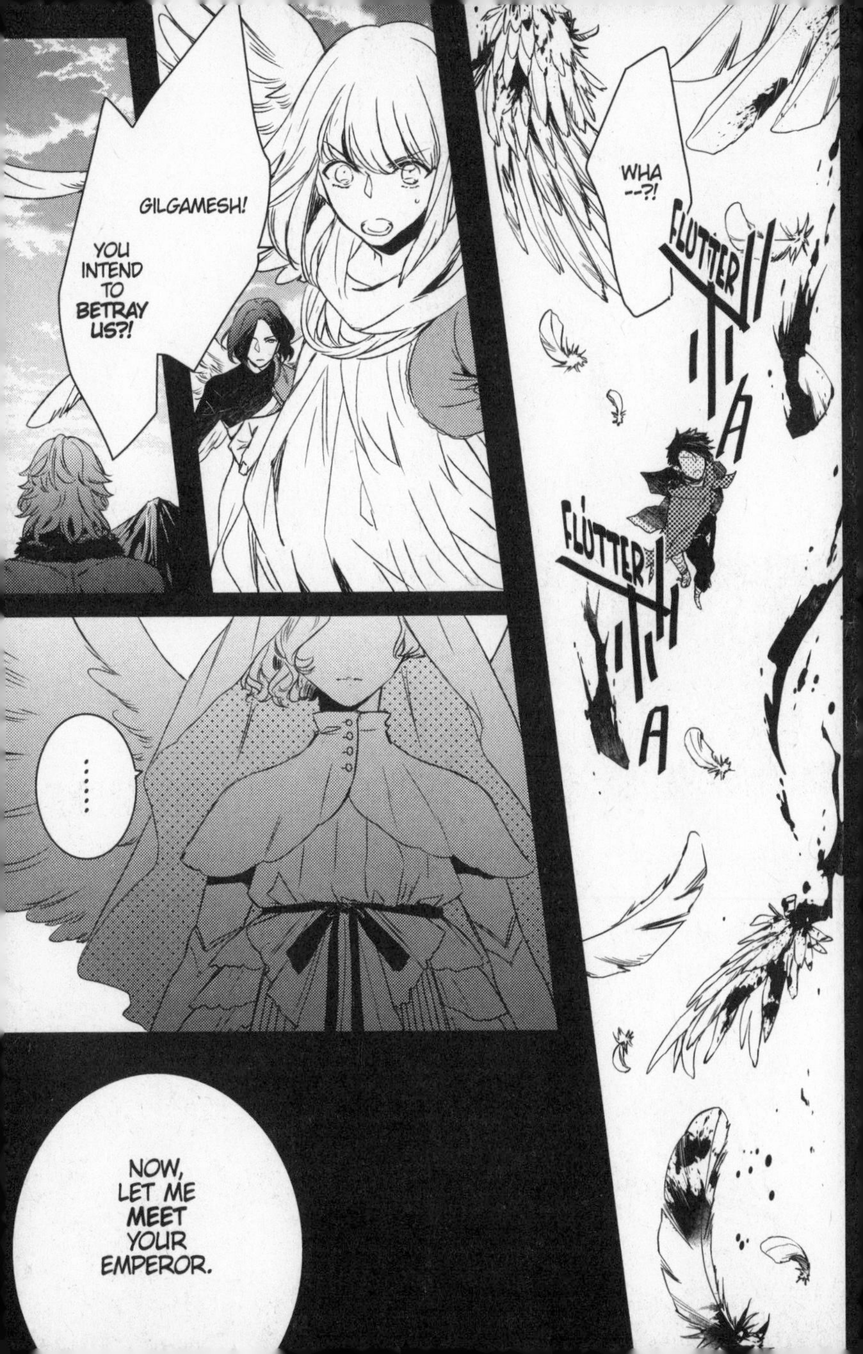
WHA--?!
FLUTTER
FLUTTER
GILGAMESH!
YOU INTEND TO BETRAY US?!
......
NOW, LET ME MEET YOUR EMPEROR.

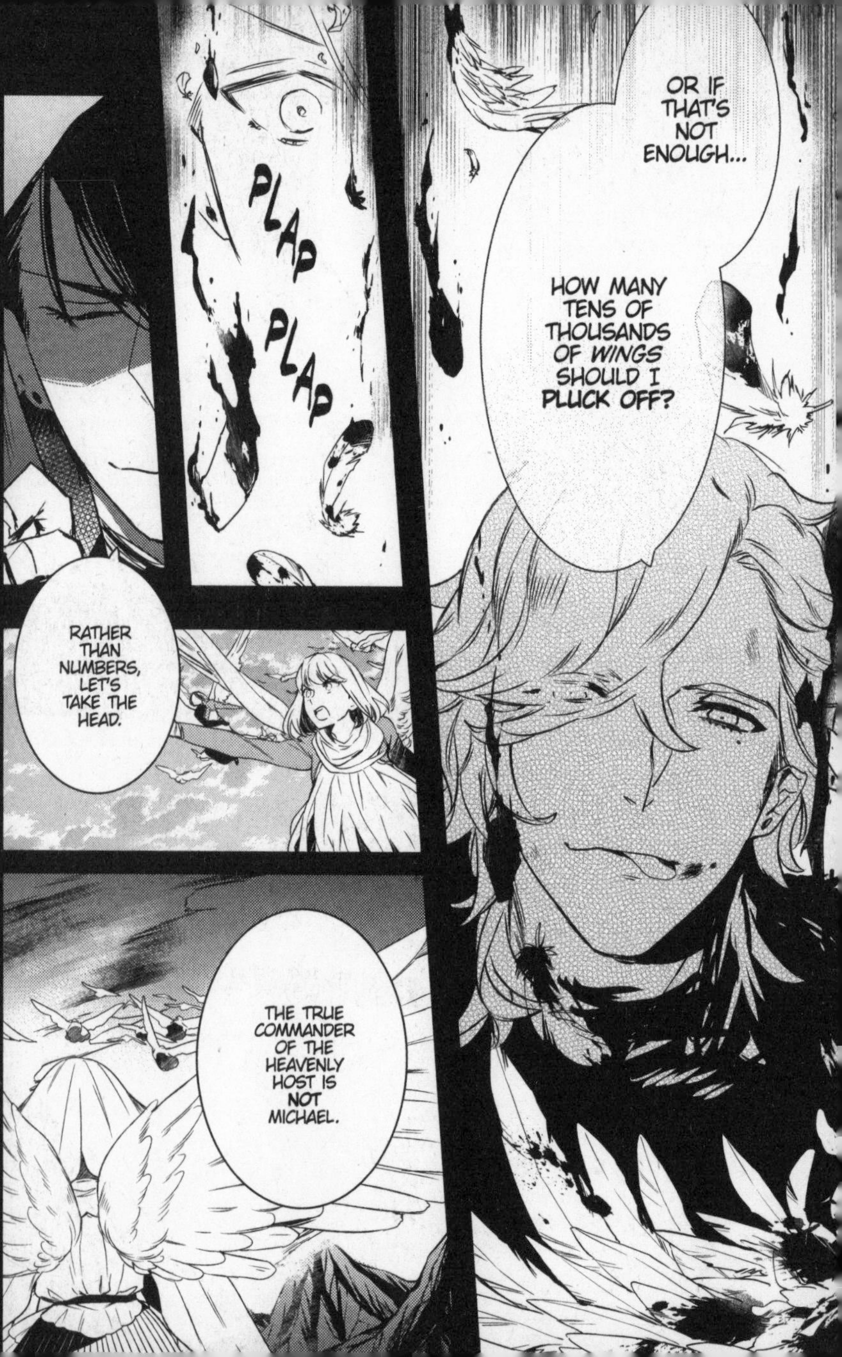
OR IF THAT'S NOT ENOUGH...
HOW MANY TENS OF THOUSANDS OF *WINGS* SHOULD I **PLUCK OFF?**
PLAP PLAP PLAP
RATHER THAN NUMBERS, LET'S TAKE THE HEAD.
THE TRUE COMMANDER OF THE HEAVENLY HOST IS **NOT** MICHAEL.

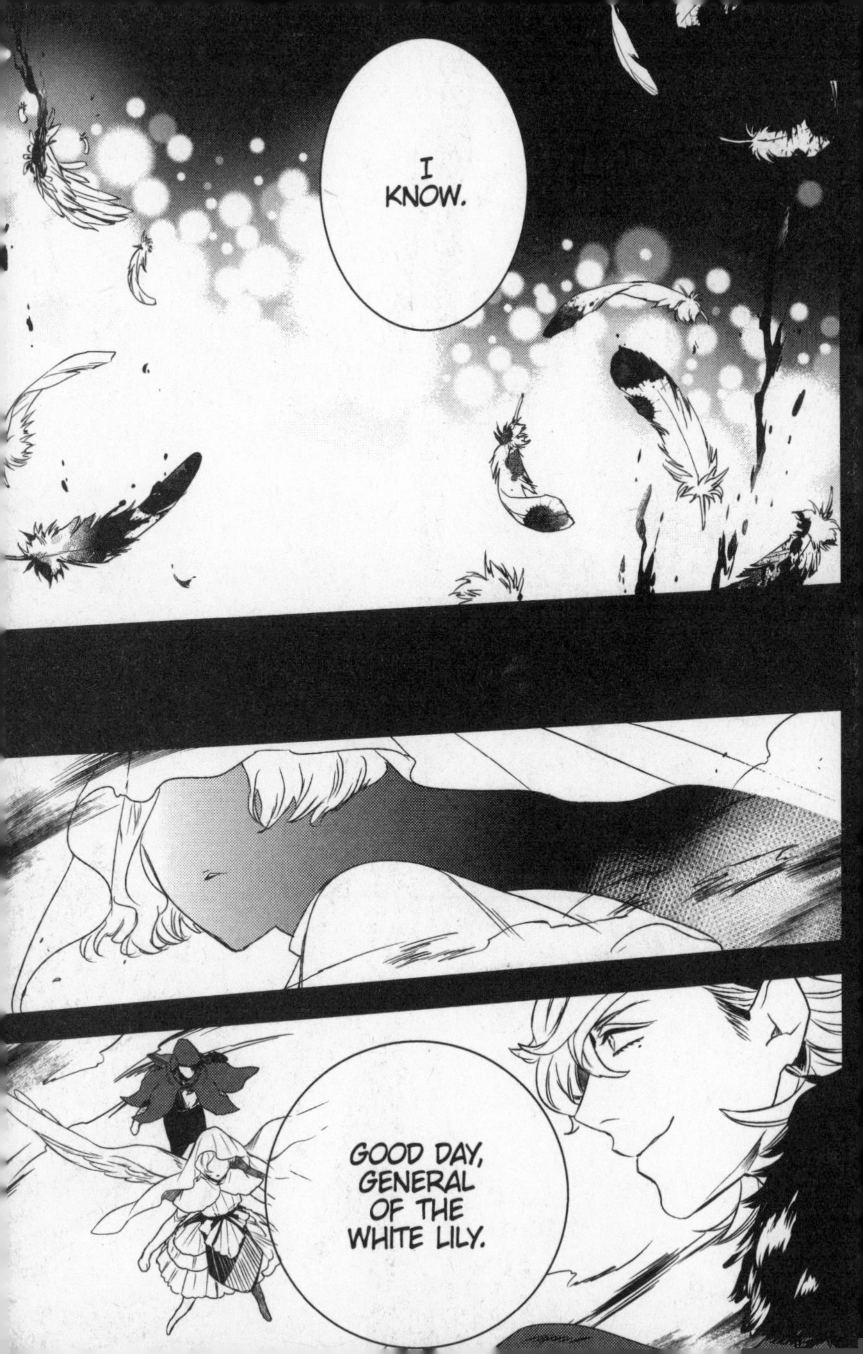
I KNOW.
GOOD DAY, GENERAL OF THE WHITE LILY.

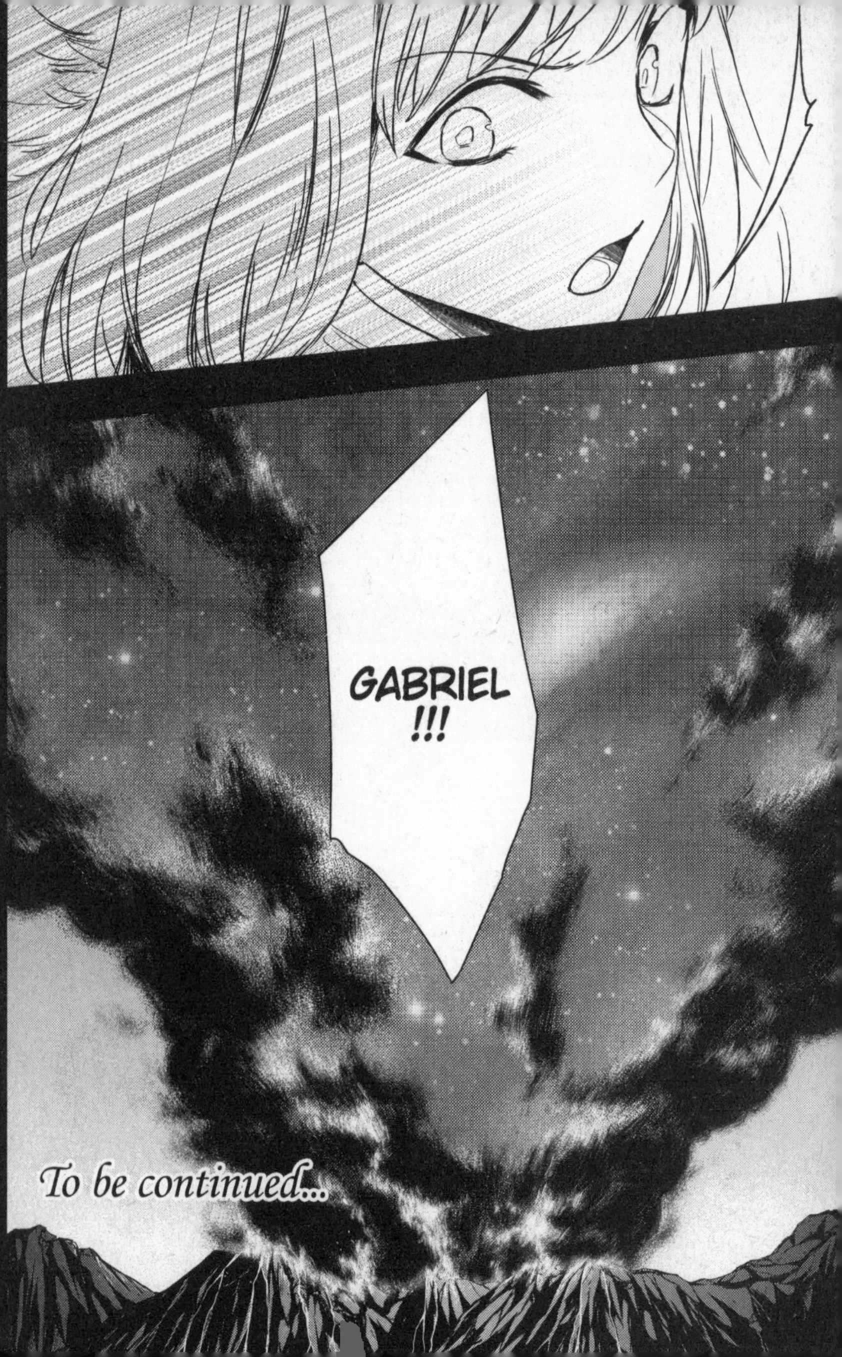
GABRIEL !!!
To be continued...

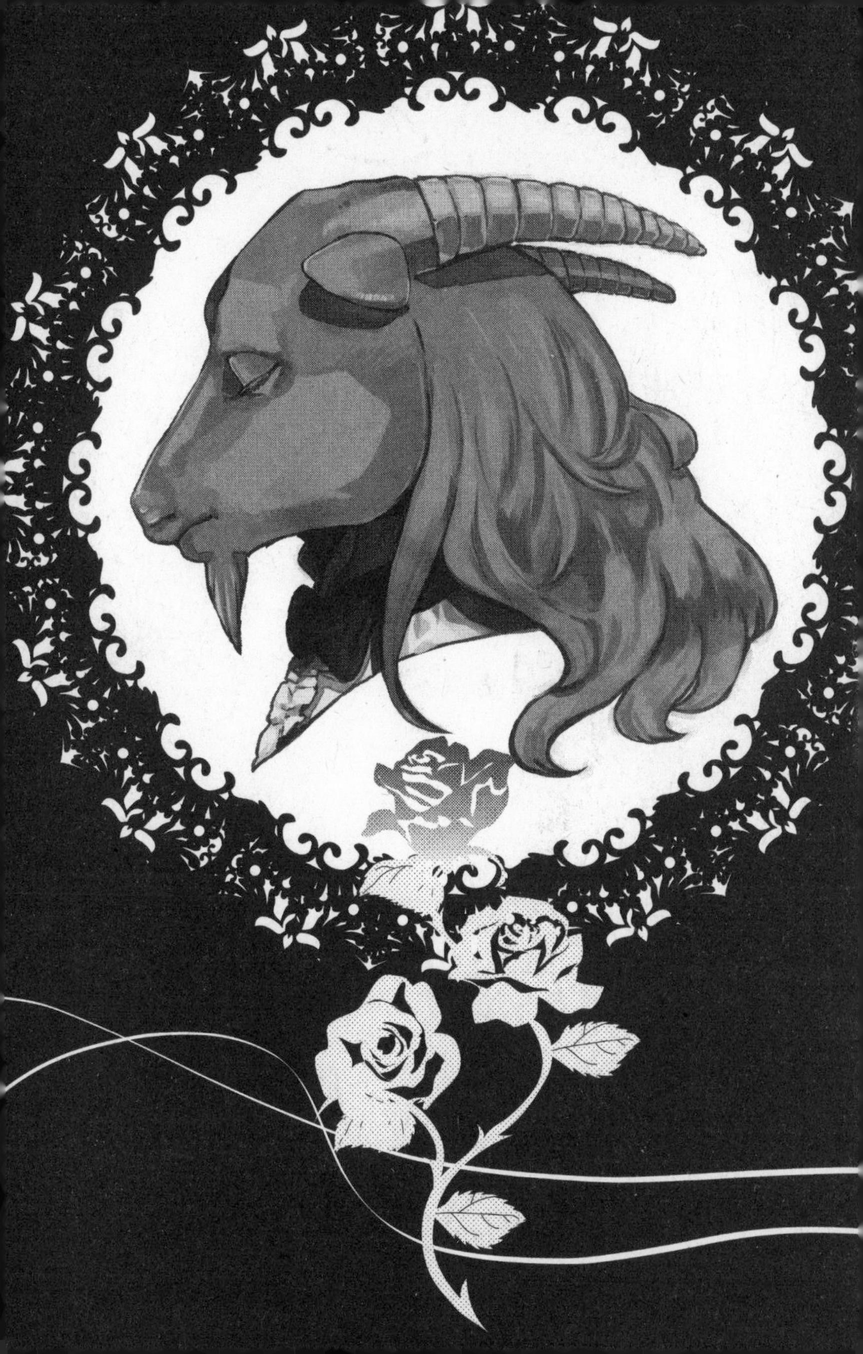

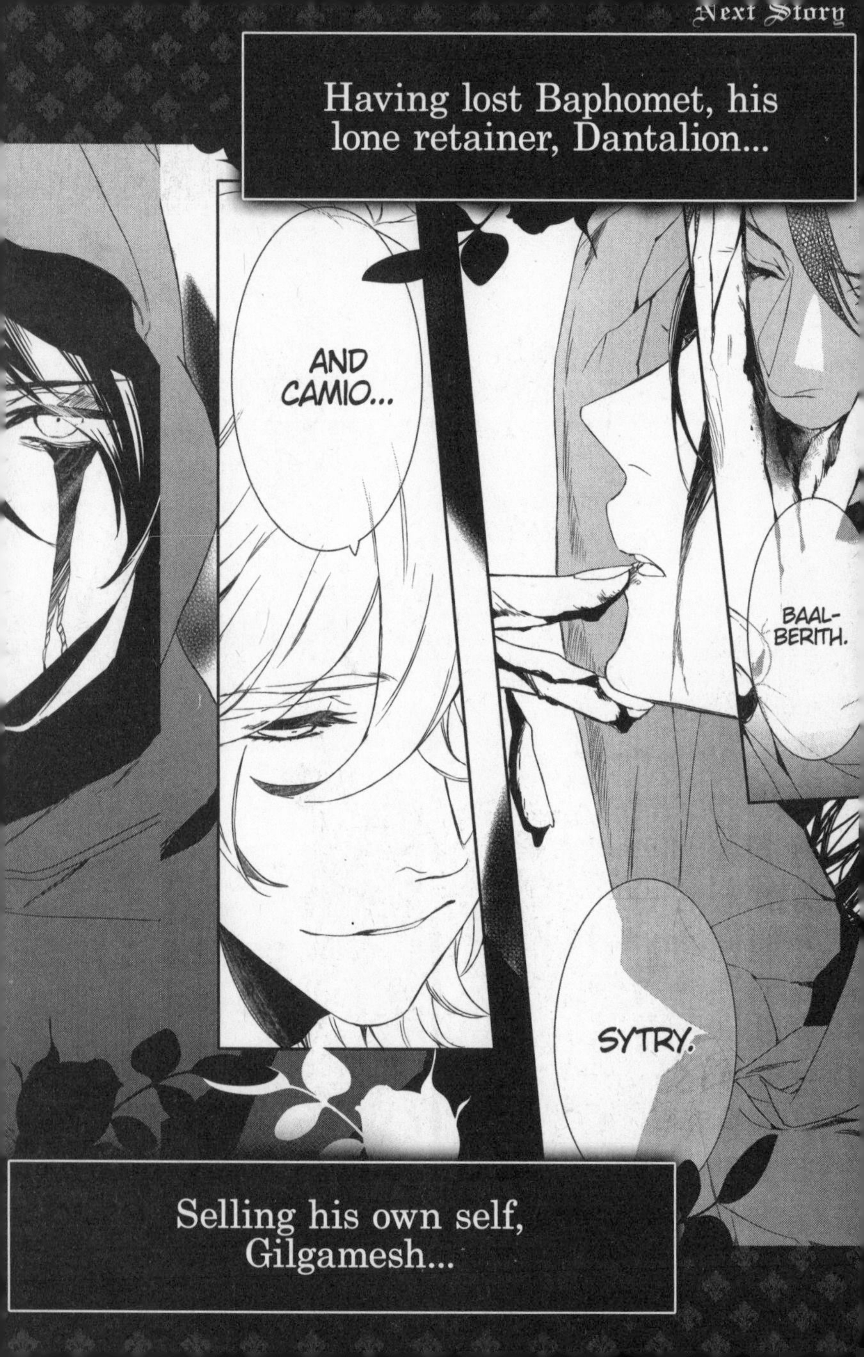
Next Story
Having lost Baphomet, his lone retainer, Dantalion...
BAAL-BERITH.
SYTRY.
AND CAMIO...
Selling his own self, Gilgamesh...

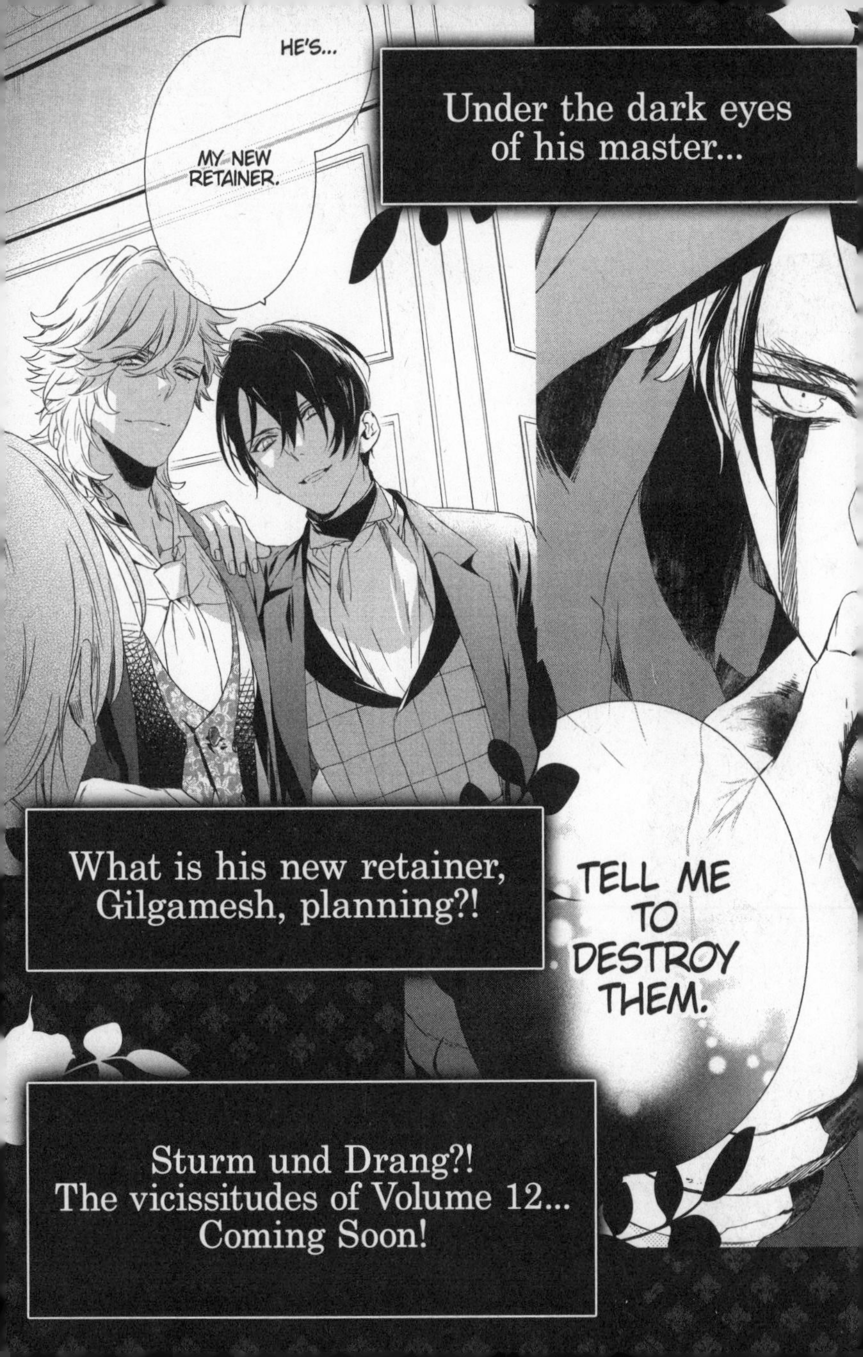
Under the dark eyes of his master...
TELL ME TO DESTROY THEM.
HE'S...
MY NEW RETAINER.
What is his new retainer, Gilgamesh, planning?!
Sturm und Drang?!
The vicissitudes of Volume 12...
Coming Soon!